Translation: Theory and Practice in Dialogue

Continuum Studies in Translation
Series Editor: Jeremy Munday, Centre for Translation Studies,
        University of Leeds, UK

Published in association with the International Association for Translation and
Intercultural Studies (IATIS), Continuum Studies in Translation aims to present
a series of books focused around central issues in translation and interpreting.
Using case studies drawn from a wide range of different countries and languages,
each book presents a comprehensive examination of current areas of research
within translation studies written by academics at the forefront of the field.
The thought-provoking books in this series are aimed at advanced students and
researchers of translation studies.

Translation as Intervention
Edited by **Jeremy Munday**

Translator and Interpreter Training: Issues, Methods and Debates
Edited by **John Kearns**

*Translation Studies in Africa: Central Issues in Interpreting and Literary and
Media Translation*
Edited by **Judith Inggs and Libby Meintjes**

Forthcoming:

Cognitive Explorations of Translation: Eyes, Keys, Taps
Edited by **Sharon O'Brien**

Self-Translation: Brokering Originality in Hybrid Culture
Edited by **Anthony Cordingley**

Words, Sounds and Image in Translation
Edited **Rita Wilson and Brigid Maher**

Translation: Theory and Practice in Dialogue

Edited by

Antoinette Fawcett, Karla L. Guadarrama García and Rebecca Hyde Parker

continuum

Continuum International Publishing Group

The Tower Building   80 Maiden Lane, Suite 704
11 York Road   New York
London SE1 7NX   NY 10038

www.continuumbooks.com

British Library Cataloguing-in-Publication Data
A catalogue record for this book is available from the British Library.

ISBN: 978-0-8264-4385-4 (hardback)
       978-0-8264-4467-7 (paperback)

Library of Congress Cataloging-in-Publication Data
A catalog record for this book is available from the Library of Congress.

Typeset by Newgen Imaging Systems Pvt Ltd, Chennai, India
Printed and bound in Great Britain by CPI Antony Rowe Ltd,
Chippenham, Wiltshire

Contents

Series Editor's Preface

The International Association for Translation and Intercultural Studies (IATIS) provides a global forum for scholars and researchers concerned with translation and other forms of intercultural communication.

The Association facilitates the exchange of knowledge and resources among scholars in different parts of the world, stimulates interaction between researchers from diverse traditions, and encourages scholars across the globe to explore issues of mutual concern and intellectual interest.

Among the Association's activities are the organization of conferences and workshops, the creation of web-based resources and the publication of newsletters and scholarly books and journals.

The Translation Series published by Continuum in conjunction with IATIS is a key publication for the Association. It addresses the scholarly community at large, as well as the Association's members. Each volume presents a thematically coherent collection of essays, under the co-ordination of a prominent guest editor. The series thus seeks to be a prime instrument for the promotion and dissemination of innovative research, sound scholarship and critical thought in all areas that fall within the Association's purview.

Jeremy Munday
University of Leeds, UK

Notes on Contributors

Jean Boase-Beier is Professor of Literature and Translation at the University of East Anglia, UK, where she teaches Literary Translation, Translation Theory, Literature and Stylistics, and runs the MA in Literary Translation. An Executive Committee member of the British Comparative Literature Association (and organiser of its John Dryden Translation Competition), she is also a translator between German and English and the editor of the *Visible Poets* series for Arc Publications. She has written a number of articles and books on translation, literature and language. Recent publications include *The German Language* (with Ken Lodge, Blackwell 2002); *Between Nothing and Nothing* (translated poems of Ernst Meister, Arc Publications 2003); *A Fine Line: New Poetry from Eastern and Central Europe* (ed., with A. Buchler and F. Sampson, Arc Publications 2004); and *Stylistic Approaches to Translation* (St Jerome Publishing 2006).

Christine Calfoglou holds an MA in Translation and Translation Theory and a PhD in Linguistics and the acquisition of L2 syntax from the University of Athens, Greece. She has taught Translation and Linguistics at undergraduate and postgraduate level at the University of Athens, has given seminars in general, has led specialized Translation Seminars in particular, and has dealt extensively with English Language Teaching pedagogy. Her research interests and published work involve literary translation and linguistics, with an emphasis on the linguistic aspects of the translation of poetry, as well as English Language Teaching, the use of translation in the language class and distance education methodology. She has been teaching on the M.Ed. course for teachers of English at the Hellenic Open University, Greece, for which she has written a volume on L2 reading and writing methodology.

Antoinette Fawcett is half-Dutch and for the first years of her life grew up speaking both Dutch and English. After education at the University of St Andrews, UK, in English Language and Literature (MA 1977) she obtained her Postgraduate Certificate in Education at the University of Durham (1978) and became a teacher of English and Drama. She spent several years teaching in the United Kingdom, obtaining an MA in English Literary Research from the University of Lancaster in 1982. Her teaching career then led her abroad, first to the People's Republic of China where she taught English at a Normal University, then to the Netherlands, Singapore and Norway. Some of her translations of poems by the Dutch poet Gerrit Achterberg have been published in *MPT*, *Poetry Review*, *Ars Interpres* and, most recently, in the *2009 Yearbook of the Achterberggenootschap* (Achterberg Society). Her own poems have appeared in *Poetry London, Acumen, Agenda, Interpreter's House, Littoral, Stand, Pitch, Other Poetry*, and *The Rialto*, amongst others. After obtaining a Master's degree in Literary Translation (UEA 2008) she is now studying at doctoral level at the University of East Anglia. The topic of her research is *Translating the Form: A Process-based Approach to Translating the Poems of Martinus Nijhoff and Gerrit Achterberg*.

Lina Fisher is a PhD student in Literary Translation at the University of East Anglia, UK. Her thesis focuses on stylistics and the effect of the author's and the translator's gender on the translations of Ingeborg Bachmann's prose works. She was one of the co-editors of volume 15 of *Norwich Papers* ('The Translator as Writer' 2007) while completing the MA in Literary Translation at the University of East Anglia.

Hiroko Furukawa is a PhD student in Literary Translation at the University of East Anglia, UK. The title of her thesis is 'New Approach to Japanese Translation as Shaper of Gender Ideology: In Search of an "Appropriate" Female Speech.' Her research interests are literary translation, with a particular focus on gender in translation, Japanese women's language as gender ideology, and East/West Exchange. Other articles include 'Representations are Misrepresentations: The Case of Cover Designs of Banana Yoshimoto's *Kitchen*,' '"Fabricated" Feminine Characters: Overemphasised Femininity in the Japanese Translation of *Bridget Jones's Diary* and a Japanese Novel *Kitchen*,' and 'Bridget Jones's Femininity Constructed by Language: A comparison between the Japanese translation of *Bridget Jones's Diary*, and the Japanese subtitle of the film.' She has experience in the fields of journalism and editing books.

Paulina Gąsior is a PhD candidate at the Faculty of Languages and Literatures at the University of Wroclaw, Poland. She is also a holder of a MA in Bilingual Translation (University of Westminster, London). Paulina works as a freelance translator, interpreter and a language teacher. Her research focuses on the cultural aspects of translation, postcolonial translation theories, dichotomies between Eastern and Western Europe and the way they affect the translation processes.

Karla Leticia Guadarrama García is a Tutor in Adult Education teaching Spanish language for adults and a freelance translator from English into Spanish. Her research areas include the translation of poetic metaphor from a cognitive linguistics and cognitive stylistics approach. She holds a BA in English from the University of the State of Mexico, Mexico. She has co-edited a volume of conference proceedings together with Rebecca Hyde Parker.

Rebecca Hyde Parker is a one-to-one Danish language teacher at the University of East Anglia, UK. She has previously been an Associate Tutor at UEA teaching Danish to undergraduates, and prior to that she held a lectureship at the University of Hull where she taught Scandinavian language and culture modules on the BA in Scandinavian Studies programme. She also holds an MA from the University of Hull, UK, in Applied Languages and New Technologies.She has had a number of articles published in the field of Translation Studies, and has also co-edited a volume of conference proceedings together with Karla Guadarrama.

Szu-Wen Kung is currently a PhD candidate in Translation Studies at the University of Newcastle upon Tyne, UK. Her thesis, entitled *Agents and networks in literary translation: A Bourdieusian and Latourian analysis of the translation of Taiwanese literature,* recognizes the shift in the recent research focus from the translator's role to translation as teamwork. It also explores the underresearched aspects of translated Taiwanese literature. More importantly, it informs Translation Studies researchers about a new development in the field, i.e. the usefulness of sociological frameworks, that of the Actor-Network Theory in particular.

Kirsten Malmkjær was lecturer in Modern English Language and MA course tutor at the University of Birmingham, UK, from 1985 until 1989, when she moved to the Research Centre for

English and Applied Linguistics, the University of Cambridge, UK. She directed the Centre's M.Phil. in English and Applied Linguistics until April 1999, when she was appointed Professor of Translation Studies and Head of the Centre for Research in Translation at Middlesex University, UK. Since August 2007 she has been Head of the Department of English, Languages and Philosophy in the School of Arts and Education at Middlesex. She is the author of a number of books and articles on Translation Studies and she co-edits the journal *Target* with Gideon Toury, José Lambert and Lieven D'Hulst.

Agnieszka Pantuchowicz graduated from the University of Silesia, Poland, and presently teaches literary theory, translation and gender studies at the Warsaw School of Social Sciences and Humanities, Poland. She wrote her master's and doctoral theses on contemporary Polish women poets. She has published in the field of literary criticism and translation. Her research interests are Translation Studies, Comparative Literature and Feminist Criticism. Currently she is working on a project concerning gender in Polish translations of contemporary Anglophone literatures. She can be contacted at *apantuchowicz@swps.edu.pl*.

Clive Scott is Professor Emeritus of European Literature at the University of East Anglia, UK, and a Fellow of the British Academy. His principal research interests lie in comparative poetics (*The Poetics of French Verse: Studies in Reading*, 1998; *Channel Crossings: French and English Poetry in Dialogue 1550–2000*, 2002 [awarded the R. H. Gapper Book Prize, 2004]); in literary translation, and in particular the translation of poetry (*Translating Baudelaire*, 2000; *Translating Rimbaud's 'Illuminations'*, 2006); and in photography's relationship with writing (*The Spoken Image: Photography and Language*, 1999; *Street Photography: From Atget to Cartier-Bresson*, 2007). He is at present engaged in the preparation of books on the translation of Apollinaire's poetry, and on the relationship between translation and reading as the source of a writing practice.

When **Elizabeth Thornton** was 9 years old, she preferred poetry's patterns to everything, excepting tabby cats and layered pastries. Since then she has had her fingers in many different pies. As a teenager, she avidly studied mathematics and physics, and nursed a secret passion for Latin. As a college freshman in Phoenix, Arizona, she was a budding young economist – that is, until she learned Ancient Greek and rediscovered good writing. Soon afterwards, she tried to talk translation down to a science. In the process she won a "Sun Angel Award" for research in the humanities, but her theory's wax wings melted when taken too far. After hopscotching along so many different career paths, she has come to suspect that success in this world, much like stealing cattle, works better when you backtrack. Accordingly, she now wrangles ancient languages in Wild West LA, pursuing a PhD at UCLA, USA, in Indo-European Studies and specializing in her first love, Poetics. She has the good fortune of working as a teacher of history, mythology, and most recently, Ancient Greek. Elizabeth thinks Hesiod was right about Memory being the mother of all Muses; to prove his point, she studies ways in which inherited poetic motifs and techniques inform the craft of later wordsmiths. She keeps track of current developments in psycholinguistics: in experimental reaction times, she discerns clues as to what makes poets young and ancient tick. In increasingly sparse spare moments she is a practicing translator, writer, Farsi aficionado and Serbian dictionary "fixer".

Preface

One of the most important questions in the discipline of Translation Studies, or perhaps in any discipline, is this: What is the relationship between theory and practice?

There are many possible forms that answers to this question might take, and it is perhaps helpful to look at such answers as relating to three pairs of opposing issues. Firstly, there are the effects of theory on practice, and the effects of practice on theory. Secondly, there is the opposition between theory as description, and theory as tool. And, thirdly, there are theories of translation, and theories from outside translation.

The first pair is in many ways the most tricky, and seems to go to the heart of what it means to link theory and practice. There is an obvious way of seeing the effect of theory on practice: you take the theory and apply it. But theories cannot always, or even usually, be applied. If a theory is a model, a mental representation of an action or set of actions, incorporating to varying degrees metaphors, ways of seeing, and also explanations, then it is difficult to see what "application" would actually mean. On a very simple level perhaps it just means that we take the picture we have of the world to be a true one and attempt to make our actions match that picture. Often, as Iser (2006: 10) points out, we have to construct a method or strategy based on this mental picture in order to apply it to a real situation. Thus our mental picture of translation might see it as violence, as a mirror, as a veil, as an appropriation, and we might attempt to formulate a method of translation that acts out, or avoids acting out, the details of our view. The converse of this approach is to consider the effects of practice on theory. If we see translation, for example, as something that causes violence to an original text, then consideration of an actual translation will help us to refine our view of the sort of violence that is done. Usually both sides work in tandem. As we try to carry out translations that fulfil our idea of what we think a translation is, we also refine our idea of what a translation is based on what is possible, or what works.

But it should be remembered that translation theories are not only theories of what translation *is*. This is certainly a fundamental question, but in fact many if not most theories take for granted (rightly or wrongly) that we know what it is, and theorize instead particular aspects of it: its ethics, its processes, its effects, its reception, the way it works in a specific culture. The vast majority of theories are partial.

The second pair of opposing ideas is related to the first. If theories describe what we do, how can they be tools? And yet that they can be tools cannot be in doubt once one has read the articles in this volume. In fact they are tools because they are ways of seeing, and ways of seeing affect how we translate. Not only is this true of metaphor-theories (a translation is an act of violence, a pane of glass, a veil) but also of theories about what we do and why: feminist texts need to be translated in certain ways; our view of an Eastern European country will affect how we translate; different views of grammar and style will lead us to judge different translations as closer or more or less literary or more or less acceptable. Because theories like these make us aware of how language works, how cultures work, how literature works, they enable the translator to take more factors into account. In this sense they are not just pictures but also tools.

And then there is the third opposition, between theories from within and from outside Translation Studies. It is striking just how many of the theories discussed here are not actually theories of translation. There are theories of meaning, of language, of style, of gender, just to name the most obvious. None of these originated as translation theories. But in the moment they interact in our minds with views of translation they become translation theories: pictures of aspects of translation.

The papers selected with such care by the editors of this volume give different answers to all the above questions, but one thing that emerges from them all is the ubiquity and the enormous importance of theory. One reason for this is simply that every translator has a theory. It is like gardening. I must have some basic idea of the seasons, of growth, of the soil and plant nutrition, or I will be unable to produce anything beyond weeds. But it is possible to go further. I can learn the constituents of soil and the different theories of its depletion and renewal. I can learn about theories of planting and the phases of the moon. Such theories may be necessary, interesting, useful, or a hindrance, depending on one's point of view. What is clear is that I cannot have no theory. That is not an option. So it is, too, with translation. The minimum requirements of anyone's theory are likely to be to do with what translation is, what it preserves, what it loses, what it is for. From this basis, theories can be built up as they interact with practice, with knowledge, with the theories of other people, with theories from outside translation studies, and with one's own theories about other things: language, culture, reading, meaning, and so on.

Theories constantly change and grow. One consequence of this is that people write books and articles about their own and other people's theories, and translators almost always tell you their theory – perhaps without realizing – in the introductions to their translations. A further consequence is that many of us – students as well as teachers – see the teaching of theory as crucial to the practice of translation and therefore to its teaching. It is only by understanding the complex interplay of theory and practice that we really benefit from studying either. It is only by changing our way of seeing translation that we can change ways of doing it and it is only by engaging with new perspectives that we can enhance the way we see. The clear message of this much-needed book is thus two-fold: theory opens out practice, allowing for innovation and experiment, and theory gives us a richer mental world with which to understand and discuss what we do.

Jean Boase-Beier
University of East Anglia, UK

Acknowledgements

The editors are deeply indebted to Professor Jean Boase-Beier not only for kindly agreeing to write the Preface but also for encouraging us to publish this volume from the outset, as well as for all her invaluable comments on the first drafts of the Introduction. We are also grateful to Gurdeep Mattu, our commissioning editor, for his enthusiasm with regard to this project and Jeremy Munday, our series editor, for his useful advice on the early drafts of the articles. We would particularly like to thank Mr P. Muralidharan, our copy-editor, and Colleen Coalter at Continuum for their support, advice, and patience throughout the editing phase of the book.

In addition, Szu-Wen Cindy Kung would like to thank her supervisors Dr. Dongning Feng at Salford University and Dr. Francis Jones at Newcastle University for their guidance and encouragement in this research project. Likewise, Lina Fisher would like to thank Professor Jean Boase-Beier for her helpful comments, and suggestions for her MA dissertation on which her article is based.

Every effort has been made to trace the copyright holders of the literary extracts reproduced in this book. The editors and publishers would like to thank the following for permission to reproduce copyright material: Maria Nikolaides, daughter of the poet Aristotelis Nikolaides, for permission to reproduce (extracts from) pages 12, 14, 20, 56, 87, 97, 229 of *Collected Poems*, by Aristotelis Nikolaides, and Anastasia Papaditsa for permission to reproduce (extracts from) pages 15, 36, 60, 135, 136, 155, 314 of 'Poetry', by Dimitris Papaditsas.

An earlier version of Chapter 8, 'Network & Cooperation in Translating Taiwanese Literature into English', by Szu-Wen Cindy Kung, first appeared in *Translation Research Projects 2* (Intercultural Studies Group, Universitat Rovira i Virgili), 2009.

Finally, we would like to express our gratitude to all our contributors for their inspiring arguments, thus, enabling us to present readers with a book which, we hope, will motivate them not only to bring fully into their consciousness the mental models lying behind their own practices and theories but also to deliberately enter into a continuous dialogue with other practices and theories and, in so doing, ceaselessly enrich and deepen theory and practice in the field of Translation Studies.

Introduction

Antoinette Fawcett
University of East Anglia, UK
Karla L. Guadarrama García
Independent Scholar, UK

. . . one has to be sensitive to the eternally changing differences that are actually to be observed within each thing, and to the unceasing emergence of new similarities and new relationships across the boundaries of various things.

Bohm 2004a: 124

This book is neither intended to give an overview of theories of translation, nor to be regarded as a handbook of translator training or of good translator practice. There are many books currently available which carry out these tasks admirably and which specifically address themselves to the presentation, description and analysis of several, often competing, theoretical models of translation, or theories which may be brought into translation from outside the discipline, or which prescribe or suggest certain translation methods or approaches to translation (see, for example, Gentzler 1993; Munday 2001; Hermans 2002; Hatim and Munday 2004; Venuti 2004; Snell-Hornby 2006; Heywood et al., 2009). Indeed, the linking and opposition of the two terms 'theory' and 'practice' in Translation Studies is so frequent, either explicitly (e.g. Nida and Taber 1969; Larson 1991; Bassnett and Trivedi 1999; Weissbort and Eysteinsson 2006) or implicitly (Chesterman and Wagner 2002; Robinson 2003), that it is almost a commonplace to argue that translation has both theoretical and practical aspects.

All commonplaces, of course, have their roots in reality and the reality implied by the collocation of these terms in the field of Translation Studies is quite simply the fact that without the actual human practice of translation there would be nothing for the academic to study. Conversely, although the practising translator may see her or his work as primarily an act, a process, a craft or an art, there may also be some awareness of grounds for philosophical and scientific enquiry into that work. Nevertheless, because the academic realm and the realm of translation practice are often, although incorrectly, viewed as being widely separated from each other, the two terms 'theory' and 'practice' may be perceived as polarities, or oppositions between doing and reflecting on doing, or as essential ways of being and thinking which are hostile rather than complementary to each other.

The question as to whether there is truly an opposition between theory and practice, and the further question as to what exactly is meant by the terms 'theory' and 'practice' in the context of Translation Studies, will, however, not be tackled in this introduction, since it is our belief that not only, as already mentioned, are there many other studies which explore these questions, but that it is in the nature of a book such as this one, a collection of essays ranging *around* the topics of theory and practice in translation from a wide spectrum of different perspectives, to leave space for readers to draw their own conclusions.

What we do suggest, however, is that an acquaintanceship with theory, and in particular with a wide range of theories, and not some single master-theory, could become a powerful tool in the hands of translators, giving them insight into the manifold ways in which their practice might be constructed. Such theories may be theories of or about translation, or may be theories from outside the field, brought in to enable both practitioner and scholar to better understand the phenomenon of translation as such. Furthermore, we also wish to suggest that practice itself inevitably will, and should, influence theory. In this respect, translation has always served to break down all apparent dualistic divides, such as those seeming to separate such categories as the creative-critical, self-other, subject-object, I-you. It will inevitably act to depolarize extremes and has the potential to be a force to unite, or, at the least, destabilize apparent opposites. By its nature then translation is interpenetrative and inter-personal, and so is, or should be, any discipline built upon its study.

With these concepts both of interpenetration and depolarization in mind, we move to an exploration of the guiding principle behind this book, which is the notion of dialogue. Dialogue as commonly understood would imply such concepts and activities as conversation, discussion, reflection, and a moving onwards through an exchange of views. In everyday dialogue two or more people have a communicative interchange in which, ideally, both sides influence and are influenced by the other. Such a process would imply that changes would occur to both sides, however subtly or subliminally these might happen.

This commonsense notion of what a dialogue between theory and practice could bring about was part of the initial concept of the present volume and is paralleled by, for example, the interesting and illuminating real-world dialogue which takes place in an earlier book between the academic Andrew Chesterman and the practising translator Emma Wagner (Chesterman and Wagner 2002). In the process of a rather lengthy discussion by e-mail on the relationship between translation theory and translation practice, in which several important themes and issues are aired, the exchange of views clearly leads to change on both sides. Wagner's initial hostility to academics and academic theories is modified by her growing realization that such theories may offer conceptual tools to the translator that are enabling rather than mystifying, whilst Chesterman's assumption of the clear relevance of theory to practice is brought under pressure by his realization that too many scholars 'talk too much to each other rather than to a wider audience' and that Translation Studies should spend more time researching into the work of 'real translators in real action' (Chesterman and Wagner 2002: 136). The present book hopes to extend on these insights not only by offering some examples of such research, but also by developing notions of what a dialogue between theory and practice might actually entail.

Knowledge of the philosophical writings of key thinkers outside the disciplines of language, translation and communication studies may deepen our understanding of the concept of dialogue. The physicist David Bohm (1917–1992), for example, in the small book which brings together many of his important ideas relating to this practice (Bohm 2004b) makes clear the importance of dialogue not only as a way of working towards an understanding of what things as such mean, but also as a method of suspending preconceptions, or ingrained thoughts and attitudes, which over the course of human development have, in his opinion, tended towards the fragmentation of something, a state of affairs or a state of being, which in spite of our misconceptions he views as being essentially whole. This recognition of an underlying wholeness does not, however, imply that different standpoints cannot, or should not, exist, but rather that each point of view, or theory, can be made explicit within a dialogic atmosphere which not only allows each to be seen as an essential part of a greater whole, but also enables the person who enters into dialogue with an open mind to see their own governing thoughts more clearly as they are held up against and contrasted with those of others. The dialogue then, becomes a space in which what is tacit, and therefore possibly dangerously unquestioned or un-theorized, can be brought into some form of explicitness (Bohm 2004b: 16).

In pointing out the etymological basis of the word 'dialogue', Bohm makes it clear that the process of dialogue is not, as may be commonly thought, necessarily a discussion between two opposing or competing parties, but rather that it can be pictured as a *'stream of meaning* flowing among and through us and between us' (Bohm 2004b: 7). *Dialogos* – dialogue – derives from two Greek words: *logos*, 'word,' and *dia* which means, as Bohm points out, 'through' and not 'two', as is commonly misconceived (Bohm 2004b: 6). As can be confirmed by any quick check in a standard English dictionary, the prefix *dia-* certainly does mean 'through' and may also signify 'across', 'during', and 'composed of' (see e.g. *Chambers English Dictionary* 1988). All these meanings – 'through-the-word', 'across-the-word', 'during-the-word', and 'composed-of-the-word' – may be seen as being relevant to the concept lying behind this book which places an implicit emphasis on the process of dialogue as a notion vital to both scholars and practitioners in the field of translation. More than this, we would claim that it is the human need for dialogue which lies behind the act of translation itself, ideally enabling a flow of meaning between languages and cultures that not only helps us to recognize and respect individual difference, but may ultimately perhaps allow us to consciously participate in that unifying and coherent whole which underlies our being in this world.

In order for dialogue to take place we believe that certain basic requirements are necessary. Firstly, that new ideas, or ideas which may at first sight seem to be antagonistic to our own, are both expressed and listened to, with a suspension of preconceived judgements which may stop us from truly hearing what is being said or even tacitly suggested. Secondly, that there is more than one point of view being expressed, that the ideas are not simply statements and re-statements of a dominant discourse, but that new and even challenging voices are heard and accepted for what they can add to the whole (see in this book the essays of, for example, Clive Scott and Elizabeth Thornton). Finally, and perhaps most importantly, that there should be a neutral ground or an open space in which all the elements of the dialogue can be heard. In the case of this book we hope that its design, which is neither that of a progressive single argument, nor that of oppositional debate, will provide that open space into which we invite the reader as a participant.

In asking the reader to consider the interplay between theory and practice as a form of dialogue, we are, therefore, drawing attention to the fact that these apparently different polarities or stances could profitably be viewed as being in continual conversation with each other, whether or not this is consciously acknowledged either by the theorist or the practitioner. In the field of translation a theorist may initially be viewed as someone who stands at some distance from the actual practice of translation but who is concerned with translation in an objective, scholarly fashion. That distance can be derived from deploying theories specifically relating to translation, language or linguistics or by bringing in, for example, philosophical, sociological, historical or psychological theories from the outside. This distinction is clearly and usefully drawn in this volume by Jean Boase-Beier's essay 'Who needs theory?'.

A practitioner, on the other hand, is clearly someone who translates, someone who at first sight may seem to be in no need of the self-awareness which a knowledge of theory provides. According to Douglas Robinson there has been 'a widespread hostility between theorists and translators' in the field of Translation Studies (Robinson 1991: xiii), one which has placed them both in a situation of rift, in which dialogue between the two sides, which he characterizes as one between feeling and thinking, may have seemed to be impossible. The notion of dialogue for Robinson is, therefore, distinct from that of Bohm, in that Robinson conceives of dialogue as a way of healing an internal psychological split between emotion and intellect, which has further split apart into types of personality or modes of operation (the feeler and the thinker, or, for example, the field of action and the field of academe), whilst Bohm's emphasis is on interrogating, challenging and understanding all that is unquestioned and pre-set in both the individual and in the larger culture or cultures. This insight is most succinctly expressed in the special meaning Bohm gives to 'thoughts' and 'felts', which he defines not as present states but as past actions or activities (Bohm 2004b: 60–1). For Bohm, therefore, without the clarification which can occur through the dialogic process we can too easily be dominated by past, inactive mental and emotional models, instead of responding to things as they actually are with present, active thinking and feeling, an insight which places a rather different emphasis on the need for dialogue than Robinson's more romantic vision. Nevertheless, like Bohm, but with specific application to the field of translation, Robinson also stresses that the ideal is to bring different perspectives into proper communication with each other. In Robinson's case the aim is to bring theorists and practitioners in dialogue, since theory and practice in his view need not and should not be 'kept artificially apart' (Robinson 1991: xiii).

In fact, as should become apparent to the readers of this collection, many theorists are also practitioners of translation, as can be seen in the essays written by Boase-Beier, Thornton, Fisher, Calfoglou and Scott, all of whom use their own translation practice either as the basis of comparison with the work of other translators, or to test theories on the ground of actual practice. In the case of both Scott and Thornton it can be said that new and often radical theories actually emerge from that practice. We can see here a process of dialogue which is both internalized and unificatory (the theoretician and the practitioner talk to each other within one and the same person) and outward-reaching (the practitioner-theorist is in contact with the individual reader of this collection and, through subtle channels of influence and ever-widening circles of dialogue, with other translators and scholars in many different parts of the globe).

An exploration of the relationship between theory and practice (as performance, production, experience or political action) is explicitly made in Homi K. Bhabha's influential book *The Location of Culture* (2004). In Chapter 1 of that book, an essay significantly entitled 'The Commitment to Theory', Bhabha advocates a de-polarization of these modes, a recognition not only that both are forms of discourse which exist 'side by side' with each other, but that they are as unified as a single sheet of paper, the 'recto and verso' of each other (Bhabha 2004: 32). Furthermore, Bhabha, although in this chapter primarily speaking of the relationship of politics to theory, expressly describes his concept of in-betweenness or hybridity, as a space in which culture is *translated*, a space where negotiation and interrogation take place, and where difference is ideally both acknowledged and respected, a shifting uncertain ground which nevertheless overlays a common ground of relatedness which is not so much the fact of our common humanity, which Bhabha radically interrogates, but the fact that humans all produce symbolic meaning through language and other media (Bhabha 2004: 32–56). This recognition of the symbolizing nature of human beings, and therefore also of their cultures, is the key to understanding both why the concept of translation is so important for Bhabha and to seeing how these ideas are, as he explicitly acknowledges, a development of his reading of Walter Benjamin's essay 'The Task of the Translator' (Rutherford 1990: 209), which in itself can be considered as one of the founding documents of modern concepts of translation. In other words, without the translation in Bhabha's mind of notions first introduced by Benjamin, that no culture, or language, is 'full unto itself' (Rutherford 1990: 210), the further notion of hybridity and the 'third space' would not, according to Bhabha, have been formulated (Rutherford 1990: 211).

A similar plea for a commitment to theory, but made specifically within the contexts of both philosophy and neurolinguistics, and with the discipline of Translation Studies acting as a Third Space in which other more abstract models of mind and language may find what is missing in their own schemas, is argued for by Kirsten Malmkjaer in this volume. Not only may the dialogue with philosophical theories of meaning and experimental empirical forms of linguistic science enrich the fields of both practice and theory in translation, but, as Malmkjaer both suggests and demonstrates, Translation Studies, with its interest in aspects of translation which are more than just language, could feed a notion of 'what else, apart from translation, is involved in translation'.

The title of this present book, *Translation: Theory and Practice in Dialogue*, has further implications which it may be useful to explore here. The most radical of these is one which has already been hinted at above: that translation itself can be seen as dialogue between theory and practice; in other words, that in this phrase the colon can be read as meaning 'is'. Thus: 'Translation *is* theory and practice in dialogue'. Looking for examples of this concept we can see an overt and conscious advocation of translation as an effective locus of such a dialogue, in, for example, those forms of translation influenced by Lawrence Venuti's concept of foreignization (Venuti 1995: 19–20), itself a development of and a response to notions discussed by German Romantic writers and thinkers, as for instance, Schleiermacher (see Snell-Hornby 2006: 145–7; Schleiermacher 2004: 49). Similarly, strong forms of interventionist feminist translation, such as discussed by Luise von Flotow (1997) and Sherry Simon (1996), present the reader with striking examples of translations which incorporate within them that dialogue between an informing theory and a performing practice.

In the present volume such innovative and renovating modes of translation and translation theory are themselves tested and brought into new dialogues, in order to prevent their radical insights themselves solidifying into new unquestioned norms. Lina Fisher, for example, through a deliberate and practical exploration of the possibilities offered by her own feminist translations of the work of Carol Ann Duffy, discovers that subversion for the sake of subversion may become counter-productive if the target culture reader is thereby shut out of any dialogue with the text. Her stress on the part that the reader will and should play in the (re-)construction of the target text ultimately leads her towards a realization that subtlety of approach, a middle way between a strongly feminist agenda-driven form of translation and an unconscious acceptance of prevailing societal norms, is more likely to create such a dialogue. By contrast, Hiroko Furukawa discovers that in an entirely different culture, that of Japan, the power of an un-theorized, over-feminizing form of translation may be so strong that it helps to construct an image of the female which at one and the same time may create and perpetuate stereotypical models of the feminine, and be at odds with the actual reality of Japanese women's behaviour and language. In effect, Furukawa shows that the lack of real dialogue between translation and developing conditions of reality has allowed older theoretical positions to perpetuate themselves, with a resulting negative and circular influence of the practice of literary writing, in both translational and source modes, on female ways of being and expression.

Thus, we can see that when the fact that translation *is* a dialogue between theory and practice is not fully apprehended it may begin to operate as such at a subconscious or even covert level, a level at which the dialogue may become not so much a stream of meaning through, among and between equal partners, but a one-way flow in which translators, because they are unaware of the nature of the dialogue, become vehicles for passing on in their work unquestioned assumptions about the nature and role of translation. In such a case, an acknowledgement of the part that unconscious theoretical models may play in our practices is needed to raise our awareness. Such a need, for example, has given rise both to radical polemicizing within Translation Studies, such as that initiated by Antoine Berman in his essay 'Translation and the Trials of the Foreign' (Berman 2004: 276–289), and to careful descriptive-analytic case studies, such as those undertaken by Furukawa and by Pauline Gąsior in this volume. The practising translator who is alerted to the several kinds of impoverishments and destructions which can be perpetrated by the act of translation on the source text, as succinctly listed and described by Berman in his essay, or to the way in which stereotypical notions of femininity, domesticity or the foreign may, in the target text, seriously damage the actual nature of the original, will almost certainly come to future practice changed in some way by their dialogue with theory. Even if such a translator continues in the same general mode there will, we contend, be more awareness of the meaning and nature of their actions. This point of view on the role that theory may play dialogically with practice, however, is clearly not a prescriptive one, that is, not one that demands that a translator should and must be conscious of this or that theory in order to be a better translator, since, at any rate, the notion of what a good translation is, or might be, is itself in flux and is subject to contextual conditions. Rather, it implies a recognition of the dynamic nature of human thought and perception which, although always subject to being trapped in the rigid structures of habit, at the same time can always, when placed in that open, neutral space in which contact with other voices may be heard, flow slowly and imperceptibly, or swiftly and dramatically, into change.

The notion that we may be trapped, rather than liberated, both by our own theorizing and an underdeveloped static form of practice, can be related to the concepts of image-schemata and mental modelling current in the Cognitive

Sciences and particularly in Cognitive Linguistics. Work by Lakoff (1987), Lakoff and Johnson (2003; 1999), and Lakoff and Turner (1989) has shown that the specific manner in which we negotiate our experiences in and of the world is always and necessarily motivated by the way in which we conceptualize them, whether consciously or not. Our conceptualizations are, in turn, never merely internal representations of properties inherent in the mental, physical, and socio-cultural worlds that we inhabit but, rather, they emerge from the correlations that we consciously or unconsciously perceive between these properties as we interact with them and with our already existing knowledge, beliefs and values, that is, the cognitive context acquired through our culture and developed individually. Such prior conceptualizations can be so internalized as to give rise to unsound responses to new situations, since it may not be recognized that in such cases we perceive through, or by means of, the mental model, rather than on the basis of what is actually there.

As an example, consider the case of the Yaquis, a group native to the Northern Mexican state of Sonora. After years of resistance to the incursions of the Spanish conquistadors, the Yaquis finally decided to sign a peace agreement in 1615 and to allow the first missionaries into their community. This was because they had seen something completely new to them: a big ship moving on the sea (Benítez 1978: 95). Given their knowledge and beliefs at the time, they could only make sense of this event by attributing tremendous magical powers to the conquistadors. Undoubtedly, the inherent properties of the Spanish ship – its size, its materials, its construction – were crucial for the way in which the Yaquis grasped and handled the experience, but their eventual decision to sign the peace agreement had less to do with the properties of the ship in themselves and more with the way in which their existing body of knowledge, beliefs and values gave conceptual structure to their perception of these properties as they came to interact with them. In this way, previous 'thoughts' and 'felts', to use Bohm's terminology (Bohm 2004b: 60–1), influenced the perception of the Yaquis to such an extent that they could not see what was actually and newly there, but instead acted on the basis of already existing mental models which effectively misinformed them and led them into a trap.

The conceptual structure we give our experiences is, therefore, not completely unconstrained, depending as it does on our cognitive drive to establish a correlation between our cognitive contexts and our perception of the elements and properties that arise from our experiences. Yet, Lakoff (1987), Lakoff and Johnson (2003; 1999) and Lakoff and Turner (1989) also suggest that, precisely because we rely on such perceived correlations, the conceptual structuring of our experience can potentially take a multiplicity of different forms, each giving rise to a mental model that prioritizes certain aspects of the experience at the expense of others. Ultimately, it is on the basis of what our mental models prioritize that we come to discern the attitudes and actions that any given experience requires of us.

It follows from this that the strategies adopted by translators at any given time are necessarily informed by the mental models, or theories, that they consciously or unconsciously bring to bear on the various aspects of their translation experience. Some of these models are entrenched to different degrees in the translators' own cultural environment in the sense that they consistently provide them and members of their culture with a means to understand and successfully negotiate their translation experiences. Behind the often apologetic Western translator's note there quite probably lies, for example, the Augustinian, the Lutheran, or the Romantic paradigm, all of them mental models upon which, according to Robinson (1991: 3–123), the edifice of mainstream Western translation theory can be seen to rest. We strongly depend upon such culturally entrenched models to perceive coherence in our experiences and to act accordingly. But, as has been argued at several points in this introduction, the deeper nature of translation in particular, and of human communication in general, is to be both dynamic and dialogic, to be open to difference, and, in fact, to have the ability to translate concepts, mental models, or schema, between one paradigm and another. A similar idea has been richly explored in, for example, Boothman's 'Translatability between Paradigms', a revealing examination of the way in which Gramsci used the concept of translation to import terms from one schema into another, thus, according to Boothman, distancing himself from a rigid paradigm (Marxism-Leninism) and opening up his own thinking, his theorizing, to outside influences (Boothman 2002: 116).

As we go about the world, therefore, there continuously emerge not only entire domains of experience which we have not encountered before, as when the Yaquis first encountered the Spanish ship, but also aspects of known experiences not accounted for by our existing mental models or inadequately accounted for by these, as when the West became aware of the multiple aspects of the translation experience that had long been misapprehended and neglected by a view that saw translators merely as the passive decoder-encoders of ideal authorial meanings[1].

Insights taken from the field of cognitive linguistics (see, for example, Lakoff 1987; Lakoff and Johnson 2003, 1999; Lakoff and Turner 1989) allow us to understand that when we face these types of situations we are prompted to build new mental models or theories by which to grasp and negotiate the experience in question. And as new mental models add to our existing body of knowledge, beliefs and values, they become, to employ a metaphor used by Boase-Beier (this volume), citing Midgley (2001: 26), 'pairs of spectacles' at our disposal through which we may comprehend and manage new domains of experience, or bring to light hidden aspects of other domains of experience with which we are already familiar, casting a different light on them if the need arises. This is, in effect, the cognitive ability which education serves to develop (Widdowson 1983: 16–20).

What we are suggesting is that as translators deliberately set out to know and comprehend different paradigms, and their deriving theories, they place themselves in the powerful position to bring fully into their consciousness the mental models that underlie their own translation practice and, in so doing, they also place themselves in the equally powerful position of deliberately confirming (as opposed to conforming to), questioning, challenging, modifying, and extending the limits of what they see as possible. It is in this sense that theory can be seen to enhance the resourcefulness, awareness, and reflectiveness that Bernardini (2004: 20–1) sees as necessary skills for the professional translator.

That the individual translator can, and perhaps should, be influenced by a dialogue with theory may be clear. Less obvious may be our claim that the opposite also holds true, that theory is also influenced by practice, although such a claim would be a further truism in fields other than Translation Studies, for example in the sciences where empirical, experimental methods inevitably work towards a moving on and redefinition of theory. Certainly when the reader is faced with the richly playful and acutely self-conscious theorizing of practitioners such as Thornton and Scott in this volume, it may be difficult to see at first sight that it is the practice that is influencing the theory and not, or not only, the other way round. Nevertheless, a dialogic openness to the creative impulses behind both the academic and translation work of these writers will, we feel, reveal their common desire to immerse the reader in a living stream, in which the text maximally engages both the body and the psyche, so that the reader too becomes part of the translation process.

Although a full history of the development of Translation Studies as an independent academic discipline has yet to be written, there are many partial and near-complete accounts of the gradual incorporation of this discipline into the academy, most of which agree in placing its commencement during the 1960s or 1970s (see e.g. Leuven-Zwart and Naaijkens 1991; Weissbort and Eysteinsson 2006; Snell-Hornby 2006; Munday 2008). Most accounts emphasize the leading role that the American writer, translator and academic James S. Holmes played in the development of the discipline and lay particular stress on his 'efforts to give direction' to its future (Leuven-Zwart and Naaijkens 1991: 1)[2]. In the context of the present book, two important aspects of Holmes's work should be noted: firstly, that, as can be seen in *Translated!*, the posthumous book of his papers on Literary Translation and on Translation Studies (Holmes 1988), his theorizing was, as also noted by Leuven-Zwart (Leuven-Zwart and Naaijkens 1991: 8), always rooted in a creative practice; and secondly, that for Holmes neither theory and practice nor pure and applied translation research should be conceived of as being in a hierarchical relationship to each other, but rather in a dialectical one. As Leuven-Zwart emphasizes in her account of Holmes's importance, much as we do in our emphasis on the dialogue between theorists and practitioners, between reader and text, between individual and community, such a relationship at its best is mutual, cooperative and interactive: 'both can flourish only if they feed each other continually' (Leuven-Zwart and Naaijkens 1991: 9).

The decades following on from Holmes' early death in 1986 have witnessed the establishment of Translation Studies as a fully-fledged academic discipline and have seen a concomitant rise in translation research worldwide. A not inconsiderable body of work now exists, for example, on the way in which different theories have modelled translation at different times in different cultures (e.g. Schulte and Biguenet 1992; Robinson 1997; Rose 2000; Gentzler 2001; Overvold et al. 2003; Venuti 2004; Chan 2004; Hung 2005; Weissbort and Eysteinsson 2006; Wang and Sun 2008; Pym 2009), and there is also an impressive number of works that set out to challenge existing paradigms while at the same time offering alternative ones (see Graham 1985; Flotow 1997; Bassnett and Trivedi 1999; Robinson 1991, 2001; Venuti 1992, 1995, 1998; Davis 2001; Bandia 2007). These latter works often draw on a multiplicity of other disciplines, in keeping with the increasing perception of Translation Studies as an 'interdiscipline' (Snell-Hornby 2006: 72). Furthermore, a wide array of printed and electronic international journals provides the scholar and the translator with a variety of platforms to discuss theoretical and methodological issues (e.g. *Target, Meta, Babel, Journal of Translation, New Voices in Translation Studies, Skase*) and year after year an equally wide number of international and interdisciplinary conferences, symposia and online discussion groups enable specialists to exchange ideas, establish collaboration networks, strengthen existing lines of enquiry and pursue new ones.

This ceaseless activity in Translation Studies has been paralleled by a noticeable increase in the number of undergraduate and postgraduate programmes aimed at the training of professional literary and non-literary translators in universities across the world[3]. Although, as noted by Schäffner and Adab (2000: vii), such programmes actually began to be offered by some European and American universities in the 1940s, their number has expanded only relatively recently, largely in response to the present day explosion of cultural, economic, and political relations as a result both of globalization and of improvements in communication technology. As pointed out by Michael Cronin in his book *Translation and Globalization* such an increase, both of the practice of translation and of the programmes which produce translators, brings with it the possibility of a stronger understanding not only of the phenomenon of translation itself, but also of the socio-technological processes of globalization and of the opposing counter-movements of anti-globalization. Cronin conceives of translation, and translators, as playing a mediating role between such forces, and therefore as having a vital role to play in developing 'contemporary self-understanding' (Cronin 2003: 1). As he stresses, 'Translation is rarely suited to the binary reductionism of polemic' (ibid.), once again placing an emphasis on the dialogic nature of translation, and by implication, Translation Studies, as such.

This is why we have come to the conclusion that instead of announcing yet another turn within the discipline, such as the 'cultural turn' predicted and promoted by Bassnett and Lefevere's influential books (1990, 1998), or the interdisciplinary turn of the 1990s (Snell-Hornby 2006: 72), or the 'sociological' turn associated in particular with the application of Bourdieusian theories to Translation Studies (see e.g. Merkle 2008: 175–7) or the 'creative turn' advocated by Nikolaou (2006), or the 'cognitive' turn (strongly signalled in works such as Tabakowska 1993), we would rather suggest that each turn (or shift in model), in keeping with our emphasis on dialogue, provides different but equally valid approaches to the study and practice of translation. In fact, we believe that a dialogic approach to the variety of such models enriches and deepens the field as a whole, and that it is not particularly beneficial to view these theoretical standpoints in either an evolutionary or revolutionary manner. The hidden metaphor of the 'turn', instead of denoting a total and complete paradigm-shift which makes it impossible to continue to work with the previous paradigm, as in the pure sciences (Kuhn 1962), may be viewed rather as a figure in a circle-dance or as dynamic movement within a choral ode. Then it can be seen that a 'turn' will inevitably be followed by its 'counter-turn', and that neither cancel the other out, but that both come to rest in the still quiet of the 'stand', where breath is gathered, where movement briefly stops. In other words, rather than proposing a Darwinian model in which each 'turn' both subsumes and supersedes what has preceded it, we propose that several schools of thought or modes of operation within and without the discipline of Translation Studies may not only profitably co-exist but that aspects of each may, and indeed already do, inform and support the other (cf. Snell-Hornby 2006).

There is, however, one turn, or important theoretical position, we have not yet fully explored, which in the light of the dialogic focus of this present volume would be an unpardonable omission. Douglas Robinson in his work *The Translator's Turn* (1991) was already laying emphasis on many of the concepts which have come to seem absolutely vital to a realistic understanding of the physical basis for translation in the body of the translator and hence not only of the translator's dialogic interaction between source-text and target-culture reader, but also of the dialogic interplay between previous paradigms of translation and the translator's own model. That kind of interplay is what we also suggest may form the most fruitful way of looking at the relationship between theory and practice, between turn and turn, between theory and theory and between reader and text. For whether we draw on existing mental models or create new ones, the conceptual structure through which we comprehend and negotiate our experiences is necessarily grounded in the correlations that we perceive between, on the one hand, the properties and dimensions of the mental, physical, and socio-cultural worlds that we inhabit as we interact with them and, on the other, our existing body of knowledge, beliefs and values. From this perspective, our mental models and our experiences simultaneously shape and are shaped by one another. It is, therefore, to this interdependence between our mental models and our experiences that the 'dialogue' in the title of this book, in part, alludes and on the basis of which its sections have been organised.

The structure of this book and some models of the dialogue between theory and practice

The parts of this book are intended to help the reader to enter into a dialogue which we can imagine both as existing between the different authors of the essays and as a dialogue between each individual author and the theories which they either draw on or reject.

Parts I and II we have conceived as being composed of essays in which their authors have been informed by the listening aspects of a dialogue. In turn, this listening to theory generates a second dialogue in which practice is in conversation with theory and in which the practitioner is in conversation with their own practice. In this way, practice is both modified by theory and in turn feeds back into theory to modify and change it. This interplay between theory and practice is illustrated in Figure 1, a micro-model which shows how mind, text and theory are in constant and complex dialogue with each other.

Contributors to these parts set out to explore the ways in which theories from outside the field of Translation Studies can be consciously brought to

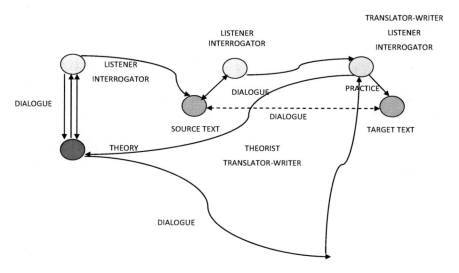

Figure 1 Model 1 is a micro-model – it shows how mind, text and theory are in constant and complex dialogue with each other

bear on literary translation practice and, as a result, help literary translators to organise their priorities and inform their strategies (Boase-Beier, Fisher, Thornton and Calfoglou) or even lead them to a complete re-conceptualization of their practice (Scott and Pantuchowicz). Some of the theoretical backgrounds interrogated and made use of here range from cognitive stylistics (Boase-Beier), to feminist and gender theories of translation (Fisher and Pantuchowicz), to rhetoric and cognitive linguistics (Thornton) and generative linguistics in the form of Optimality Theory (Calfoglou). Scott, on the other hand, rather than using one specific theoretical background from which to listen to and interrogate both theory and practice, brings a radical, personalized element to his insistence that the act of translation is both performative and readerly, and that we should see such an act as a translation *into* the literary, rather than as a translation of the already literary.

Part III has been conceived as a form of dialogue in which scholars in the field of Translation Studies are, as it were, in conversation both with source and target texts and with current discourses in the field. This can be illustrated by Figure 2, a micro-macro model which shows how individual research can be situated between source and target cultures, languages, texts and theories, is influenced by both, and is potentially influential to both. This is explored from the perspective of three researchers from very different source culture traditions: the Eastern European; the Sino-Taiwanese; and the Japanese.

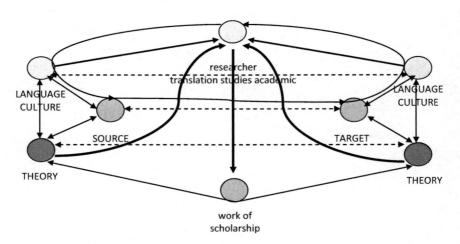

Figure 2 Model 2 is a micro-macro model – it shows the way in which individual research dialogues with both theory and the source and target languages, cultures and texts, and how potential lines of influence might flow between them

The contributors to this part of the book set out to unveil the mental models behind the translation and the metatextual strategies of the Target Text against the context of asymmetrical relationships of power between source and target culture (Gąsior and Kung) or within the translating culture itself (Furukawa). In so doing, they manage to bring into focus what current discourses in Translation Studies have failed to address (Furukawa) and question the validity of some of their premises (Gąsior and Kung).

Part IV does not offer a conclusion to the two forms of dialogue between theory and practice in the previous parts but instead asks the reader to return to basics, to examine the need for a philosophy of translation in Translation Studies and, conversely, the need for the insights provided by Translation Studies to disciplines such as Philosophy and Linguistics, by which such disciplines can, as it were, be made to talk to each other. Malmkjær's chapter attempts to arrive at a basic understanding of translation that empowers the translation theorist and the translation practitioner to challenge the view that sees translation as an impossible enterprise. Our view of the dialogic implications of this chapter is illustrated in Figure 3, a macro-model in which it is shown how the discipline of Translation Studies can add texture to theories which might otherwise be perceived as being separate from its concerns.

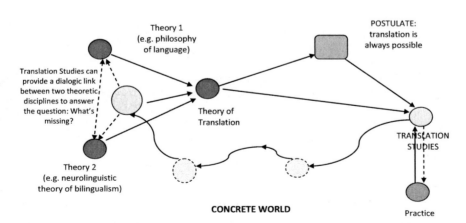

Figure 3 Model 3 is a macro-model showing how translation studies interacts with both the concrete and abstract worlds, how it can add texture to theory, filling in missing elements because of its privileged knowledge of specific practices

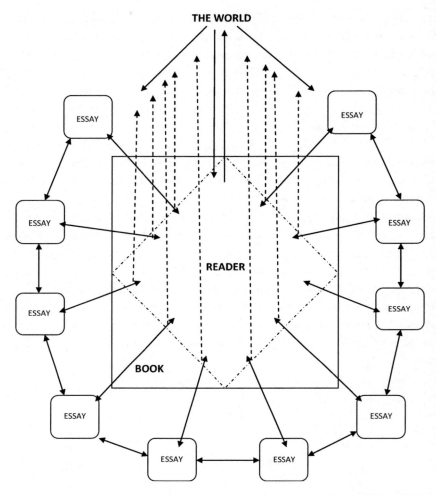

Figure 4 Model 4 imagines reading both as a form of dialogue and as an actualization of the book in the real world. Until the reader reads the book and enters into a dialogue with it, and with each text or essay within it, it does not exist in anything more than potential. The central space in such a dialogue is, therefore, both the book itself and the mind of the reader. This is also the space where the dialogue between theory and practice will translate itself into real and unpredictable actualities

Finally, as we have stressed from the outset in our vision of this book, the reader too may be conceived of as forming an essential element in the dialogue. We believe that readers will inevitably configure their own constellations of meaning from those presented in this volume, and will then take those meanings into the world outside the text, thereby further modifying existing structures and even this book itself. We offer a model in Figure 4, therefore, which is that of the open space in which the reader is both affected by and affects the dialogues which take place.

This book, in its emphasis on dialogue, does not attempt a cancellation or suppression of difference, but is an invitation to see and hear those differences in articulation, to hold them in suspense in order to perceive them clearly for what they are. It admits contradictions and ambivalences, as well as the impossibility of determining clear boundaries between theory and practice, between the world and the text.

The contributors and the editors hope that the reader of this book will find in its chapters not only an informative source but also a motivation to bring fully into their consciousness the mental models behind their own practices or theories and to confirm, question, challenge, modify, and extend the limits of what they see as possible.

Notes

1. When did the West become aware of this? We would argue that this awareness is still ongoing but that its roots lie in the development of the academic disciplines of language, linguistics and communication studies, and, in particular, of Translation Studies, in the second half of the twentieth century. We have already pointed to important specific examples of scholars who have played a role in changing and developing common perceptions of translation, including Lawrence Venuti, Sherry Simon and Luise von Flotow. Further examples are discussed throughout our introductory essay.

2. This is not to devalue the pioneering role of Eugene Nida in the development of translation theory, but simply to point out that the acceptance of Translation Studies as a discipline in its own right can be dated, generally speaking, to the late 1960s / early 1970s. Nida's work, and that of other scholars in linguistics and literary theory, can be seen as paving the way for, and then being incorporated into, the discipline of Translation Studies. As pointed out by Susan Bassnett-McGuire in *Translation Studies*, itself 'an attempt to demonstrate that Translation Studies is indeed a discipline in its own right' (1991: 1), the 'systematic study of translation is still in swaddling bands' (ibid.).

3. Consider, for example, the facts and figures presented by universities from all over Europe in the 2009 European Masters' in Translation Conference held by the European Commission in Brussels, http://ec.europa.eu/dgs/translation/external_relations/universities/emt_conference2009_en.htm. See also Caminade and Pym 1998: 284.

Bibliography

Bandia, Paul F. (2007) *Translation as Reparation: Writing and Translation in Postcolonial Africa*, Manchester: St Jerome.

Bassnett, Susan and Trivedi, Harish (eds) (1999) *Post-colonial Translation: Theory and Practice*, London; New York: Routledge.

Bassnett, Susan and Lefevere, André (1998) *Constructing cultures: Essays on Literary Translation*, Clevedon: Multilingual Matters.

Bassnett, Susan and Lefevere, André (eds) (1990) *Translation, History and Culture*, London: Pinter.

Bassnett-McGuire, Susan (1991) *Translation Studies (Revised Edition)*, London; New York: Routledge.

Benítez, F. (1978) *Lázaro Cardenas y la Revolución Mexicana, El Cardenismo*, México: Fondo de Cultura Económica.

Benjamin, Walter (trans. Harry Zohn) (2004) 'The Task of the Translator: An Introduction to the Translation of Baudelaire's *Tableaux Parisiens*', in Lawrence Venuti (ed.) *The Translation Studies Reader (Second Edition)*, New York; London: Routledge, 253–63.

Berman, Antoine (trans. Lawrence Venuti) (2004) 'Translation and the Trials of the Foreign', in Lawrence Venuti (ed.) *The Translation Studies Reader (Second Edition)*, New York; London: Routledge, 276–89.

Bernardini, S. (2004) 'The Theory Behind the Practice: Translator Training or Translator Education?' in K. Malmkjær (ed.) *Translation in Undergraduate Degree Programmes*, Amsterdam; Philadelphia: John Benjamins, 17–29.

Bhabha, Homi K. (2004) *The Location of Culture*, London; New York: Routledge.

Bohm, David (2004a) *On Creativity*, London; New York: Routledge.

Bohm, David (2004b) *On Dialogue*, London; New York: Routledge.

Boothman, Derek (2002) 'Translatability between Paradigms: Gramsci's Translation of Crocean Concepts', in Theo Hermans (ed.) *Crosscultural Transgressions: Research Models in Translation Studies II: Historical and Ideological Issues*, Manchester, UK; Northampton, MA: St Jerome Publishing, 103–19.

Caminade, Monique and Pym, Anthony (1998) 'Translator-Training Institutions', in M. Baker (ed.) *Routledge Encyclopedia of Translation Studies*, London; New York: Routledge, 280–5.

Chambers English Dictionary (1988) Edinburgh; Cambridge; New York; Melbourne; W. and R. Chambers Ltd and Cambridge University Press.

Chan, Tak-hung L. (2004) *Twentieth-century Chinese Translation Theory: Modes, Issues and Debates*, Amsterdam; Philadelphia: John Benjamins.

Chesterman, Andrew and Wagner, Emma (2002) *Can Theory Help Translators?* Manchester, UK; Northampton, MA: St Jerome Publishing.

Cronin, Michael (2003) *Translation and Globalization*, London: Routledge.

Davis, Kathleen (2001) *Deconstruction and Translation*, Manchester, UK; Northampton, MA: St Jerome Publishing.

Flotow, Luise von (1997) *Translation and Gender: Translating in the Era of Feminism*, Manchester: St Jerome Publishing.

Gentzler, Edwin (2001) *Contemporary Translation Theories,* Second Edition, Toronto; Sydney: Multilingual Matters.

Gentzler, Edwin (1993) *Contemporary Translation Theories,* London: Routledge.

Graham, Joseph F. (1985) *Difference in Translation,* Ithaca, NY: Cornell University Press.

Hatim, Basil and Munday, Jeremy (2004) *Translation: An Advanced Resource Book,* London; New York: Routledge.

Hermans, Theo (ed.) (2002) *Crosscultural Transgressions: Research Models in Translation Studies II: Historical and Ideological Issues,* Manchester, UK; Northampton, MA: St Jerome Publishing.

Heywood, Louise, Thompson, Michael and Hervey, Sándor (2009) *Thinking Spanish Translation: A Course in Translation Method: Spanish to English.*

Holmes, James S. (1988) *Translated! Papers on Literary and Translation Studies,* Amsterdam: Rodopi.

Hung, Eva (2005) *Translation and Cultural Change: Studies in History, Norms and Image Projection,* Amsterdam: John Benjamins.

Kuhn, Thomas S. (1962) *The Structure of Scientific Revolutions,* Chicago, IL; London: University of Chicago Press.

Lakoff, George (1987) *Women, Fire and Dangerous Things: What Categories Reveal about the Mind,* Chicago, IL; London: University of Chicago Press.

Lakoff, George and Mark Johnson (2003) *Metaphors We Live By,* Second Edition, Chicago, IL; London: University of Chicago Press.

Lakoff, George and Mark Johnson (1999) *Philosophy in the Flesh: The Embodied Mind and its Challenge to Western Thought,* New York: Basic Books.

Lakoff, George and Mark Turner (1989) *More than Cool Reason: A Field Guide to Poetic Metaphor,* Chicago, IL; London: University of Chicago Press.

Larson, Mildred L. (ed.) (1991) *Translation: theory and practice, tension and interdependence* (American Translators Association scholarly monographs, 5), Binghampton, NY: State University of New York.

Leuven-Zwart, Kitty. M. van and Naaijkens, Ton (1991) *Translation Studies: The State of the Art: Proceedings of the First James S. Holmes Symposium on Translation Studies,* Amsterdam; Atlanta, GA: Rodopi.

Merkle, Denise (2008) 'Translation Constraints and the "Sociological Turn" in Literary Translation Studies', in Anthony Pym, Miriam Shlesinger and Daniel Simeoni (eds) *Beyond Descriptive Translation Studies: Investigations in Homage to Gideon Toury,* Amsterdam; Philadelphia: John Benjamins, 175–186.

Midgley, Mary (2001) *Science and Poetry,* London: Routledge.

Munday, Jeremy (2008) *Introducing Translations Studies: Theories and Applications,* London: Routledge.

Munday, Jeremy (2001) *Introducing Translation Studies,* London: Routledge.

Nikolaou, Paschalis (2006) 'Notes on Translating the Self', in Manuela Perteghella and Eugenia Loffredo (eds) *Translation and Creativity: Perspectives on Creative Writing and Translation Studies,* London; New York: Continuum, 19–32.

Nida, Eugene A. and Taber, Charles R. (1969) *The Theory and Practice of Translation,* Leiden: E. J. Brill.

Overvold, Angelina E., Priebe, Richard K. and Tremaine, Louis (2003) (eds) *The Creative Circle: Artist, Critic and Translator in African Literature,* Trenton, N.J: Africa World Press.

Perteghella, Manuela and Loffredo, Eugenia (eds) (2006) *Translation and Creativity: Perspectives on Creative Writing and Translation Studies*, London; New York: Continuum.

Pym, A. (2009) *Exploring Translation Theories*, New York; London: Routledge.

Pym, Anthony, Shlesinger, Miriam and Simeoni, Daniel (eds) (2008) *Beyond Descriptive Translation Studies: Investigations in Homage to Gideon Toury*, Amsterdam; Philadelphia: John Benjamins.

Robinson, Douglas (2003) *Becoming a Translator: An Introduction to the Theory and Practice of Translation*, London; New York: Routledge.

Robinson, Douglas (2001) *Who translates?: Translator Subjectivities Beyond Reason*, Albany, NY: State University of New York Press.

Robinson, Douglas (1997) *Western Translation Theory: from Herodotus to Nietzsche*, Manchester: St Jerome Publishing.

Robinson, Douglas (1991) *The Translator's Turn*, Baltimore, MD; London: Johns Hopkins University Press.

Rose, Marilyn Gaddis (ed.) (2000) *Beyond the Western Tradition: Translation Perspectives XI*, Binghampton: Center for Research in Translation.

Rutherford, Jonathan (1990) 'The Third Space: Interview with Homi Bhabha', in Jonathan Rutherford (ed.) *Identity: Community, Culture, Difference*, London: Lawrence and Wishart, 207–21.

Schäffner, Christina and Adab, Beverley J. (eds) (2000) *Developing Translation Competence*, Amsterdam: John Benjamins.

Schleiermacher, Friedrich (trans. Susan Bernofsky) (2004) 'On the Different Methods of Translating', in Lawrence Venuti (ed.) *The Translation Studies Reader (Second Edition)*, New York and London: Routledge, 43–63.

Schulte, R. and Biguenet J. (1992) *Theories of Translation: An Anthology of Essays from Dryden to Derrida*, Chicago; London: University of Chicago Press.

Simon, Sherry (1996) *Gender in Translation: Cultural Identity and the Politics of Transmission*, London: Routledge.

Snell-Hornby, Mary (2006) *The Turns of Translation Studies: New Paradigms or Shifting Viewpoints?*, Amsterdam; Philadelphia: John Benjamins.

Tabakowska, Elżbieta (1993) *Cognitive Linguistics and Poetics of Translation*, Tübingen: G. Narr.

Venuti, Lawrence (ed.) (2004) *The Translation Studies Reader (Second Edition)*, London: Routledge.

Venuti, Lawrence (1998) *The Scandals of Translation: Towards an Ethics of the Difference*, London; New York: Routledge.

Venuti, Lawrence (1995) *The Translator's Invisibility*, Abingdon, UK; New York: Routledge.

Venuti, Lawrence (ed.) (1992) *Rethinking Translation: Discourse, Subjectivity, Ideology*, London; New York: Routledge.

Wang, Ning and Sun, Yifeng (eds) (2008) *Translation, Globalisation and Localisation: A Chinese Perspective*, Clevedon: Multilingual Matters.

Weissbort, Daniel and Eysteinsson, Ástráður (2006) *Translation: Theory and Practice: A Historical Reader*, Oxford: Oxford University Press.

Widdowson, Henry G. (1983) *Learning Purpose and Language Use*, Oxford: Oxford University Press.

Part I
Knowing Why We Do What We Do

Who Needs Theory?

Jean Boase-Beier

University of East Anglia, UK

Chapter Outline

1. What is theory and how does it affect practice?

One way in which theory can be useful for translators is that it encourages a certain amount of freedom from too narrow a view of the source text and this can be an aid to creativity. I discussed this possibility in an earlier article (see Boase-Beier 2006b), and explored how translation theory can enable us to go beyond a naïve, unquestioning view of translation as involving an unspecified but obvious equivalence to the source text.

Things that are unspecified do not always give freedom: we have a tendency to go for the safe and obvious. Theory, on the other hand, can give us the confidence to try out other methods, explore other types of equivalence, or question degrees of closeness. In this chapter I want to take up again the issue of how theory interacts with practice, how we use it, and whether we need it.

The short answer to the last question, and the question in the title of this article, is that everyone needs theory, because any act which is not a reflex or purely the result of intuition (and perhaps even then) must be based on a theory, which is simply a way of looking at the world (cf. Gutt 2005: 15).

When I walk carefully over an icy patch on the pavement, carrying on my back a heavy rucksack filled with marked students' essays, I walk in a way which seems, to my mind, in my view of the world, to take into account the new centre of gravity lent me by the rucksack, the degree of slipperiness of the pavement, the readiness of my muscles to counteract a sudden slide of my soles, and so on. It is, of course, only a partial theory. It is unlikely to take account of the degree of friction between the soles and ice, and the adjustments I make for the weight of the essays or the slope of the pavement will only be approximations. But if I had no theory at all, because I had never met an icy pavement or never carried a rucksack before, then it would be much more difficult to act and I might hesitate, uncertain how to proceed. So the theory helps, but I need to remember that it is partial, built up out of experience and the way each new experience makes me adjust my mental picture of the world. If I apply the same theory when the road is not icy as when it is, or when carrying a child in my arms as when carrying a bag on my back, I will fall.

A theory is a partial description (mental or perhaps written down) of a segment of perceived reality, and so the attempt to apply it to any new situation has to be approached with extreme caution. This is especially true in the humanities, according to Iser (2006: 5–7), who maintains that theories here do not embody laws that make predictions, but rather search for metaphors adequate to the description of the phenomena in question in order to understand them. Furthermore, he makes a distinction between those theories that can be applied and those that cannot. Similarly, Andrew Chesterman argues in his interview with Emma Wagner (Chesterman and Wagner 2002), that it is a mistake to assume that theories can be directly applied because in fact their job is to describe, not to prescribe. If we take this view, we might say that the only reason to apply a theory in the humanities is to test the theory itself against the phenomena it describes. Thus the critical readings in a book like Castle's *The Blackwell Guide to Literary Theory* (2007), for example, could be seen to tell us a great deal about the usefulness of each theory as a description of how we read a literary text, but they might not be expected to tell us anything new about the texts themselves, or about how to read them.

Within the discipline of Translation Studies, an understanding of theory as essentially descriptive, and the descriptive practices that go with this understanding, form the basis for the type of approach known as Descriptive Translation Studies (see e.g. Toury 1995). This type of approach is especially concerned with observing what people do and documenting it. But theory that is descriptive generally aims to explain as well as to describe; for this reason Toury refers to work done within Descriptive Translation Studies as 'descriptive-explanatory' (1995: 15). And it is because of this explanatory function of theories, even in the humanities, that they affect the way we approach tasks in the particular area that has been explained. They become part of our cognitive context, of what we know and think about a particular area, so that they act as what Mary Midgley calls 'pairs of spectacles through which to see the world differently' (2001: 26; see also Culler 1997: 4). Thus structuralist theories of the text allowed us to see literary texts as sets of relationships within the text and with 'large abstract issues' (Barry 2002: 41) in the world outside the text; post-structuralist theories (though 'not theories', according to Iser 2006: ix) have taken the notion of relationship and difference further, and have helped us see to what extent the text might be free from the real world's context and the author's intention (cf. Barry 2002: 66); theories of the reader (such as those by Fish 1980 and Iser 1974) helped us to focus on the reader as part of the context of a literary work; and cognitive poetic theories (e.g. Stockwell 2002) have allowed us to see the reader's mind as part of the context and the context as itself in the mind. Because theories teach us that there are different ways of seeing, knowledge of theory makes us more able to question conventional views. Thus, for example, Toury's distinction between adequacy and acceptability made it clear that we can view a translated text in relation to its source text or in relation to the receiving culture, and that those two relationships will be different.

Because, then, theories are partial, descriptive, and represent different ways of seeing, they should enable us to free ourselves from naïve conceptions of what translation is. And because they are explanatory they become part of the way we approach the world in a very practical sense. They may not dictate practice, but they will certainly influence it.

So how do we assess whether their influence on translation practice is good or bad, whether it narrows or broadens? I would argue that the danger of naïve application, which treats theoretical description as though it had the status of a law, is less acute with theories from outside the area in question. A theory of translation is potentially more dangerous to translation practice than a theory of meaning, of literature, of the text, or of the reader. This is especially true when that theory is based on a metaphor: translation is like performing on a stage, like melting and re-freezing an ice cube, translations are windows, not veils; these are metaphors used by Willard Trask (Honig 1985: 14), Margaret Sayers Peden (1989: 13) and Eavan Boland (2004: 11) respectively. The purpose of such a metaphor, according to Iser is that it 'triggers associations' (2006: 6). It is therefore a starting point for further theories, a partial view which tells us something, but not everything, about the process it refers to. But unfortunately it is extremely tempting to try and actually carry out a translation that conforms to whatever partial view of the act such metaphors suggest. This temptation, and the nature of translation metaphors like those given above, which suggest its effects are not radical or interesting, are some of the reasons for much of the disquiet felt by translation critics such as Venuti (2008) or Berman (2000), who feel that the invisibility of the act and its agent has become written into the performance.

If, however, the theories we use are theories of the text, such as Halliday and Hasan's (1976) theory of coherence discussed by Malmkjaer (2005: 134–45), or of communication, such as the relevance theory of Sperber and Wilson, discussed by Gutt (2000), or of reading, such as the reader-response theory integrated into Díaz-Diocaretz' (1985) approach to translation, then the danger of an encompassing, simplistic application is automatically reduced.

2. The limits of the window metaphor

Venuti (1995: 1) criticises American translator Norman Shapiro for suggesting that 'a good translation is like a pane of glass' (Kratz 1986: 27), in that it does not attract attention to itself. As Venuti goes on to suggest in this book and later in his 1998 book, one danger of such an approach is that, as the act of translation disappears, so the 'foreignness of foreign cultures' (1998: 189) is obscured.

Venuti has done an enormous service to translation theory by linking the notion of 'transparency' (1998: 12) to ethics. Making the translated text read like a text originally written in the target language can today no longer be viewed as a merely linguistic issue, if indeed it ever was. Venuti spoke his warnings more than ten years ago, and foreignization has become part of the discourse of Translation Studies. When I formulated the introduction to my series

Visible Poets in 2000 (see, for example, Elsworth 2000), I argued that aiming not to hide but to reveal the original poems should also 'render visible the translator's task', thus suggesting that the window metaphor, if not subjected to scrutiny, is a dangerous half-truth. My words, and the title of the series, were in part a response to Venuti's warning.

I am not convinced, though, that the practice of translation has been very good at taking on board the notion of the foreignness of the translated text and perhaps it never will. It is certainly true that we have generally become less wary of talking about translation, and we have become more accepting of alternative renditions, especially in poetry. For example, in the ten years between 1997 and 2007, there appeared at least five new editions of Rilke's poems, by different translators, as well as the 2007 *Agenda* issue devoted to translations and discussions of Rilke's work. This suggests a view of translations as alternative rather than definitive versions. And yet, though this looks hopeful, it still seems to be the case that theory has too often been ignored by practitioners or has been somewhat naïvely applied.

Don Paterson, for example, in the 'Appendix' to his 2006 translation of Rilke's *Sonnets to Orpheus*, distinguishes something he calls a 'version' from a 'translation', thus suggesting that a translation is not a version, but rather something that aims for 'the smooth elimination of syntactic and idiomatic artefacts from the original tongue'; something, then, that aims to achieve elegance rather than poeticity of style, that does not aim to be a poem in its own right (p. 73). This is not a view of translation that is easily recognisable to scholars of translation today, as we have seen, nor does it reflect what translators think they do. Connolly, for example, in his 'Preface' to his translations of Kondos (2003), speaks of the 'intrinsic poetic quality' the translation must have, and Terry comments on the importance to him of other poets hearing his translations so they could tell him if he had 'produced a good poem in English' (2004). It should be noted that both these translators, like the many others in the *Visible Poets* series, have subscribed to the view that they must both reflect the foreignness of their original poet *and* write a good poem themselves. Such poet-translators appear, therefore, to be writing something they regard as a translation, but which contains many characteristics of what Paterson calls a version, something Paterson would no doubt regard as an attempt to 'serve two masters' (2006: 74). Paterson's view of translation – his theory – has the virtue of making a neat distinction between two different processes. But the extent to which this theory would be accepted by most good translators or most contemporary theorists is open to question.

Eavan Boland in her 'Preface' to *After Every War: Twentieth-Century Women Poets* (2004), takes a different approach, saying that she tries 'to be as faithful as possible to the original text', not to 'add anything', to create translations which are 'windows, not veils' (2004: 11). By contrasting the window image with that of a veil, I presume she means that she aims for two-way vision: the original poem can look out but the reader can also still see it. Understood in terms of a foreignizing approach, there might seem to be nothing wrong with this. Understood in terms of the invisibility of the act of translation, one would have to say that, if this is Shapiro's window, or pane of glass, then the window and the veil inevitably become the same: if the act of translation is invisible, if it has added nothing, then the original is lost to view, just because the original was a poem, and the result will not be.

Part of the problem is the inherent contradiction in the window metaphor, that becomes evident if you do try to apply it. If you foreignize in the sense that you allow the foreign text to be visible in your translation, then your translation is a window. And this causes exactly that invisibility of the translation against which Venuti argues. The way out of the contradiction is to remind oneself that Venuti never says that foreignization is a mimetic process, in which the translation does nothing and is nothing, so that the text somehow appears as it was in the source language. He goes to great lengths to explain that he is talking about experimental writing that signals 'the linguistic and cultural differences of the foreign text' (1995: 311). Windows and veils will not help us here: they are simply irrelevant. What is needed is an approach that sees translation as art, and thus by nature not mimetic (or only in certain aspects). The way to truly make us aware of the original is to transform it.

It is surprising how often Venuti's foreignizing is taken to mean mimicry of the foreign text. If we take it in its intended meaning of experimental rewriting (see Venuti 2008: 18–20), it allows all the elements of alienation in the target text to come into play. Foreignization or defamiliarization in this sense derives directly from the *ostranenie* of Russian Formalist critic Shklovsky (1965: 4: 13ff.). The target text is foreignized, and in being foreignized does justice to the foreignness of the source text. But what *is* the foreignness of the source text? Beyond the simple fact that it is in a foreign language, it has special elements that characterize its particular type of defamiliarization as a literary text that differs from all the other texts in its source culture. We still need something to help us decide what the source text does and how it does it.

Rather, then, than focus on what translation is, lest we fall into the trap of trying to translate in a way that satisfies that view, we should, I argue, focus on the style of the text. It is this that will allow us to understand how texts in general work, how the particular text to be translated works, and also how the translated text works.

3. A theory of poetic style and its effects on translation

I argue that the focus should be on the style of the text both from a concern for the communicative function of literature – how it says what it says – and from a concern to distance myself from an essentialist view of the nature of a literary work. The problem with such a view, which maintains that there is something intrinsic to the form of literary texts which makes them literary, is that it has been repeatedly shown to be false. Many works in stylistics, from Fowler (1996) to Simpson (2004) have illustrated this. Metaphors occur in advertisements as much as in novels, and ambiguity will play as great a role in politics as in poetry. There will be senses in which literary language tends to differ from non-literary, but these are merely tendencies, to do with the main difference, which is one of style.

Style is not a set of formal features, but it is those elements of the text the reader takes to represent the attitude or state of mind of the reconstructed figure of the author, narrator, or character. It is the style of the text that indicates how it is to be read, and literary reading does differ from non-literary reading, as a number of studies (e.g. Miall and Kuiken 1998) have shown. Taking a cognitive view of style, which is the view that we can relate stylistic choices in a text with the structure of the mind and its processes (cf. Semino and Culpeper 2002: ix), we can say that reading a text as literary involves making the following assumptions about its style:

- it conveys attitude and cognitive state and these will be more important sources of meaning than reference
- it allows the reader to create meaning out of the text
- it affects the mind of the reader by changing her or his views, adding to knowledge, giving new ways of seeing, causing consternation or puzzlement and creating the need to search for meaning
- it goes beyond the text to include cognitive context
- it is as much constituted by connotation, suggestion, implicature and absence as by what is actually and obviously there.

It would be quite impossible to apply such a theory of style directly to an act of translation. However, it is a theory which will help determine priorities, will indicate a way into an understanding of the text, will suggest that some methods of translation are better than others, and will, inevitably, also have its own limitations.

Let me illustrate by attempting a translation of the following poem by Ingeborg Bachmann:

Botschaft
1. Aus   der leichenwarmen   Vorhalle   des   Himmels tritt   die Sonne.
   out-of the corpse-warm ante-chamber of-the heaven steps   the   sun
2. Es   sind   dort   nicht   die   Unsterblichen,
   there are   there   not   the   un-dying
3. sondern die   Gefallenen,   vernehmen   wir.
   but   the   fallen   notice   we
4. Und Glanz kehrt   sich   nicht an   Verwesung.   Unsere   Gottheit,
   and   shine bothers itself   not about   decay   our   god-ness
5. die Geschichte,   hat   uns   ein   Grab   bestellt,
   the   history   has   us   a   grave   ordered
6. aus   dem   es   keine Auferstehung   gibt.
   out-of which there   no   resurrection   is

(Bachmann 1964: 20f.)

In my 2006 book I maintained that reading for translation is different from reading not intended as a prelude to translation (Boase-Beier 2006a: 24f.). By reading for translation I mean a reading that not only takes the style into account, as any close critical reading will do, but that also hears in the text echoes of the translation it is about to become. Reading Bachmann's poems on this basis we note at least the following five points:

(i) Each stanza begins with a long line, and there are parallels between these two first lines. Line 1 iconically (see Boase-Beier 2006a: 101ff.) echoes the movement of the sun emerging from the antechamber in an awkward, stumbling rhythm. The verb *tritt* (steps) comes very late in the sentence and it is emphasized partly because the voiceless [t] of *tritt* following the voiced [z] of *Himmels* is awkward to pronounce. Line 4 (the first line of stanza 2) is a similarly long and irregular line, and also has a pause towards the end, before *unsere Gottheit*. *Leiche* (corpse) in line 1 is echoed by *Verwesung* (decay, especially of bodies) in line 4. *Sonne* (sun) in line 1 is echoed by *Glanz* (brilliance) in line 4. *Himmel* (heaven, sky) in line 1 is echoed by *Gottheit* (divinity, godhead) in line 4. Both lines 1 and 4 suggest a statement which can be understood in several ways (the sun has brought the corpses to life or has failed to do so; brilliance is undulled by decay or does not care to overcome it, or is ignorant of it) and the two short lines following in each stanza highlight one of these ways: the corpses remain dead; decay does not give way to resurrection. If we want the reader of the translation to first consider the situation, and only then discover the answer, we will need a similar structure in the translation.

(ii) There is a sequence of movements or states that result from movement:

> *tritt* (line 1) – steps – is actually a movement
>
> *Gefallenen* (line 3) – fallen – is a past participle used as an adjective and nominalized; it is negated
>
> *kehrt sich nicht an* (line 4) – literally 'does not turn round because of' but idiomatically meaning 'not to care about'
>
> *Auferstehung* (line 6) – resurrection – a deverbal noun, literally 'getting up',
>
> both the action and the resulting state; also negated.

These verbal expressions are spaced evenly throughout the poem, suggesting a reiterated staticity, as all but the first – *tritt* – are negated.

(iii) There is an abundance of words to do with death; one occurs in each line: in line 1 there is *Leichen-* (corpse-); in line 2 there is *Unsterblichen* (immortals), a word which contains the stem *sterb-* (die) and is reinforced by being twice negated: *not* the *un*dying; in line 3 (not) the fallen, in line 4 decay, in line 5 a grave, in line 6 (no) resurrection. Death, then, is the main theme of the poem.

(iv) There are repeated sounds in **Lei**chen-, Gott**hei**t, **kei**ne, evenly spaced in lines 1, 4 and 6, and in **G**efallenen, **G**lanz, **G**ottheit, **G**eschichte and **G**rab, giving a dense mass of sound repetition in such a short poem.

(v) There is a weak semantic chain of religious imagery: *Himmel* in line 1 is 'heaven' but it is weak because the word also means 'sky', and the appearance of the sun three words on weakens its religious sense further. *Die Unsterblichen* are those who, in religious terms, are saved and find eternal life, but lines 2 and 3 tell us this is not what we find in the antechamber of the heavens. *Gottheit* in line 4 is the quality of being God, but it stands in apposition to *Geschichte*, history, and is even alliterated with it, making the link closer: history is what determines our fate, divinity is historical rather than universal. And *Auferstehung* in line 6 is, as previously noted, negated: no resurrection is possible. And as though this were not clear enough, *Sonne* in line 1 and *Gottheit* in line 4 are in the same, line-final position, suggesting even more strongly that *Himmel* is both the heaven of God (though the latter is merely history) and the sky in which the sun resides.

These, then, are the meanings I read into, and out of, the style of the German poem, and my translation attempts to capture these elements:

Message
1 Out of the corpse-warm antechamber of the heavens steps the sun.
2 There lie not the undying,
3 but the fallen, we realise.

4 And brilliance has no time for decay. Our Godhead
5 history has left us a grave
6 from which we can never arise.

It will be obvious in most cases why I have chosen to translate like this. I want to preserve the argument of the poem in the long ambiguous statements of those first lines and the comment which follows. I aim to keep both the echoed movement of the sun in line 1 and the echo of our thought process in line 3. My translation arises out of the view of poetic style outlined above. If I compare its first two lines with Eavan Boland's 'Out steps the sun / Out of the corpse-warmed entrance hall to the sky' (Boland 2004: 95), I can only assume that what she has done is to locate the meaning of the poem in its reference and not its style: the position of 'steps' does not matter, nor does the iconic rhythm of that line, nor does the way the argument is structured.

Yet this is clearly not Boland's theory of poetry. If it were, she could not write the wonderful poems she does (see, for example, Boland 1987, 1990, 1994). It is almost as though her translations come from a different place: a place where there is no iconicity, no carefully-crafted imagery, no textual cohesion, and above all, no playing with the reader. There is no waiting for the verb 'steps', and no waiting to see what steps out, because the sun steps into the poem at the start. There is no playing with the heaven-sky ambiguity, because it is just the sky. There is no echoing of our thought-processes, because line 3 begins with 'What we perceive', rather than ending with it, though this attempt to follow the process of perception is evident in three other translations, by Anderson (1968: 55), Friedberg (2005: 339) and Filkins (2006: 45). But there are other reasons for the stylistic choices in my translation: the mention of the sun, the dying, and warmth suggests an echo of Wilfred Owen's poem 'Futility' (1990: 135). In that poem the body is still warm, but the sun does not warm it further. Here the antechamber is 'corpse-warm' (warm as corpses), not 'corpse-warmed' (warmed by corpses) as in Boland's version. It is a subtle difference but an important one. The antechamber in Bachmann's poem is as warm as a corpse which has just died, but it will be cold when the sun steps out, just as a corpse will cool when life has left. The comparison in 'corpse-warm' thus suggests this further comparison. But the adjective 'corpse-warmed' has no comparative basis, there is no metaphor, and so no further comparison of the sun leaving the chamber and life leaving the body is triggered in the reader's mind. Lines 3 and 6 have been made to rhyme in my version, to reflect the assonance in lines 3 and 6 of the German in vernehmen wir/Auferstehung gibt. But another reason for 'arise' in line 6 is to create an allusion to Blake's youth and maiden who, in 'Ah! Sunflower' (Blake 1958: 51), do in fact arise from their graves but, having done so, merely aspire to go where the sunflower wishes to go, which is the place where they already are. Death is not overcome in Blake's poem, because it represents an entirely circular movement (cf. Freeman 1976). Bachmann's poem, too, in my reading, is a poem in which death is not overcome, the fallen remain fallen and the dead remain dead, and the allusion is welcome. It could also be seen as a questioning (at the very least) of Christian belief in which the sun is often associated with Christ as symbol and agent of rebirth (Biedermann 1992: 330). Here there is no such triumph. And I have tried to strengthen the association with a Christian view by translating Gottheit as 'Godhead', a word used in Christian hymns ('veiled in flesh the Godhead see'; Dearmer 1936: 45), but not in everyday discourse as, indeed, Gottheit in German is not. But the main reason to use 'arise' as the final word where Boland uses 'resurrection' (as do both Anderson and Filkins) is to keep the sense of movement – 'steps', (not) 'fallen', (never) 'arise' – because the transparent nature of German morphology (as in Auf-ersteh-ung 'up-arise-ing') allows us to see the verb in the nominalisation and foregrounds the pattern of negated movement. English 'resurrection' being morphologically opaque, loses the intransitive verb and thus loses the movement, and so it also loses the negation of movement which is so striking in this poem.

4. What does all this mean?

Is there not, though, a danger that such close attention to the text might do what I argued against in 'The limits of the window metaphor'? That it might tie the translator into slavish reproduction? Not if what the translator is concerned with is style in its full cognitive sense rather than merely with form, if stylistic devices are seen as having a counterpart in the mind, so that reading the text involves the elements and processes mentioned in 'A theory of poetic style and its effects on translation'. A concern with style in this sense avoids an understanding of foreignizing which involves mimicking the German, putting assonance or alliteration where the original has it, echoing *Glanz* with one of the common Germanic synaesthetic stock of words in 'gl' – that relate to light, such as 'glow', 'gleam' or 'glitter', or repeating 'out' because the German repeats *aus* and they are etymologically connected.

Such imitative foreignizing has its place, and it has led to interesting sound experiments such as the Zukofskys' translations of Catullus (1969). But it is inappropriate to a method of translation influenced by a view which sees sound and other formal aspects of the text as meaning little in themselves, but rather as gaining their meaning by virtue of the fact that style encompasses the mental pictures the words convey and the cognitive effects they elicit.

What I am principally arguing against is a view that translation is a window whose only function is to be transparent. In fact, no such static metaphor seems adequate to describe what is surely a dynamic communicative act, which recreates both an initiator (the voice behind Bachmann's poem) and a recipient (the reader who will engage with the translated poem), on the basis of a dynamic communicative and cognitive view of style. In this approach, that possibility of engagement by the readers of the translation is of paramount importance. Ideally they should be able to go through an infinite number of thought processes and changes of mind, to relate the poem to Blake, Owen, Christian hymns or any other English literature as well as to an original poem by Bachmann. They should be able to experience some of the pessimism that the reader feels in the original, and they should be encouraged to think who the fallen are, and what history is being referred to. It might be the history of the last war, or any other war, something which Boland suggests when she titles this collection of the work of twentieth-century women poets *After Every War*. More generally, I am suggesting that we view all metaphors of translation with caution. I am arguing against the naïve, unconsidered application of theory, and even against any direct application of translation theory to the act of translation. Such theories are not meant to be sets of instructions and they serve translators, including the best poet-translators, badly when so used. Let us instead take on peripheral theories: of the text, the context, the reader, the effects of history, the nature of literature. They are more interesting, more useful, and far less dangerous.

5. Bibliography

Agenda: A Reconsideration of Rainer Maria Rilke (2007) 42, 3–4.

Anderson, M. (trans.) (1968) *In the Storm of Roses: Selected Poems by Ingeborg Bachmann*, Princeton, NJ: Princeton University Press.

Bachmann, I. (1964) *Gedichte, Erzählungen, Hörspiel, Essays*, München: Piper.

Barry, P. (2002) *Beginning Theory: An Introduction to Literary and Cultural Theory*, Manchester: Manchester University Press.

Berman, A. (2000) 'Translation and the Trials of the Foreign', in L. Venuti (ed.) *The Translation Studies Reader*, London; New York: Routledge, 284–97.

Biedermann, H. (1992) *The Wordsworth Dictionary of Symbolism*, Ware: Wordsworth.

Blake, W. (1958) *A Selection of Poems and Letters*, (ed.) J. Bronowski, Harmondsworth: Penguin.

Boase-Beier, J. (2006a) *Stylistic Approaches to Translation*, Manchester: St Jerome Publishing.

Boase-Beier, J. (2006b) 'Loosening the Grip of the Text: Theory as an Aid to Creativity', in M. Perteghella and E. Loffredo (eds) *Translation and Creativity: Perspectives in Creative Writing and Translation Studies*, London; New York: Continuum, 47–56.

Boland, E. (1987) *The Journey and Other Poems*, Manchester: Carcanet.

Boland, E. (1990) *Outside History*, Manchester: Carcanet.

Boland, E. (1994) *In a Time of Violence*, Manchester: Carcanet.

Boland, E. (2004) *After Every War: Twentieth-Century Women Poets*, Princeton, NJ: Princeton University Press.

Castle, G. (2007) *The Blackwell Guide to Literary Theory*, Oxford: Blackwell.

Chesterman, A. and Wagner, E. (2002) *Can Theory Help Translators? A Dialogue Between the Ivory Tower and the Wordface*, Manchester: St Jerome Publishing.

Connolly, D. (trans.) (2003) *Yannis Kondos; Absurd Athlete*, Todmorden: Arc Publications.

Culler, J. (1997) *Literary Theory: A Very Short Introduction*, Oxford: Oxford University Press.

Dearmer, P. (ed.) (1936) *Songs of Praise*, London: Oxford University Press.

Díaz-Diocaretz, M. (1985) *Translating Poetic Discourse: Questions on Feminist Strategies in Adrienne Rich*, Amsterdam; Philadelphia: John Benjamins.

Elsworth, B. (trans.) (2000) *Michael Strunge: A Virgin From a Chilly Decade*, Todmorden: Arc Publications.

Filkins, P. (trans.) (2006) *Darkness Spoken: Ingeborg Bachmann, The Collected Poems*, Brookline: Zephyr Press.

Fish, S. (1980) *Is There a Text in This Class?* Cambridge, MA: Harvard University Press.

Fowler, R. (1996) *Linguistic Criticism*, Oxford: Oxford University Press.

Freeman, D. (1976) 'Iconic Syntax in Poetry: A Note on Blake's "Ah! Sunflower"', *University of Massachusetts Occasional Papers in Linguistics* 2, 51–7.

Friedberg, L. (trans.) (2005) *Last Living Words: The Ingeborg Bachmann Reader*, Los Angeles: Green Integer.

Gutt, E.-A. (2000) *Translation and Relevance*, Manchester: St Jerome.

Gutt, E.-A. (2005) 'On the Impossibility of Practising Translation Without Theory', in J. Peeters (ed.) *On the Relationships Between Translation Theory and Translation Practice*, Berlin: Peter Lang, 13–21.

Halliday, M. A. K. and Hassan, R. (1976) *Cohesion in English*, London: Longman.

Honig, E. (ed.) (1985) *The Poet's Other Voice: Conversations on Literary Translation*, Amherst, MA: University of Massachusetts Press.

Iser, W. (1974) *The Implied Reader: Patterns of Communication in Prose Fiction from Bunyan to Beckett*, Baltimore, MD: Johns Hopkins University Press.

Iser, W. (2006) *How To Do Theory*, Oxford: Blackwell.

Kratz, D. (1986) 'An Interview with Norman Shapiro', *Translation Review* 19, 27–8.

Malmkjær, K. (2005) *Linguistics and the Language of Translation*, Edinburgh: Edinburgh University Press.

Miall, D. S. and Kuiken, D. (1998) 'The Form of Reading: Empirical Studies of Literariness', *Poetics* 25, 327–41.

Midgley, M. (2001) *Science and Poetry*, London: Routledge.

Owen, W. (1990) *The Poems of Wilfred Owen*, London: Chatto & Windus.

Paterson, D. (2006) *Orpheus: A Version of Rilke's 'Die Sonette an Opheus'*, London: Faber & Faber.

Peden, Margaret Sayers (1989) 'Building a Translation, The Reconstruction Business Poem 145 of Sor Juana Ines de la Cruz' in J. Biguenet and R. Schulte (eds) *The Craft of Translation*, Chicago, IL: Chicago University Press, 13–27.

Semino, E. and J. Culpeper (eds) (2002) *Cognitive Stylistics: Language and Cognition in Text Analysis*, Amsterdam; Philadelphia: John Benjamins.

Shklovsky, V. (1965) 'Art as Technique', in L. T. Leman and M. J. Reis (trans) *Russian Formalist Criticism: Four Essays*, Lincoln, NE: University of Nebraska Press, 3–60.

Simpson, P. (2004) *Stylistics: A Resource Book for Students*, London; New York: Routledge.

Stockwell, P. (2002) *Cognitive Poetics: An Introduction*, London; New York: Routledge.

Terry, A (tr.) (2004) *Gabriel Ferrater: Women and Days*, Todmorden: Arc Publications.

Toury, G. (1995) *Descriptive Translation Studies and Beyond*, Amsterdam; Philadelphia: John Benjamins.

Venuti, L. (2008) *The Translator's Invisibility: A History of Translation*, London; New York: Routledge.

Venuti, L. (1998) *The Scandals of Translation*, London; New York: Routledge.

Venuti, L. (1995) *The Translator's Invisibility: A History of Translation*, London: Routledge.

Zukofsky, C. and Zukovsky, L. (trans) (1969) *Catullus*, London: Cape Goliard Press.

Horace's Hyperbaton: Wrapping One's Head around 'Word Warps' and Patching Up a Gaping Language Gap

Elizabeth Thornton
University of California, USA

Chapter Outline

Is Horace a master wordsmith? Or is he an old 'fuddy-duddy' whose labyrinthine lines could only be an eyesore (or earworm) for us moderns, now 'enlightened' and relieved of the burden of stylistic artifice? You may say: the question is brutal and biased; the scales are already tipped, with an army of adjectives aligning themselves in the condemnatory camp. True enough; but less sententious sentences would quite literally 'gloss' over the gruff opposition which admirers of Horace often encounter – and still fail to counter. However strong our instinctive appreciation of this Roman poet's intricacies, we lack entirely a verbal arsenal to repel criticisms. I became interested in translation as the best possible kind of 'lexical renewal', remedying once and for all this loss for words.

When I found that my style handbooks lacked any terminology to describe Horace's ambiguity-inducing tactics, I sought out good English versions which would illustrate the effect his poetry might have on ears exposed from birth to the Latin tongue. Upon discovering that within my university's entire library there was not even one translation which mimicked the wiles of Horace's word usage, I endeavoured to try my own hand. My lyre was attuned to linguistics; theory and translation existed in a symbiotic relationship revolving around the search for a principle of functional equivalency: a descriptive and pragmatic common ground uniting Latin hyperbaton and orderly English, quelling any condemnations that might arise from simple misunderstanding. As a litmus test for this brew of apparently opposing principles, I submit the modern Muse that is their product: I will end with an English rendering of Ode IV 1 that transmits the Horatian spirit in a form more amenable to contemporary eyes and ears.

1. Introduction to Horace: the form and function of 'warped' word order

Up to this day I have not had an artistic delight in any poet similar to that which from the beginning an Ode of Horace gave me. What is here achieved is in certain languages not even to be hoped for. This mosaic of words, in which every word, by sound, by placing, and by meaning, spreads its influence to the right, to the left, and over the whole; this minimum in extent and number of symbols, this maximum thereby achieved in the effectiveness of the symbols, all this is Roman, and believe me, elegant par excellence.[1] Nietzsche, 'What I Owe the Ancients' Twilight of the Idols, I. (as cited in Commager 1995: 50)

Horace (Quintus Horatius Flaccus, 65–8 BC) was the first poet – ancient or modern – to ever take my breath away. In his *Odes* I saw form fused seamlessly with function. The parallel lines on the page – and the spaces in between – acted as a kind of *warp*, isolating words from clarifying bits of context and changing their meanings in the process. Then, sense and sentence were bent back into shape as the reader's mind stitched in between the lines. I remember exactly when I first began to detect the separate threads of Horace's '*text*ile,' and the shifty subtext woven by their interplay. I was reading the following verse from the celebrated 'Soracte' ode (Carmen I.9; syntactic siblings are put in the same font):

Nunc	et	**latentis**	*proditor*	*intimo*
now	and	hiding-of	betrayer	intimate-from/of

Gratus	**puellae**	*risus*	ab	*angulo*
Grateful	girl-of	laughter	from	corner-from

One can translate these lines together to mean, 'Now too, from an intimate corner, grateful laughter, betrayer of a hiding girl.' However, one can also pause in between the lines and take the first verbal thread on its own. In that case, *latentis* refers to a hiding *person* rather than specifically a hiding girl; *proditor* 'betrayer' might refer to a sinister traitor rather than to telltale laughter; and *intimo* could be from the noun *intimus* 'intimate friend' [2] instead of serving as an adjective modifying *angulo* 'corner'. In that case, the first line on its own would literally mean 'Now too, from intimate friend, a traitor of a man in hiding' – in other words, 'Here also a friend of a man in hiding becomes his traitor.' In the next line, each word is reunited with its syntactic twin – its clarifying context – and the overall meaning emerges. Read thread-by-thread, the text first presents us with a scene of military espionage, which only afterwards *transforms* into a late-night tryst. An English translation which comes nearer to capturing this ambiguity might go as follows:

They uncover a sleeper,[3] betrayed by an intimate

Laughter – she's cornered
and grateful –

The irreverent implication of this thematic confusion is that these activities are at bottom one and the same: interchangeable, incidental outlets for youths' restlessness. Slowly it sunk in that this sly, slanted perspective was in fact a satirical squint from millennia-old eyes. I thought: who needs the pomp of séances when you have Latin lessons!

2. An unnerving interpretive oversight: the 'pattern for the sake of pattern' prejudice

This euphoria lasted for exactly one day – right until the next class discussion. My amusement at this mischievous metaphor was dampened by the flood of complaints from my classmates, who insisted they had never read such a boring piece of so-called 'literature'.

For them, only the overall meaning of the lines existed. Consequently, the words appeared unnecessarily scrambled. Communing with this ancient must have felt something like doing jigsaw puzzles at a retirement community. It was a charitable act of remembering one's elders; a kind of piety. It might improve your character; it would definitely improve your college application. But in practice, it meant mind-numbing hours spent piecing scattered bits of information together (be they puzzle pieces or strangely arranged words). The less than spectacular end result of all this toil was a commonplace scene or conventional poem: depicting picnics along the river; battle scenes; sailboats in the sea and so on.

I turned to my professor for support like a panicked pilgrim to a cleric. She quickly quoted the Nietzschean chapter and verse that is quoted earlier; but from that moment on the day's session was spent hashing out the literal translation rather than exploring multiple layers of meaning. So, that afternoon, I scanned the standard 'scriptures' on my own: I went through the appendices of every grammar and reader I owned, searching for terminology that could describe the aesthetic contribution of the spliced syntax in these and other Horatian lines. I wanted a quick fix to patch up the gap in understanding between my classmates and myself; I presumed that I could find some venerable label, 'stick it to them,' and end the debate there.

To my surprise and dismay, all the terms that I found – chiasmus (symmetrical, 'Matryoshka doll' word order); golden line and silver line (see the following argument); or synchysis (interlocked or alternating order) – merely described the visual *form* of the word order configurations found in Latin poetry, and made no reference to their ambiguity-inducing *effects*. I suddenly wondered whether I was reading too much into Horace's lines: perhaps poets valued these patterns in and of themselves, rather than as a means to a double meaning. Then came the straw that seemed to break the back of my pet theory on Horatian polysemy: namely, the heinous term *hyperbaton*. If you look up hyperbaton in the (Basil Gildersleeve terminological) dictionary, you really will find Horace there. You will also find the following unforgiving appraisal of his stylistics: 'a violent displacement of words' (Gildersleeve and Lodge 1989: 436). To think that Horace's verbal *warps* had bewildered even eminent philologists into preserving this Greek term – which comes from a verb meaning 'to transgress' – to describe what they view as a literal perversion of the proper progression of phrases! These scholars' message seemed clear: warped word order was a mere decorative device, which decadent Augustan authors like Horace often employed in excess.

Granted, I did eventually find more euphemistic descriptions of Horace's inventive word orderings: for example, Daniel H. Garrison's buoyant take on hyperbaton as 'a leap-frogging of normal word order . . . to allow for the artful arrangement of words found in inclusive or interlocked word order, chiasmus, and the golden line' (Garrison 1991: 389). Garrison's words, while thankfully replacing sharp criticism with sympathetic whimsy, still write-off the idea of *meaning*-driven mutations of the unmarked word order. In other words, he seems to assume that Roman poets appreciated intricate patterns in the placement of words *only* as decoration and not to encourage multiple interpretations.

Even favourable remarks motivated by this 'patterns for patterns' sake' perspective deepened my disappointment with the discourse on Horace: I realized that they seemed different from my classmates' complaints only by 'virtue' of their proponents' greater degree of masochism. Both parties agreed that Horace's lines appear unnecessarily 'scrambled'; only, one group *rebelled against* this practice and the other *revelled in* its abstrusities.

3. Not all that is golden glitters, and some difficulties run deeper than our terminological reservoir: the interpretive anachronism of the 'patterns for the sake of patterns' perspective, and the single possible antidote of translation

Luckily, recent research suggests that the Romans did not share our preoccupation with palliative word patterns; rather, we have inherited this assumption from the Middle Ages, a time in which Latin's status as a purely scholarly language (rather than a truly 'living' one) no doubt contributed a certain artificiality to stylistic norms. In particular, Kenneth Mayer (see as follows) traces the history of the term 'golden line'.

In an ubiquitously quoted quip, John Dryden defines the golden line as 'two substantives and two adjectives with a verb between to keep the peace' (from a preface to *Sylva*; quoted e.g. Garrison 1991: 388). For example: examine the following war-torn phrases written by Ovid, Horace's younger contemporary (Ovid Metamorphoses 2.607):

Candida	*puniceo*	perfudit	*membra*	*cruore*
Shining-white	punic red-with	flooded	limbs	blood-with
a	*b*	C	A	B

'[The arrow] flooded shiny white limbs with punic-red blood'

Here, the 'peace' is (rather poorly) kept by *perfudit*, with the syntactic phrases *candida membra* and *puniceo cruore* rearranged to create the characteristic 'golden line' pattern abCAB. (Note that the author is obviously trying to extract a 'visceral' reaction from his audience by presenting gory details. It would be an odd time to be focusing on harmonious abstract structural properties; already we must wonder whether the overall word order pattern was really the poet's primary goal.) An additional, subsequently coined term – 'silver line' – describes *any* line with the general pattern ABCAB.

In fact, the term 'golden line' seems to be no older than Dryden's seventeenth century contemporaries, and appears to be a specifically English phenomenon (Mayer 2002: 139). As for the pedigree of the word order pattern itself: Diomedes, the first grammarian to mention something *similar to* the 'golden line' under the term *teretes versus* 'rounded verses,' probably wrote his treatise a full 350 years after Horace's prime (Mayer 2002: 141, 148). The supposed pre-eminence of this particular structure – what promoted it all the way from 'round' to 'golden' – likely dates back to the Venerable Bede (c. 772–735 CE), a famous English monk who stressed the importance of hyperbaton as a formal stylistic trait, and especially preferred the separation of adjectives from their host nouns (Mayer 2002: 142).

The shift in perspective identified in these formal treatises on style plays out in poetic practice, with 'golden' and 'silver' lines being around ten times as frequent in medieval authors compared to most mainstays of the classical canon (Mayer 2002: 161)[4]. Definitely then, the overvaluation of these formal patterns seems to be an accident of their transmission from antiquity to the modern Anglo-American textbooks.

Can the same be said for ornamental word order in general? Mayer notes that the first obvious critique we get of patterns for patterns' sake – authored by the Roman poet Martial, who lived only a hundred years after Horace and the rest of the Augustans – suggests that contemporary eyes viewed such a technique contemptuously. To quote the poem (Martial 2.86) and Mayer's translation (Mayer 2002: 140–141):

Quod nec carmine glorior supino	Although I don't boast a verse supine
Nec retro lego Sotaden cinaedum	Nor read Sotades' backward behind,
Nusquam Graecula quod recantat echo	Although Echo never sings back like a Greek,
Nec dictat mihi luculentus Attis	Nor cute Attis offer me
Mollem debilitate galliambon :	a galliamb soft and weak
Non sum, Classice, tam malus poeta.	All the same, Classicus, I'm not such a bad poet.
Quid si per gracilis vias petauri	**What, would you force a sprinter to squeeze**
Invitum iubeas subire Ladan?	**Into the delicate mesh of a circus trapeze?**
Turpe est difficiles habere nugas	**Complicated hobbies are a crass way to go,**
Et stultus labor est ineptiarum.	**And putting effort into ephemera is stupid and slow.**
Scribat carmina circulis Palaemon	**Let Palemon write poems in popular circles,**
Me raris iuvat auribus placere	**I'd rather please the ears of those in the know.**

Not all that is golden glitters; and the theory that ubiquitous, gratuitous hyperbaton was prized by Roman poets is losing currency altogether. Mayer and others convinced me that pinpointing the function of Horatian phrasing would entail more than putting my finger on scholarly-sounding misnomers, which poorly matched not only my instincts but also the reality of Roman sensibilities.

Now the 'disconnect' took on another dimension. No longer was it my instincts versus those of my classmates; now there were the anachronisms of certain Classicists to combat as well. It occurred to me that this growing lingual and cultural chasm – between Horace's hinting hyperbaton on the one hand and the straitjacket of English rigid word order and restrictive scholarly presumptions on the other – might be narrowed in the same way as others: by 'commissioning' artisans of words, who stitch across language gaps and word warps for a living. That is, I hoped to find translations which excited the same amusement from literarily inclined English speakers as the Latin had from me. If I could not describe my impressions in terms time-honoured and unimpeachable, I could at least use these translations to inculcate them in others. Repeated concomitant reading of an effective English rendering along with the Latin original would create conditioned reactions, in almost the Pavlovian sense: the student would begin to associate the English versions' turns of phrase with Horace's winding words. (Of course, the goal is not to be 'Pavlov's dogs', but to become empowered readers!) The proof would be in the 'pudding' of recognizable wordplay; my classmates were sure to eat their words and Horace's too.

4. 'Pattern for patterns' sake' and translation attempts: 'dank and dropping' verbal weeds, frivolous formalities and unapologetic departures

What would it mean to find an effective translation? I was soon to discover that poets, despite their usually superior instincts, seemed to have no more of an answer than I did. Obviously, a word-for-word translation of Horatian hyperbaton is impossible in most instances: for instance, in English, adjectives simply cannot appear a line before their nouns (as they did in the Latin lines quoted at the beginning of this chapter). The results of directly rendering even less drastic 'disruptions' of word order are infamous to all those who have encountered Milton's famous translation of Horace's 'Pyrrha' ode. I will quote only the end:

> Hapless they
> To whom thou untry'd seem'st fair. Me in my vow'd
> Picture the sacred wall declares t' have hung
> My dank and dropping weeds
> To the stern God of Sea.[5] (Horace I.05.12–16)

We have already seen that in Horatian ambiguity, two contradictory meanings crystallize at different times in the text, creating a tension more 'telling' than his attitudes are tacit. In contrast, the syntactic uncertainties in this translation merge into a single indecipherable blur, a sprawling syntactic tree whose only 'fruit' is the frustration of the uninitiated reader. 'Dank and dropping weeds' indeed! Such a result convinces nearly all that Milton's minimalist technique should not be tried again.

The inability to mimic the form of Horace's phrases is only the beginning of the problem: what really ties the tongues of translators is an imprecise understanding of the purpose of Horatian word order patterns. Because many of these poets do not know what meanings they are losing, they make no effort to preserve them; rather than deftly bending a modern weft around Horace's warped words, they start from scratch with a more amenable new formal framework.

They may choose the sentence rather than the metrical phrase as the smallest unit of thread, and in so doing piece together a prose translation (e.g. Rudd 2004). In this case the dynamism of the poem is lost, with the separate contributions of each warp-strand obscured by the finished façade of the text as a whole. They may elect to render Horatian poems into their own particular style, twisting both meter and meaning to serve their own bent (e.g. McClatchy 2005).

Finally, they may decide to change fabrics altogether: opting for a rhyme scheme in which arbitrary phonetic echoes replace syntactic and semantic affinities as the patterns that connect line to line (e.g. Michie 2002; Sydenham 2004). But whereas shifting syntactic and semantic alliances – created by the alternating isolation *from* and reconciliation *with* clarifying bits of context – cause multiple meanings to arise between the lines, rhyme schemes are very often patterns for the sake of patterns only. This is not to deny the pleasing aesthetic of rhyme, or to ignore its potential ability to suggest extra-syntactic associations between words. Precisely because of its aesthetic appeal, rhyme is a favourite *palliative*; when so employed, it is bound to impoverish the poetry onto which it is imposed. The relationship between an ambiguous Horatian ode and its randomly rhyming ersatz could be compared to the difference between one of Escher's optical illusions and a checker-patterned quilt.

Those who knowingly eschew the formal features of the Latin in favour of unadorned prose or their own designs likely do so in the service of a purpose other than my own. The former crowd likely aims to produce a literal translation; the latter aspires to compose self-reflective adaptations with a large degree of autonomy from the original. They work in the service of students, fellow poets or their own drive towards self-discovery; so, their translations have a definite use attached to them. It is aimless, arbitrary adaptations which are to be avoided. Concocted in the formal vacuum created by the failure of the word-for-word technique, they are a callous cakewalk over Horace's grave.

We can only escape this travesty by relying on *functional* rather than formal equivalence:[6] by finding a way to unravel the exact implicatures of Horace's convoluted verses and then repack them into English phrases. Here we encounter an even more enormous obstacle: how can we possibly nail down all the nebulous nuances of an ancient text? Translators of any ancient literature must first of all deal with the withering 'warp' of time: a lack of native speakers and a lapse of millennia seem to reduce texts to a few ghostly threads of meaning. Combine that with Horace's inimitable hyperbaton, and one starts to feel as if his Latin lines must be so distorted by the distance in lingual and cultural shifts as to be self-contained and isolated by their own curvature. We would seem to be digging ourselves into a wormhole, in the vain attempt to access a parallel universe inaccessible to modern perusal.

5. The light at the end of the microscope: linguistic treatments of wordplay

We need not surrender ourselves to the cosmic forces conspiring for miscomprehension. It is true that the precise *cultural* reference of any given line can be lost with time; but a verse's *linguistic potential* for literary wordplay can be evaluated in a vacuum. That is to say, the 'baseline' linguistic ambiguities that are the foundational fulcrum of double meanings are not a matter of 'culture' in the expansive sense: they are a matter of the relative frequency of word meanings, phrases, and syntactic attachments – facts of usage which are often preserved provided an extensive corpus still exists.

To understand the difference between literary wordplay and 'baseline' linguistic ambiguity, let us analyse the English pun 'peace of paper'[7]:

i. Figure of speech: baseline linguistic ambiguity

No context is needed to grasp the polysemy of this phrase; even when presented in isolation,[8] it seems to mean at once 'peace -'and also '*piece* of paper'.

Nor do we need a formal theory to understand the ambiguity; but it will help to go through the exercise of analysis, because here our instincts can serve as feedback to our conceptual framework. Just like turns of phrase spun around the threads of Horace's warp, these two meanings evolve at specific times within the text.

The first relevant moment is immediately after the mind reads the word 'peace'. 'Peace' is on the one hand a visual symbol – connected in writing to other words, abstract symbols and images all representing harmony, rest, or the absence of conflict; it is also a stand-in for a sound [pis] – which, in addition to being connected to all the aforementioned ideas, is linked to the alternate meaning / part of a whole /. When the word 'peace' is read, the semantic associations of both the *visual iconograph* 'peace' *and* the sound [pis] are activated.[9] However, only one interpretation crystallizes in the conscious mind: the one based on the visual graph. This is likely because the associations flowing through the aural word [pis] are more numerous, including both / part of a whole / and / harmony /: the mind, tottering between two meanings, takes twice as long to arrive at either.

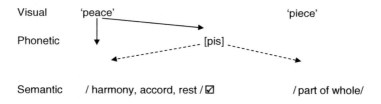

This visual/aural dichotomy might seem like too much 'machinery' for a relatively simple lexical decision task. Before jumping to this conclusion, examine what happens after the reading of the complete phrase 'a peace of paper'. This time, the aural path of associations is the decisive one. The visual phrase 'peace of paper' is a non-standard collocation both in terms of surface graphs and semantic ideas. In general, phrases like '- of paper' which feature an (aptly named) partitive genitive are associated with words like 'piece' that designate parts of a whole; but the appearance of 'peace' contradicts this. As a result, when the mind tries to follow associations based on the phrase's *visual* form, it falls victim to the same 'tottering' phenomenon that we saw on the aural end before. On the other hand, because of the typical meaning of the phrase [pis əv peɪpər], adding [əv peɪpər] to the mind's inner ear encourages the association of [pis] with /part of a whole/. So this time, the meaning /part of a whole/ is activated first, via the everyday utterance [pis əv peɪpər].

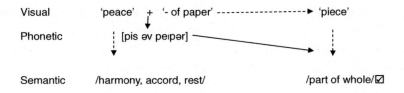

Note that dissecting this pun required no cultural context whatsoever: we just needed to know the status of 'peace' as a graph unambiguously connected to the meaning /harmony, accord, rest/, and the ability of the phrase [əv peɪpər] to narrow the associations of [pis] by completing the lexicalized phrase [pis əv peɪpər].

ii. Figure of thought: cultural context and the culmination into wordplay

Culture is what transforms this and other instances of spontaneous, 'baseline' polysemy into full-fledged wordplay. The conflicting interpretations will typically be related to real-world circumstances or mindsets that are highly salient within a given discourse. By way of this association, these subtle ambiguities become 'hot-buttons,' rekindling the embers of an incendiary dispute with the slightest of nudges.

The basic linguistic ambiguity in 'peace of paper' has taken on at least two drastically different bents in the service of thematic context:

In Asad's Syria it became popular to exclaim that any peace made with Israel was from the Syrian perspective merely a peace on paper (*salam al-waraqa*) and not a peace from the heart (*salam al-qalb*) (Cook 1996: 43). In an apparent case of a pun being *gained* in translation, since the late 1990s Israelis and others have frequently used the literal rendering of the phrase *salam al-waraqa* – 'peace of paper' – to refer to a shaky, half-hearted verbal commitment between Israel and one of its neighbours. The conflict between the two meanings 'peace-' and 'piece of paper' mirrored the contradiction between the lofty, perhaps airy ideal of peace and the few and flimsy tangible steps made in its direction. In this case the double meaning could be paraphrased as, 'This peace is only a piece of paper.'

In a quite distinct context, 'peace of paper' has been used to describe the sending of a thousand paper cranes to a group of 'afflicted' individuals (with the most recent example in my memory being Virginia Tech college students). There the pun was used to emphasize just how important seemingly insignificant gestures can be, with the meaning 'piece of paper' referring to the cranes themselves and the 'peace- ' connoting the comfort they are known to provide. Here the double meaning could be paraphrased as, 'Though they are only pieces of paper, these cranes can restore some sense of peace.'

As this example shows well, the 'punch' a pun packs – or the consolation it contributes – can vary widely with the thematic context; but the baseline linguistic ambiguities persist unchanged as long as the literary corpus does. If linguistic ambiguity exists in a vacuum, there is no reason why Horatian wordplay should languish in the wasteland of our cultural *lacunae*.

In what follows, we will try to analyse Horace in the same fashion: highlighting the ambiguities which assuredly arise within the text, and only later consigning ourselves to culture-dependent speculation about the precise thematic focus of each turn of phrase.

6. 'Activation cost', ancient poetry and an equivalency principle for use in translation

Of course, we will have to systematize this method somewhat before projecting it onto ancient poetry: there we do not have instincts strong enough to intuitively discriminate between better and worse theoretical descriptions. We should start by explicitly laying out the hallmark assumptions of our treatment of the pun 'peace of paper':

1. *Incremental, iterated processing: the mind interprets a given phrase multiple times, at different stages in its progression.* In our example, multiple meanings arose because the mind initially interpreted a sub-segment of the phrase ('peace') independently of context and only *subsequently* tackled the string of words as a whole.
2. *Parallel processing: the mind processes different interpretations in tandem.* Since the mind cannot know in advance what factors will be most relevant to disambiguating a phrase, the only way for the visual pathway to prevail in one round and the aural in the other is if the mind pursues both avenues both times.
3. *Limit to the resources of memory: divided attention causes an attenuation of each interpretation.* In our discussion of the 'tottering' effect, we assumed that competing interpretations along the same pathway slowed down the

pace of processing, and lessened the strength of each association. That is to say, we supposed that we have a finite amount of resources to allocate to establishing any given kind of connection between words, and the greater number of alternatives we must keep in our heads, the less the chance that our minds will pursue any of them aggressively.

4. *Survival of the strongest association: 'frequency' and 'compatibility' each play a role.* The winning route was the quickest one to form a strong association between the word forms and *one* specific meaning. In other words, a given interpretation crystallizes in the conscious mind when a definite *favourite* emerges among possible meanings. The two factors which enabled different interpretations to cross the threshold of consciousness might be termed 'frequency' and 'compatibility'. The more 'frequent' – and in this case, exclusive – association of the visual word 'peace' with the meaning / harmony, accord / guided the mind's first context-free guess at the meaning of this word. But the partitive phrase 'of paper' / [əv peɪpər] was highly 'compatible' with the / part of a whole / interpretation on the aural end.

These bare-bones principles – incremental processing; parallel processing; survival of the strongest association; and the identification of frequency, compatibility and the limited resources of memory as factors which affect the development of an interpretation – already place us well within the bounds of a particular linguistic theory, known as the 'activation cost'/ 'activation threshold' framework (Vosse and Kempen 2000; Gibson 1998).

According to this theory, at any given moment as we listen to a sentence, without our necessarily being aware of it, different interpretations are jockeying for supremacy in our mind. The mind works to activate, or reinforce, a particular interpretation beyond a certain level, called the 'activation threshold'. Crossing the activation threshold means crossing the threshold of consciousness, becoming an interpretation the reader or listener is aware of considering rather than a dim potentiality which is quickly suppressed. The speed with which a given potential interpretation approaches this all-important threshold depends on 'activation cost' – a measure of how difficult it is for a particular interpretation to win the mind's conscious consideration. In the example above, the relative activation cost of two competing interpretations of the phonological word [pis] associated with the graphic representation 'piece' changes from one stage of processing to the next. When quantified, this concept can reliably predict whether test subjects will be able to parse an ambiguous sentence at first glance, and what their interpretation will be. However, we are concerned with *metrical* poetry whose inherent prosodic cues already suggest a specific piecewise strategy of interpretation. All that is left is to determine whether the mind will take these hints, and how far it will go with them: that is, how likely it is that the independent interpretation of each prosodically-circumscribed line segment will cross into consciousness. This simpler task requires a less formalized survey of the factors which increase or decrease activation cost.

Already we have identified three of the four factors commonly claimed to affect the activation cost of a particular interpretation. The first is 'frequency' in the sense discussed above.[10] If a word has multiple meanings, the more frequently occurring meaning will have a default prominence in the mind of the speaker; in the present jargon, it will *ceteris paribus* acquire a higher level of 'activation' in the mind. For example, in the sentence 'Yesterday I had a date,' speakers will automatically activate the primary meaning of 'date' – 'social engagement' – rather than the perfectly possible meaning 'a kind of dried fruit'.[11] Similarly, if a word can take on different syntactic roles in a sentence, then the most frequent role has the lowest activation cost. This is the cause behind the confusion in sentences such as this: 'The dog walked to the park was chasing the squirrel' (Gibson 1998: 3). The verb 'walk' is more frequently intransitive, with the result that the word form 'walked' will be interpreted as a finite past tense form rather than a passive participle (which requires a transitive meaning); that is, the 'activation cost' of the finite interpretation is smaller.

The second factor – also no surprise – is 'compatibility'.[12] If I were to change one of the above sentences to 'Yesterday I had a *tasty* date,' the less frequent meaning of 'date' would automatically acquire dominance, because its activation has been reinforced by a compatible adjective.[13] Similarly, a sentence 'The dog which was walked to the park . . .' contains no ambiguity, despite being based on the less frequent passive participle interpretation of the form 'walked'; this is because the presence of an auxiliary verb 'was' is compatible only with that interpretation. Compatibility with other data, then, also decreases the activation cost of a given interpretation.

The third factor – memory cost – refers to the 'tottering effect' – the exhaustion the mind experiences when it is forced to consider multiple potential associations at once.[14] Memory cost *increases* the activation cost of all interpretations, because fewer cognitive resources are left to pursue each potential association when so many possibilities must be retained and rehearsed. Consequently, the mind works slower or gives up altogether. Consider the way that working memory tends to break down when confronted with sentences like this:

> The administrator who the intern who the nurse supervised had bothered lost the medical reports. (Gibson 1998: 3)

The analogue in spoken speech is a long string of words uttered in rapid succession and without prosodic differentiation – say, at a time when the speaker is flustered. Aside from explaining why competing associations[15] slow down the general task of processing, 'memory cost' puts limits on the size and complexity of well-formed phrases. In general, memory cost will rule out the possibility that Horace's complex sentences would be the first stop in sentence comprehension. Instead, metrically-prescribed pauses would be pronounced, reducing the number of initially possible parses reflected in the written form. These pauses would help the mind 'pace' itself, establishing smaller phrases as separate stages of interpretation.[16]

Finally, we need the related idea of *locality*,[17] which turns out to be quite important for the task of interpreting poetry. Locality refers to the extreme expense associated with preserving the memory of potential syntactic and semantic associations over long distances, and the resultant tendency of the mind to let them decay at a fairly quick clip unless the arrival of new compatible words reinforces them. This decay is distinct from the poor performance induced by high memory costs: it is a function not of the number of incompatible words encountered, but rather of the time that has lapsed after the introduction of a word and the initial activation of its potential interpretations.

This means that *pauses* of the kind found in metrical poetry can have a profound effect on the interpretation of the verses they enclose. Pauses not only give time for words to be interpreted in isolation (i.e. for an initial interpretation to cross the threshold of consciousness without the influence of subsequent context); by facilitating this process of decay, they can also isolate phrases from prior context. In other words, one can theoretically interpret every single metrically-isolated phrase in isolation, provided the activation cost of that phrase is low enough.[18]

Of course, these phrases will not be interpreted *only* in isolation; in keeping with the idea of *iterative* interpretation, metrically isolated sentence chunks will eventually be reconciled with one another. Following Morton Ann Gernsbacher (1990) and others, I will assume that this integration phase is an automatic part of the mind's structure-building process, and that it occurs at least during the pauses in between each large sub-segment of the sentence – in this case, in between each metrical unit or 'prosodic phrase', as I will term metrically isolated strings of words for the sake of this chapter.

From this descriptive framework, we can (finally!) derive a definition of Horatian wordplay which paves the path for an English equivalent. Horace uses word order and metrical pauses to configure his verses into small, sub-sentential units with a low enough activation cost to be interpreted independently of context. Within each of these prosodic phrases, the activation levels of given potential interpretations differ greatly from their levels within the broader context of the sentence as a whole. Horace exploits the natural power of pauses, allowing these discrepancies in activation to heighten into ambiguity on the conscious level. Within English free verse, line breaks and blank spots can have the same slowing effect as the Latin's metrical pauses; we are already paving a path towards translation.

7. One example: baseline ambiguity and cultural reciprocity; the poet's patronage

The time has come to apply this theoretical framework to an age-old ambiguity, like the one which presents itself in the following lines (Odes I.12 lines 37–40):

Regulum et Scauros   animaeque magnae
Prodigum Paulum   superante Poeno
Gratus insigni   **referam Camena**
Fabriciumque

-*Literal translation, including only the final interpretation:* 'Regulus, the Scauri, and Paulus: generous with his great soul while the Phoenician was winning – **grateful, I will relate [them] with distinguished poetry** – and Fabricius too.'

-*Parse of the sentence in bold based on this interpretation:*

Gratus	*insigni*	referam	*Camena*
Grateful	distinguished-with	I will relate	poetry(/poetry goddess)-with

As with the analysis of 'peace of paper', a distinction will be made between the linguistically undeniable 'figure of speech' and the culturally predicated 'figure of thought.'

i. Figure of speech

Here we will deal only with the line in bold, in which an ambiguity arises involving the grammatical status of *insigni* (ablative or dative? adjective or substantive?). The prosodic phrases listed below are prescribed by the meter; I make note of the interpretations with the lowest activation cost *within* each separate phrase, and explain what factors heightened their activation; then, I show how activation levels change when each phrase is reconciled with context. (A check indicates that the phrases are interpreted as self-contained units.)

1) ☑ [Gratus insigni]
   -*Syntactic compatibility.* The word form *insigni* is morphologically ambiguous between the dative and ablative (i.e. the 'to _' and 'with_' cases). The adjective *gratus* often takes a dative complement. Hence, the dative interpretation of *insigni* would be reinforced. This leads to an overall interpretation of the phrase as 'grateful to an excellent (individual).'
   -*Semantic compatibility: gratus* immediately narrows *insignis* down to its positive meaning 'eminent' as opposed to neutral 'notable for, characterized by – '. This reduces the memory cost of the phrase as a whole.

2) ☑ [referam Camena]:
   -*Syntactic frequency:* this is a syntactically transparent phrase, a verb with a (morphologically unambiguous) adverbial ablative of means.
   -*Semantic compatibility:* to repeat (*referare*) a tale or a grand deed was the main task not only of the historian or the town crier, but the poet as well; so the meaning *Camena=* 'work of poetry' acquires prominence over the meaning 'goddess of poetry'.

3) Final reanalysis /Gratus insigni referam Camena/
   ☒ Gratus insigni
   ☑ /... insigni Camena/
   -Higher *syntactic frequency:* Latin's penchant for substantives notwithstanding, the specific word *insignis* is not often used alone to mean 'distinguished person'. Instead, it typically appears with a noun, even when it refers to the most inferable of entities, a man (in which case *homo* or *vir* is used). So, as soon as the mind becomes aware of a suitable candidate noun like *Camena*, it will be inclined to associate the two words.

-Semantic compatibility: inanimate and abstract things are often called *insignis,* and Perseus quotes an instance of the phrase *verba nove et insigniter dicta.* So the use of *insignis* to modify *Camena,* 'poetry,' should be immediately attractive to the mind of a Latin speaker.

A short summary of the interpretations is as follows:

1) First prosodic phrase and interpretive phase: /[Gratus *insigni*]/
2) Second prosodic phrase and interpretive phase: /[referam Camena]/
3) Integration, third interpretive phase: /Gratus referam *insigni Camena*/

ii. Figure of thought: syntactic transition symbolizing a social transaction

What could Horace's target audience possibly be expected to make of a flighty modifier floating from one host word to another? Well, if we count both interpretations as equally important, we are not talking about a flight but an *exchange* or transferal of the quality of excellence between a notable person to whom the poet is grateful (*gratus insigni*), and the poetry through which the bard retells this person's exploits (*referam insigni Camena*).

All this is to say that a Roman audience would have detected in this low-level linguistic shift an allusion to a social institution as old as collective memory: the poet-patron relationship. Essentially, the idea was that both poet and patron could gain a kind of immortality through the creation of verse. They were dependent upon each other: the heroic patron needed the poet's elegant verse, the only vehicle powerful enough to convey his name across the millennia; and the poet needed a story to tell (not to mention food to eat, to insure he would not reap the benefits of his certain immortality prematurely). Word and deed go hand in hand; without either kind of excellence there is no 'glory imperishable'.[19] This poet-patron relationship was still alive and kicking in Horace's day. Many of his odes refer to it in one way or another; in particular, the *interdependence* of poet's word and patron's deed is explicitly stressed in Carmen IV.8. This theme is as prominent in Horace as elsewhere in the ancient world; and the ritual of praising the famous in Carmen I.12 would immediately bring it to mind. So, provided the reader detects this syntactic ambiguity, he will find in it an allusion to the transfer of excellence in the poet-patron relationship – where *Camena* (here, 'poetry') snatches up *insigni*, the quality of excellence, and gives it new life as the *insignis* [*homo*] ('distinguished man') himself vanishes without a trace.

iii. Translation strategy

To find an English equivalent in the sense discussed above, we need a phrase which in isolation seems to describe Horace being inspired by an eminent figure, but which in the broader context has him claiming ownership of that very excellence we thought came from another. My solution was as follows:

> *Star-struck* – I will supply
> *My* heaven-sent lyricism –

The frequent, idiomatic meaning of 'star struck' is 'flustered by the presence of a famous person'. However, the semantic affinities between being struck by a star and receiving one's lyric talent from 'heaven,' combined with the stress on 'my' in the latter phrase, make it seem as if both phrases refer to traits which Horace innately possesses and 'supplies' to others.

8. Conclusion

We have made some seemingly paradoxical discoveries: To augment our *intuitions* about ancient texts, *formal* theory is required. Native speakers' spontaneous reactions are the *only* aspects of a poem which are (more or less) reconstructible across the millennia. Most surprisingly of all, meaning can find its way from the labyrinthine 'hedging' of Horace to the less landscaped world of modern English verse. The difference between the Latin original and a modern translation does not have to be a matter of apples and oranges; instead it can be a matter of well, apples and eggs (*mala* et *ova*)[20]: of crafting a well-rounded rendering with the same turns of phrase from the beginning to the end-stages of interpretation.

To end on the best 'note' possible, I have included in the endnotes the promised translation of Carmen IV.1, with a literal prose translation for comparative reference.[21]

9. Notes

1. This translation is oft-quoted among Classicists. I cannot track down its origin; see Edwards 2002:
   101 for a partial list of appearances. The Commager citation is given as being the most likely
   source.

2. With the ablative case ending -*o* being interpreted in an origin/material sense, employed to indicate what this Benedict Arnold was before he shifted his allegiances: '[a traitor]*from/of a friend*.'

3. The sharp-eyed observer will have noticed that in the English version, the girl is a 'sleeper' instead of a 'hider'. I have used a word with more overtly double-edged semantics ('sleeper cell' vs. sleeping girl) to compensate for the suggestive syntactic ambiguity of the original (*latentis* 'hiding (man)' hence 'covert agent' versus *latentis puellae* 'hiding girl'. The syntactic trick was of necessity lost in translation.

4. Compare the following statistics from Mayer, showing the percentage of golden or silver lines to overall lines in a few important classical and medieval works:

Horace, Satires and Epistles: .	.45 per cent
Vergil, Aeneid	.61 per cent
Ovid, Metamorphoses	1.28 per cent
Adhelm, Carmen de virginitate	7.27 per cent
Caelius Sedilius, Paschale 1	7.95 per cent
Ennodius, Itinerarium	11.54 per cent

5. My own rendering: Latin original:

And me? well, I've been 'served'

> Me tabula sacer
> votiva paries indicat uvida
> suspendisse potentis

By your venerated court
ship: broken, but alive – now I'm
hung over

> vestimenta maris deo

Literal translation:

Your mantle – in an image, an iconic

> The sacred wall shows that I have
> hung up my wet clothes in honour of the powerful

Wreck – fulfilling vows
with the accustomed lines:

> deity of the ocean

(Principal ambiguities exploited: *tabula* can mean a legal

'Behold – I've given up my – wine-
-dark sea-stained wardrobe –

> document or a votive tablet; *sacer* can be a term of abuse
> for a foe – here, a litigious '*ex*' – or simply mean 'sacred';
> *suspendisse* can mean 'have hung up' or 'have stopped';

Hung my hat – and habit – out to dry – I
offer up it all – to my *Almighty*

> *uvid*- can mean 'drunk', but here refers to wet clothes;
> *potens* can be used absolutely to refer to a god, *but in fact*
> modifies a sea(-born) god(dess))

Goddess – of the deep.'

6. The term 'functional equivalence' was of course coined by Eugene Nida (see Nida 1964 in full); but its meaning in practice has been debated ever since.

7. Rachel Giora mentions this pun in her brilliant work on the linguistic basis of wordplay *On Our Mind* (Giora 2003: 16). However, I have opted for a different explanation of the double meaning as it unfolds.

8. The phrase would have to be presented through a visual medium to be ambiguous, of course.

9. The idea that both the direct (orthography to semantics) and the phonological (orthography to phonology to semantics) are simultaneously involved in activating semantic data during silent reading is not controversial – although accounts of the specific distribution of labor during the time course of reading still vary. See Harm and Seidenberg: 2004 for a literature review and a connectionist model of the two pathways' interplay.

10. See Gibson 1998: 9: 'Higher frequency items require fewer energy resources to become activated than low frequency lexical items do. As a result, high frequency lexical items can be activated by the resource pool more quickly. Relatedly, structures representing plausible meanings require fewer energy resources to become activated than structures representing implausible meanings.' In Vosse and Kempen's mathematical formula (Vosse and Kempen 2000: 118), this factor is expressed via the 'initial activation value' of each syntactic interpretation (discussed on p. 116). This initial or default value reflects relative frequency in the mental lexicon.

11. Of course, if the speaker is, say, a happily married individual in his or her 60s, the mind will have no trouble suppressing this interpretation before it passes the threshold of consciousness. Initial, automatic activation is just the first step towards crossing the activation threshold. One interpretation is given a head start, but other contextual factors may later undermine it.

12. Gibson 1998:9: 'If all the constraints favour one structure for the input, then that structure will quickly receive a high activation. If there are two competing analyses for the input which are similar in heuristic value, then it will take longer to bring one of the representations over the threshold.' 'Compatibility' effects are expressed in the formula of Vosse and Kempen by the factor labelled $p^{foot\ incr.} + p^{root\ incr.}$. The 'root' and the 'foot' are two ends of a potential syntactic interpretation trying to coalesce in the conscious mind (e.g. the possible 'direct object' interpretation of a noun and the 'governing head' interpretation of a nearby transitive verb). Hence, the variable $p^{foot\ incr.} + p^{root\ incr.}$ is the sum of the continued activation of two compatible words participating in the same interpretation.

13. Those who are fond of the 'spicier' fringes of human experience and verbal expression will object that the other kind of 'date' can be tasty, too. As in the previous example, extra-linguistic contextual factors such as the identity and tastes of the speaker would determine whether an initially favoured interpretation would be later suppressed. Since these factors remain more or less constant in poetry of single authorship, I have omitted them in this discussion of linguistic ambiguity. (For an in-depth argument as to why the interpretive process can be described in terms of initial activation followed by (intra- and extra-linguistic) context-based adjustments, see Giora 2003 in full.)

14. See Gibson 1998: 3, 6, etc. In Vosse and Kempen, memory cost is reflected by the fact that all competing associations exert an inhibiting force on the development of a given interpretation. The sum of the competitors' inhibiting forces on a given interpretation u_i is expressed as $\Sigma u_j I_{i,j}$ in their formula (Vosse and Kempen 2000: 118).

15. This sentence is not globally ambiguous the way a line of Horatian poetry might be; when I speak of competing associations, I mean on a local, incremental level (such as multiple potential subjects for the second verb in a sea of centre-embedded clauses).

16. An analogy can be drawn between the smaller phrases defined by metrical pauses and the *intonation unit* of spoken speech, which is said to be the fundamental level at which separate thoughts

are communicated. On the latter, see Chafe 1994: 95; on connections drawn between the intonation unit of spoken speech and other traditions of ancient poetry, see Bakker 1990 or Edwards 2002 in full.

17. The example sentence is taken from Gibson 1998:8. Vosse and Kempen factor in a default decay of activation *d* (see Vosse and Kempen 2000: 116) which is greater in proportion to the time elapsed since an initial interpretation was activated: that is to say, to the distance in phonemes and breaths since a given word was comprehended.

18. The reader may have noted that the role of pauses in creating different interpretive possibilities was treated somewhat differently above: there, pauses were said to 'define the segments of interpretation', like official road signs alerting the travel-weary mind that an interpretive 'rest-stop' is at hand. These two accounts do not contradict each other, but rather treat sentence processing from both the 'top down' and 'bottom up' perspective. The present 'bottom up' account shows how pauses automatically effect an essentially passive processor; the former 'top down' account shows how pauses function when we consciously, attentively employ them as an interpretive cue.

19. 'Glory imperishable' is an English translation of one of the precious few poetic formulas which we can date back to the proto-Indo-European period (a claim made on the basis of the sound-by-sound equivalency of Greek κλέος ἄφθιτον and Sanskrit śravas akṣitam, verified via systematic correspondences between each respective phoneme in a slew of other cognate words). See Watkins 1995: 173–8 for a history of this formula. The phrase is used to describe the fame a fallen warrior receives when his story is retold throughout the ages. So, the poet-patron relationship was a cultural phenomenon with extremely deep roots, which still anchored and oriented the sensibilities of bards in Horace's day. See Watkins 1995: 68–84 for expressions of this relationship in various traditions of verbal art; and in particular p. 70 for a pair of lines in which the word κλέος exhibits a sort of polysemy similar to that of *insignis* in Horace's lines.

20. A famous Latin proverb *ab ovo usque ad mala* – 'from apple to eggs' – literally refers to the traditional beginning and ending of Roman feast, and figuratively describes something done thoroughly from beginning to end.

21. Literal translation:

Venus, why do you again enjoin the battles which had been called off for a while? Spare me, I beg you, I beg you. I'm not the sort I was once under the reign of good Cinara. Stop bending someone of around fifty years, who is now hard to soft commands, o mother of savage desires. Go away to where the flattering prayers of young men call you. You will more successfully carouse your way into the house of Paulus Maximus, aloft on purple swans, if you seek a heart fit to burn. For he is noble and comely, and he is not silent on behalf of his agitated clients, and he is a boy of a thousand arts; he will bear your flag far and wide. And when he mocks the gifts of a grandiose rival, he will put you up in marble underneath a cedarwood roof near the Alban lakes. There you will lead much incense up to your nose, and you will be entertained by mixed songs of the lyre and the oriental flute, not without a pipe. There twice a day boys along with young virgin girls, while praising your name, will stamp the ground with their shining white feet three times in the manner of the Salii. Neither woman nor boy can help me, nor a believable hope of a kindred soul, nor vying with wine nor binding my temples with new flowers. But why, Ligurinus, why does a rare tear drip down my cheek? Why does my facile tongue slip in between the words with an unbecoming silence? I hold you captive in my night-time dreams, then

I follow you, swift, through the grasses of the field of Mars, through the waters, you hard-hearted, fickle boy.

In this ode, baseline ambiguities echo and are amplified by the power struggle that is the main theme. They reflect confusion – or perhaps self-deception – concerning questions like the following: who has the upper hand in this relationship? Who broke up with whom? Who is hard of heart and who is heartbroken? Is the 'Venus' mentioned a demanding goddess or a dependent gold-digger?

Translation based on our new equivalency principle:

Venus, I have broken down
And up with you,
And *now* you call me back –
to arms?

Just spare me. Please!

I'm not the type
I was – for good

Cinara – when she was around to hold
sway over me

Stay where you are –
sweet Mother of all

Poison darts – with tickle feathers –

Don't you try to sway me – I

Am five times
ten years
in your service, tired

Of bearing that

Quiver –

Go where young men's flattering

Prayers will trail you –
where you'd be less
unfashionably late, and more

At home – with Paulus
Maximus: the eldest son,

The heir:
Sitting pretty, in the purple

Chariot
drawn by swans,
parade your way in – if your heart is burning

For a man who's 'set', who's 'made'
To be inflamed –

He's got blue blood,
and very noble

Stature, when he stands up

For the poor
saps that he represents in court –

He'll fight your battles –
even bear your standard

Expectations – he's
an errand boy 'of many counsels' –

Giddy from the empire he's built –
with the bribes of colleagues

Far beneath him,
he'll put you on a pedestal

At his lakeside villa
overshadowed by his shrine
of cedarwood

Your upturned nose
will take in all –

The incense floating in the air –
the lyres all choice – and oriental

Flutes – will treat you –
like Cybele –

With music melting in a pot –
and muddled to the ears –

With shepherd's reeds
intruding in –

Adoring adolescents
will serenade your

Highness,
twice *each* day, with tender strains

Of little virgin girls –
all pounding their immaculate young feet,
as if they were initiates of Mars –

Enough!
I'll not be helped by women, boys –

I simply have no soul
mate – probably

I'm done with all those
drinking games –

With letting trophy
'wreaths'
get in my hair.

Ligurine – my little tenor –
why, oh why, when

Someone special
sheds me –

A tear – or two

Will trickle down my cheek?

Why is it my smooth-
talking tongue

Stumbles through the lines and –
stops –
all too soon?

In my dreams
I hold a captive –

You –

And then I'm at
his heels –

Running through the field
of Mars – soon I'm swimming

Darting, swaying
changing

With the tide.

10. Bibliography

Bakker, E. J. (1990) 'Homeric Discourse and Enjambement: A Cognitive Approach', *Transactions of the American Philological Association*, 120, 1–21.

Chafe, Wallace (1994) *Discourse, Consciousness, and Time: the Flow and Displacement of Conscious Experience in Speaking and Writing*. Chicago, IL: University of Chicago Press.

Commager, Steele (1995) *The Odes of Horace: A Critical Study*, Norman, OK; London: University of Oklahoma Press.

Cook, Steven A. (1996) 'On the Road in Assad's Damascus', *The Middle East Quarterly*, III, 4, 39–43.

Edwards, Mark W. (2002) *Sound, Sense, and Rhythm: Listening to Greek and Latin Poetry*. Princeton, NJ: Princeton University Press.

Flaccus, Quintus Horatius and Wickham, E. C. (1922) *Q. Horati Flacci Opera*, New York: Oxford University Press.

Garrison, D. H. (ed.) (1991) *Horace: Epodes and Odes, a New Annotated Edition*. Norman, OK: University of Oklahoma Press.

Gernsbacher, Morton Ann (1990) *Language Comprehension as Structure Building*. Hillsdale, MI: Lawrence Erlbaum Associates.

Gibson, Edward (1998) 'Linguistic complexity: locality of syntactic dependencies', *Cognition*, 68, 1–76.

Gildersleeve, B. L. and Lodge, G. (ed.) (1989) *Gildersleeve's Latin Grammar*. Wauconda, IL: Bolchazy-Carducci Publishers, Inc.

Giora, Rachel (2003) *On our Mind: Salience, Context and Figurative Language*. Oxford: Oxford University Press.

Harm, Michael W. and Seidenberg, Mark S. (2004) 'Computing the Meaning of Words in Reading: Cooperative Division of Labor between Visual and Phonological Processes', *Psychological Review*, 111 (3) 662–720.

Martial (1993) *Epigrammata (Oxford Classical Texts Series)*, New York: Oxford University Press.

Mayer, K. (2002) 'The Golden Line: Ancient and Medieval Lists of Special Hexameters and Modern Scholarship', in C. Lanham (ed.) *Latin Grammar and Rhetoric: Classical Theory and Modern Practice*. London : Continuum Press, 139–79.

McClatchy, J. D. (ed.) (2005) *The Odes: New Translations by Contemporary Poets*. Princeton, NJ; Oxford: Princeton University Press.

Michie, James (trans.) (2002) *Odes: with the Latin Text*. New York: Modern Library.

Milton, John (1900) *The Poetical Works of John Milton*, ed. H. C. Beeching, Oxford: Clarendon.

Nida, Eugene A. (1964) *Toward a Science of Translation*. Leiden: E. J. Brill.

Ovidi, Nasonis P. (2004) *Metamorphoses (Oxford Classical Texts Series)*, ed. R. J. Tarrant, New York: Oxford University Press.

Rudd, Niall (trans.) (2004) *Horace: Odes and Epodes*. Cambridge, MA: Harvard University Press.

Sydenham, Colin (2004) *Horace: The Odes; New Verse Translation with Facing Latin Text and Notes*. London: Duckworth.

Vosse, T. with Kempen, G. (2000) 'Syntactic Structure Assembly in Human Parsing: A Computational Model Based on Competitive Inhibition and a Lexicalist Grammar', *Cognition*, 75, 105–43.

Watkins, Calvert (1995) *How to Kill a Dragon: Aspects of Indo-European Poetics.* New York: Oxford University Press.

Theory and Practice of Feminist Translation in the 21st Century

3

Lina Fisher

University of East Anglia, UK

Chapter Outline

1. Introduction

This chapter explores a new approach to feminist translation. I will use my own translations of poems published in Carol Ann Duffy's collection *Mean Time* (1993) to illustrate what I understand as feminist translation. I examine the issues in three broad sections: reader-response theories, feminism, and examples from my translations.

Feminist translation in the twenty-first century, in my view, is the practice of basing one's approach on advances made in the fields of translation, linguistics, literature and reader-response theories. It is regrettable that feminist translation does not receive the attention it did in the 1970s and 1980s as it is still possible to demonstrate the effect of sexist language on women's lives: a 2007 study found that after listening to sexist jokes men are less likely to donate money to women's charities (Ford 2008). Kramarae's Muted Group Framework (1986) still provides a structured analysis of the unbalanced power relationship inherent in discourse and will be discussed in the translation context that follows.

In my translations, I will implement changes suggested by German feminist linguists, rather than feminist translation strategies. The German language is particularly useful for an endeavour such as this as it uses grammatical gender and, until a few years ago, the generic masculine.

Feminine experiences and perspectives play a central role in Duffy's writing and she has stated that 'I doubt I would now write a poem in the male voice' (Forbes 2002: interview with the *Guardian*). According to another interview, Duffy does not define herself as a woman poet (Winterson 2005), perhaps fearing that such a limited label would reduce readings of her poetry to a single aspect. Nevertheless, it is not clear whether Duffy sees herself as a feminist author, and, in any case, reader-response theories have moved criticism on from concentrating on the author's intent. I will thus support my strategies through theories of reading and authorship, especially the notion of the 'inferred author' (Boase-Beier 2004: 279) and the position of the feminist reader (see Flynn and Schweickart 1986).

The shift in the perception of the reader's degree of involvement has helped to elevate the status of the translator, and can empower the translator, especially if s/he has political convictions that play a role in the target text production.

i. My approach

The main issue at the outset of this project was whether I was justified in using feminist (translation) strategies. Most feminist translation theory is concerned with subverting texts written by male authors (especially the Canadian theorists de Lotbinière-Harwood 1995; Flotow 1997; Simon 1996) or translating feminist texts (Flotow; Simon; Díaz-Diocaretz 1985); the same is true of feminist reader-response theories (Mills 1994).

In some cases I expect clear translation choices to present themselves since nouns, grammatically neutral in English, can take the feminine, masculine or neuter gender in German. It is interesting to note that grammatical gender in German does not always conform to biological gender, so that 'das Mädchen' [the girl], for example, takes the grammatical neuter form. Where an English noun can be translated with either a feminine or a masculine noun in German, I will use the feminine as the generic form.

One could say that changing certain aspects of the language used by Duffy could be a form of censorship, but my translations are simply one of many possible readings of Duffy's poetry. The realization that 'reading is a form of translation' and that 'translation is in turn a form of critical reading, and a concrete realisation of that reading' (Boase-Beier and Holman 1999: 14) played a central role in this project. Post-modern theories of language further helped me understand the feminist translator's role: '[t]he recognition of translation as a form of *écriture*, as a production rather than a mere recovery of someone else's meaning [. . .] is a key factor for politically active, feminist translators' (Arrojo 1994: 149). However, feminism is often derided (Aune 2003; Toller et al. 2004: 89), and as a consequence an overtly feminist text might alienate readers so that they would either not read it at all or not notice other important elements such as striking themes or stylistic devices. A more subtle approach would enable me to make a feminist statement where possible, but without distorting the poems or risking antagonizing readers. Of course, it is impossible to please all readers, but rather than addressing a particular readership with my translations, I decided to attempt to find out how far one could take the introduction of feminist elements without allowing them to take centre stage.

2. The role of the reader

Views on the role of the reader have changed considerably over time. The translator, apart from being a text creator, is a source text reader; hence it makes sense to examine various theories regarding this aspect. In this section I will give an overview of the changing roles of author and reader and the effects they have on the position of the translator.

The Classical perception of the reader was based on the representation of the mind as a passive recipient of information provided by the outside world: Plato, in his *Theaetetus* (ca. 360 B.C.), compares the mind to a wax tablet which receives impressions (see Jowett 1953: 191), while Locke in 1690 thought of the mind as a 'white paper, void of all characters, without any ideas' (Locke 1961: 109). However, this view allows the reader a minimal role as 'the possibility that different readers might legitimately extract different messages from the same words is not acknowledged' (Crawford and Chaffin 1986: 3). This view evolved somewhat over the course of the centuries that followed, so that in stylistics from the 1960s onwards, the model of an 'implied author' (Booth 1961: 138) was assumed, defined by Booth as the actual author's 'second self' (ibid.) and described by Suleiman as 'the shadowy but overriding presence who is responsible for every aspect of the work and whose image must be constructed (or rather, reconstructed) in the act of reading' (Suleiman 1980: 8). Thus, whereas in the Classical view the mind was seen as completely passive, from the 1960s it was seen to take a slightly more active role in the reading of the text. But the idea of the 'implied author' and its counterpart, the 'implied reader', still limits the reader's involvement in the creation of meaning since 'a successful reading experience requires (1) a correct identification of the implied reader's values and beliefs [. . .] and (2) an identification *with* the implied reader' (Suleiman 1980: 9). This view seems to suggest that when the reader cannot identify with the implied reader, a successful reading experience cannot take place, which can be an issue especially in the case of political texts or readers with political convictions: a text which overtly addresses a certain readership is likely to alienate readers whose values differ from those of the implied reader or implied author.

Barthes provides another milestone in the evolution of reader-response theories by questioning the elevated status given to the author in the creation of meaning: '[t]he *explanation* of a work is always sought in the man or woman who produced it' (Barthes 1977: 143), just as in a Christian world view God is the creator of all things in existence. From this position Barthes sets out to criticize the God-like role assigned to the writer, the position of 'Author-God' (146), who one might say was implied by Booth's statement '[t]he author [. . .] makes his reader as he makes his second self' (Booth 1961: 138). Barthes extends his comparison:

> literature [. . .], by refusing to assign a 'secret', an ultimate meaning, to the text (and to the world as text), liberates what may be called an anti-theological activity, an activity that is truly revolutionary since to refuse to fix meaning is, in the end, to refuse God. (Barthes 1997: 147)

It seems that as Western readers brought up in a traditionally Christian environment, it is in our nature to seek explanations in a superior being so that the author as hitherto regarded was the result of the deistic nature of our culture, and it may be that these literary developments were foreshadowed by the philosophical advances of the 1960s: just as advised by Sartre's Existentialism, we have to reject (the author-) God and make sense of the world and the text by ourselves. As a consequence, the author becomes a figure to rebel against: by disagreeing with the interpretation which seems to present itself as most obvious we can find our own.

A very significant advance concerning the role of the reader, and by extension that of the translator, was made by Wimsatt in his development of the 'Intentional Fallacy' (Wimsatt 1954). In short, 'knowledge of an author's intentions will not help the reader or critic to interpret a text' (Boase-Beier 2006: 33). Of course the author has an intention when composing a text, but there is no way for the reader to know what it is; all s/he has at her/his disposal is the text. We can scrutinize the author's biography to learn more about her/his life, it may even help us shed light on previously obscure references in the text, but at the same time it is important to know that we are merely constructing an 'inferred author' (Boase-Beier 2004: 279). This is an important distinction: an implied author is seen as implied by the text, the reader simply has to perceive her/him, whereas an inferred author is constructed by the reader, thus a shift in emphasis has taken place.

ii. Consequences for translation

The understanding of the author as just described has serious implications for the translator: if a text is seen to hold meaning as intended by the author, the translator's task is merely to transfer this meaning. This makes translation seem to be a rather menial task: '[a] strong view of meaning as the author's suggests the simplest view of translation' and is 'the least fruitful as it denies the translator, as reader, much involvement in the process' (Boase-Beier 2006: 35). Subscribing to the view that the reader plays no role in the creation of meaning implies that the translator's task is merely to transfer the author's message into the target language and does not take into account aspects, such as style, which are not always the result of conscious choice.

These developments now let theorists state, 'readers read the poems they have made' (Schweickart 1986: 36); they also elevate the status of the translator so that s/he is now seen as

> an agent (subject, person) whose receptive disposition to the act of reading is the act of writing, and whose discursive production will be a new chain of significations and responses in the RT [receptor text] that perhaps does not belong to the original response. (Díaz-Diocaretz 1985: 8–9)

Literary translators now enjoy a greater freedom: they are no longer seen as mere slaves of the source text and its author but instead are entitled to their own interpretation, which they then transfer. Thus, it seems that the liberation of the reader and translator may enable minorities to reach bigger audiences. This, of course, is especially useful for translators who entertain political convictions, such as feminism, which they aim to demonstrate in their target text production.

3. Feminism

iii. Feminist stylistics

'[Feminist stylisticians] study the ways in which images of women are constrained by language, and work towards a critical feminist awareness, which might lead to resistance and, ultimately, linguistic and/or social change' (Weber, 1996: 5). Agreement with this point depends on whether one believes that language influences social realities. In my view, it seems logical that language would influence society. According to Mills,

> it is necessary to stress that as well as keeping people in their place, language can also be one of the many ways that they can question their position; awareness of the ways in which language is used as a stabilizing mechanism can be a step in the direction of liberation. (Mills 1995a: 14)

Mills mentions language reform as a way of stopping sexism in society (Mills 1995a: 85). What this means for the translator is clear: if the translator is aware of patriarchal linguistic structures, s/he can question as well as change them. Duffy's poetry seems particularly suitable for this as language and how it influences our experiences is a theme in many of her poems, demonstrated especially by the poem 'Litany', an example of 'Duffy's rendering of the perceived marriage of words and things' (O'Brien 1998: 165) which describes the world of 1950s housewives who have a 'tribal fear of invoking something by naming it' (ibid.). Consequently, embarrassing words are 'broken / to bits' (Duffy 1993: 9; line 12–13) and no one has 'leukaemia, which no one could spell' (ibid; line 16) as 'language embarrassed them' (ibid; line 6). Rowland further notes that Duffy's 'amorous lyrics are rooted in debates over the function of language, and the difficulties in formulating "experience"' (Rowland 2001: 200).

iv. Feminist language issues

Kramarae examines the concept of patriarchal language as part of the Muted Group Framework, a theory examining women's relation with language. According to her,

> the language of a particular culture does not serve all its speakers equally, for not all speakers contribute in an equal fashion to its formulation. Women (and members of other subordinate groups) are not as free or as able as men to say what they wish when and where they wish, because the words and the norms for their use have been formulated by the dominant group, men. (Kramarae 1981: 1)

The theory of muted groups describes situations of asymmetrical power relationships and proposes the hypothesis that the dominant group controls language and the norms for its use. The experiences of the muted group must use language derived mainly from the dominant group's perception (see Crawford and Chaffin, 1986: 21). While von Flotow does not explicitly refer to the Muted Group Framework, she nevertheless acknowledges women's 'gendered exclusion' from the 'dominant patriarchal code' (Flotow 1997: 12) by drawing a connection between women's language and translation:

> translation has long served as a trope to describe what women do when they enter the public sphere: they translate their private language, their specifically female forms of discourse, developed as a result of gendered exclusion, into some form of the dominant patriarchal code. (Flotow 1997: 12)

As a result of the existence of such processes, some experiences will inevitably be 'lost in translation' and thus 'remain unvoiced, and perhaps unthought, even within the muted group' (Crawford and Chaffin: 1986 21).

Several insights can be gained from these two extracts: language has been formulated by men, hence it is unsuitable to express feminine experiences; women have to 'translate' their discourse so that it conforms to the patriarchal norms. Furthermore, the absence of a linguistic system to encode female experiences could lead to an inability of women to think certain thoughts.

This realization can be linked to the notion of Linguistic Relativity (often used by feminist linguists such as Mills, Samel and Pusch in order to draw attention to the importance of gender-inclusive language): if language does not take into account the existence of women in certain parts of society, it will be difficult for them to move into those areas. Mills mentions the example of sex-unbiased job advertisements which encourage more female applicants than advertisements using the generic masculine (Mills 1995a: 85). Thus, it could be said that patriarchal language damages women.

Few would now agree with Sapir's statement that 'the "real world" is to a large extent unconsciously built upon the language habits of the group' (1949: 69). However, a more moderate or limited Whorfianism, namely that 'there is *at least some* causal influence from language categories to non-verbal cognition' (Gumperz and Levinson 1996: 22), is more acceptable. It is thus clear that language plays a role in the position of women in society, and perhaps even their mental well-being.

Linguistic expressions may need to be changed in order to accommodate feminine idioms which reflect women's experiences; I am thinking especially of expressions which equate masculinity with strength and femininity with weakness. This cannot be achieved in the short term: radical changes may result in writing becoming incomprehensible, and this would not help the feminist goal as such a strategy might lead to alienation rather than acceptance and would consequently be only short-lived. Feminist writers of the 1970s and 1980s subverted patriarchal language and concepts by producing very experimental texts that have been criticized for 'limit[ing] oppositional culture to the reading and writing experiments of an intellectual elite' (Felski 1989: 6). Poetry may be seen as experimental by nature and may achieve greater effects in the reader by making her/him work harder in processing different possible readings (see Boase-Beier 2003: 257), but in my view a balance has to be found in order for the text to have the desired effect.

Extremely experimental translations that at the same time proclaim their feminist aim could easily alienate readers. The writing of authors such as Nicole Brossard, Helene Cixous and Barbara Godard can be described as radically feminist and experimental. These writers used new words, spellings, grammatical constructions, metaphors and images in an attempt to move beyond the conventions of what they saw as patriarchal language detrimental to women's wellbeing. In her translation of Brossard's *Sous la langue* (1987) Susanne de Lotbinière-Harwood quite literally makes the feminine visible: 'Fricatelle ruisselle essentielle aime-t-elle dans le touche à tout qui arrondit les seins la rondeur douce des bouches ou l'effet qui la déshabille?' becomes 'Does she frictional she fluvial she essential does she in the all-embracing touch that rounds the breasts love the mouths' soft roundness or the effect undressing her?' (quoted in Flotow 1997: 23). The repetition of the French 'elle' [she] and the English 'she' in the translation reinforces the feminine context of the text (Flotow 1997: 23) while leading to the creation of several neologisms. It thus becomes apparent that experimental feminist writing and translation is more concerned with sound than with meaning, associations often playing a pivotal role.

Research in gender identity and attitudes toward feminism indicates that 'in men, increased masculinity [is] associated with negative attitudes toward feminism, negative attitudes toward non-traditional gender roles, and unwillingness to consider oneself a feminist' (Toller et al., 2004: 87) while 'more feminine women [...] may [view] feminism and nontraditional gender roles as masculine' (ibid. 89). Thus, presumably, masculine men and feminine women, representing two extremes of my translations' potential readership, who might be seen to rely on their gender image for their sense of self-worth, might have difficulties identifying with the poet or her personae if they identify a text as feminist, or they might be unwilling to be open to the text's implicatures.

This is why, in my translations, I have attempted to make changes mostly on a lexical level: replacing words denoting women that are used in a pejorative sense (as in the translation of 'Never Go Back'). I chose to make changes on a lexical level rather than a graphological or phonological level because these alternatives are more likely to result in texts which are incomprehensible to a non-specialist reader: rather than producing a totally experimental poetic structure I decided that a focus on systematically changing lexis was more productive, and less antagonizing, from the standpoint of introducing the desired political position to the reader. While this raises serious issues relating to the use of the text to further my own political aims, these are, in this case, as I will show with the example of 'Never Go Back' below, secondary to the wider translation endeavour and given the writer's own political stance, discussed above, not significant here. In my translation of 'Small Female Skull' I made changes on a grammatical level by referring to 'Schädel' [skull], a noun taking the masculine gender in German, as 'sie' [she] (see explanation below).

The choice of text to translate can further help convey a political message: according to Schweickart, 'the feminist inquiry into the activity of reading begins with the realization that the literary canon is androcentric, and that this has a profoundly damaging effect on women readers' (Schweickart 1986: 40). If one subscribes to Chesterman's view that 'translators are agents of change' (Chesterman 1997) and that '[t]ranslations change the state of the world, by adding new texts' (Chesterman 2000), choosing to translate a text written by a woman author means that the target language literary canon becomes less androcentric through this addition. Thus, a feminist translator can achieve her aim of propagating her political message by consciously choosing to translate mainly texts written by women.

Issues concerning language must have consequences for the translator. Although Schweickart's view that '[l]iterature acts on the world by acting on its readers' (Schweickart 1986: 39) could be seen as idealistic, literature is nevertheless a means by which to influence people and therefore is useful for the propagation of feminist strategies and viewpoints.

Boase-Beier states that '[i]f language use is not autonomous, then neither literature itself nor literary style can simply be seen as closed off from the influences of society' (Boase-Beier 2006: 17). The idea that literature can be seen as being closed off from societal influences would, according to Burton, 'merely naively [support] and [demonstrate] the (largely unseen and unnoticed) political bias of the status quo' (Burton, 1996: 225). By extension, however, what Boase-Beier's statement means for the translator of literature is that on the one hand, s/he realizes, through knowledge of the relation between text production and society, that choices in translation, and hence the target text style, are influenced by society. On the other, the translator can make political choices and thus subvert the status quo, as far as this can realistically be combined with publishers' demands. This can be difficult to achieve as 'publishers have clear ideas about what they can market' (Mills 1995a: 32) while

> constraints on publishers, because of the nature of multinational ownership of publishing firms by companies whose main interests are not in literature or writing, can also have a great effect, so that profit motives are at the fore in the choice of which authors to engage and which not. (Mills 1995a: 32)

If the choice of author is determined by these factors, the choice of translator is likely to be constrained in similar ways, so that an overtly feminist translator might not be employed in order to ensure that the book remains as marketable in the target language as it is in the source language.

4. My translations

v. Feminist interpretations

Duffy was born in Glasgow 1955 and grew up in Staffordshire; *Mean Time* was published in 1993. The collection explores several of Duffy's most prevalent themes such as time ('Mean Time', 'Brothers', 'Before You Were Mine'), religion ('Confession', 'Prayer') and displacement ('Close', 'Oslo', 'Never Go Back'). While gendered perspectives clearly play a role in Duffy's poetry, she does not seem to define herself as a woman poet. Díaz-Diocaretz explains that '[a] poem written by a woman is not necessarily female-identified; when the text is ambiguous, only the reader's act of inferencing can determine whether the persona, or the speaking subject is a woman' (Díaz-Diocaretz, 1985: 45). In Duffy's writing it is often not clear whether the personae of her poems are male or female; this sense is heightened by the fact that the majority of the experiences explored in *Mean Time* can occur in both women and men's lives.

My translations were not done with the aim of publication, but rather as an experiment to find out if feminist elements could be included without overshadowing the poems' other elements such as Duffy's rich imagery or subject matter as I did not want to make choices that I saw as without foundation in the source text. Although the idea of 'faithfulness' in translation is long outdated, I nevertheless felt an obligation to preserve what I interpreted as Duffy's style or as elements in the text put there by her in order to produce a certain image or story in the reader's mind.

a. 'The Windows' – 'Die Fenster'

Duffy's poem 'The Windows' could detail events witnessed by a male passer-by: if one believes the scenes pictured to be appealingly homely and assumes that women turn houses into homes while their husbands are excluded from family life because of long working hours, then it certainly seems logical to see the 'stranger passing your gate' (Duffy 1993: 47) as a man. But it is also possible to imagine a woman: on a more abstract level, the stranger could be seen to represent all women, looking in on the privileged and more fortunate life they were denied as a result of gender politics and the wage gap. It could even be a child, rejected by her/his own relatives, watching joyful family scenes on Christmas Eve.

Although I consider these three interpretations to be supported by the text, I had to find a way to translate 'the stranger' into German with its grammatical gender markers. My initial, instinctive, reaction was to choose 'der Fremde' [the stranger; masculine form], but then I realized that there was no reason to give this form preference over 'die Fremde' [the stranger; feminine form] and that this was precisely what feminist linguists aimed to avoid with their reforms.

One might say that I eliminated a possible interpretation through my decision: that of a male stranger passing the gate; however, it is still possible to interpret 'die Fremde' as a child and it was my aim to represent women in the text.

b. 'Small Female Skull' – 'Kleiner Frauenkopf'

Feminist translation strategies can, to a certain extent, be seen as akin to Venuti's foreignization approach: 'Venuti (2000) specifically links the stylistic nature of the target text to political questions' (Boase-Beier 2006: 68). According to him, 'fluency masks a domestication of the foreign text that is appropriative and potentially imperialistic, putting the foreign to domestic uses which, in British and American cultures, extend the global hegemony of English' (Venuti 2004: 334). If domestication is imperialistic, hence if composing a translation that reads fluently can be seen to contribute to English erasing traits of other cultures, then using patriarchal elements such as the generic masculine in a German-language target text means translating in a way which supports and confirms patriarchal linguistic structures and also, possibly, societal structures.

Thus, the 'ethical politics of difference' (Venuti 2004: 483) Venuti advocates could be used for feminist purposes. This insight was especially useful for the translation of 'Small Female Skull': it justifies my decision to translate 'it', referring to the skull, as 'sie' [she] where grammatically appropriate. Thus I am using the generic feminine as suggested by German feminist linguists (see Pusch 1984; Samel 2000). *Splitting*, the practice of referring explicitly to women and men (e.g. *Studenten und Studentinnen* [male students and female students]), and one of the measures suggested by feminist linguists in order to make the German language more gender-inclusive, is now widely accepted in German-speaking societies. However, the generic feminine might still surprise readers of my translations as it is not widely used but rather the polar opposite of the previously accepted usage of the generic masculine. In fact, the generic feminine was never seen as a serious suggestion for reform as such a change would clearly be an exaggeration, though not without a laudable objective. Pusch thought that although men would never agree to this as they feared nothing more than total feminization, they might agree to a less drastic but equally effective transformation (Samel 2000: 76). Using the generic feminine in my translations thus means that my texts do not read fluently in Venuti's sense.

Margitt Lehbert in her 1996 collection of Duffy translations *Die Bauchrednerpuppe* uses 'er' [he] to refer to 'Schädel' [skull], as it is a masculine noun. However, the poem's title is 'Small *Female* Skull' and given that the poem can be interpreted to describe a woman suffering violence at the hands of a male perpetrator, it is clear that it would not be in the interest of the poem to use masculine forms. In my view, one loses the connection between the skull of the title and what the skull represents within the poem by changing the gender to match the object's grammatical gender.

Lehbert's translation is also rather literal as she uses 'Glasche Glier' to translate 'gottle of geer':

> 'take it to the mirror to ask for a gottle of geer'
> (Duffy 1993: 25; line 11)

> 'nehme ihn   mit   zum   Spiegel,   um eine Glasche Glier zu erbitten'
> take   it/him with-me to-the mirror in-order a   gottle   geer to ask-for
> (Lehbert 1996: 89; my gloss)

> 'gehe zum   Spiegel, geb vor ich   wäre   der Puppenspieler'
> go   to-the mirror pretend I   would-be the puppet-master
> (my translation and gloss)

I didn't use 'Glasche Glier' as I had never heard this expression used in German before and it had no connotations of ventriloquism. It seemed more appropriate to attempt to translate my interpretation of Duffy's peculiar wording in order to then re-encode it in a way understandable to a German audience.

Ventriloquism is a common theme in Duffy's poetry: it is also mentioned in 'The Dummy' and 'The Psychopath' (both *Selling Manhattan*, Duffy 1987: 20; 28) and seems to be a widely known form of entertainment in the UK, but while 'Bauchredner' [stomach speakers] are a traditional attraction at German annual fairs, they do not use puppets. The control the ventriloquist exerts over the dummy suggests one person speaking for another. This connotation cannot be expressed by using a phrase referring to 'Bauchreden' and I thus had to find an image that would,

1. express a person being in control of another,
2. preserve the possibility of a feminist interpretation and
3. be understood by a German audience to mean 1) and 2).

The doll metaphor offered itself and I was able to use an image involving marionettes (well known in Germany). Marionettes are attached to strings that allow a puppet master (slightly sinister connotations) to control their every move. This image expresses the plight of women who can be chained to the house by their husbands, chained to the husband by being forbidden to speak to certain people or restricted to move only within certain social strata by societal conventions.

Changing the image used here in the source text can be seen as a domesticating choice: a German audience will be familiar with marionettes, and indeed they are an image commonly used to describe a situation one would hint at by muttering 'gottle of geer'. Thus I am effectively 'mov[ing] the author towards [the reader]' (Schleiermacher in Venuti 1991: 129), to quote Schleiermacher's well-known words. It might seem inconsistent to advocate the use of foreignizing choices, that is, the use of the generic feminine, while also choosing to domesticate 'gottle of geer'; however, using the metaphor of the puppet master in a way which is clear to a German audience means that I am able to ensure that the political message is more likely to be inferred. Furthermore, in Venuti's view, domestication and foreignization are not used as general strategies, they are merely 'tendencies' (Venuti 1995: 309), later also referred to as a 'practice' (Venuti 2008: 23). Although I believe that feminist aims can easily be combined with the aims of a translator striving for recognition by using foreignizing strategies, achieving the translator's and women's visibility in the process, in this instance I decided that the image used by Duffy would be lost on a German reader if I did not domesticate it to some extent. Doing this allowed me to preserve the political message I interpreted to be contained in Duffy's writing. This cultural domestication means that my translation would be less likely to alienate German readers; thus a subtle approach will prevent the poem's political element of the feminization of the text from being rejected.

c. 'Never Go Back' – 'Geh Nie Zurück': Sexist Language

The main issue in the translation of this poem was the rendering of 'whore' in the line 'for a drenched whore to stare you full in the face' (Duffy 1993: 30; line 40). I first considered using the term 'Freudenmädchen', an archaic word meaning 'prostitute' (Wahrig: 501) because 'Freude' means 'joy' and 'Freudenmädchen' hence seems to have slightly more positive connotations. On the other hand, Duffy may have used the term 'whore' in order to increase the feeling of bleakness this poem conveys: death and decay are central themes, and the breakdown in society (excluding areas where prostitution is legalized) that leads to prostitutes roaming freely in an area contributes to an air of desolation. However, in my view, a desolate atmosphere could just as well be preserved by using 'Bettler' [beggar] instead. It seems that choosing to make a political point here, such as reclaiming the term 'Freudenmädchen', would be to the detriment of Duffy's style as it would negate what I interpret as a carefully constructed image of two contrasting worlds. This might not be an issue for a reader who can access both source and target text as s/he might be able to follow my reasoning, but to a reader who relies solely on the translation, it may seem odd to include the vaguely positive term 'Freudenmädchen' in a poem otherwise pervaded by hopelessness. Altering this thematic structure could also be confusing: in my interpretation, 'Never Go Back' describes the situation of a person reluctantly returning to the place of her/his childhood where everything appears like the set of a horror film. This place is described in entirely negative terms, whereas the new home, 'wherever you live', seems warm and inviting, signalled by the lights and fires. There thus seems to be a great distance between these two places, perhaps remarking on the impossibility of fully returning to the place of one's childhood after leaving the nest. This distance would not be preserved if there were positive elements in the parts relating to the former home.

In some instances feminist choices are relatively easy to implement, a clear alternative to the use of masculine forms or arising out of metaphors used by Duffy. In other cases where there seems to be a choice between an overtly political choice and preserving part of what I saw as a poem's essence, as in the case of 'Never Go Back', I chose not to disturb the world I found to be constructed by the poem according to my interpretation.

It seems that although I attempted a feminist translation in all cases, this is not always possible to carry through.

5. Conclusion

At the start of this project I was unsure of whether it would be possible to use feminist strategies in my translation. I endeavoured to make a political point wherever possible, but also to preserve the elements that I saw as essential to my interpretation of the story a poem told, even if it would lessen the feminist elements.

I was influenced by theories concerning reading, translation and stylistics in order to understand my position as a feminist translator. The attempt to feminize Duffy's writing made me question my interpretation and translation as I wanted to ensure that I did not add elements that were not in some way provided by the texts themselves. In most cases, this testing of my choices resulted in the discovery that I reduced the possible understandings of Duffy's poetry.

Had I placed my political aims above the notion of some degree of faithfulness to my interpretation, it might have been possible to feminize Duffy's poems to a greater extent. It might be necessary to construct entirely new poems in order to portray feminine rather than masculine experiences.

The strategy one chooses for a project such as this depends on one's convictions and their relation to the chosen text. Some texts might be easier to adapt for feminist aims, others might cause a strong reaction in female translators and be easily adaptable for that reason. Feminist translators more radical than me might have no qualms about appropriating the source text entirely, and there is no reason why they should not.

6. Bibliography

Arrojo, R. (1994) 'Fidelity and the Gendered Translation', *TTR* 7 (2) 147–63.

Aune, K. (2003) 'Who Says Feminism is Dead?', *The Guardian* 17 April 2003.

Barthes, R. (1977) (trans. S. Heath) *Image – Music – Text*, London: Fontana Press.

Boase-Beier, J. (2006) *Stylistic Approaches to Translation*, Manchester: St Jerome Publishing.

Boase-Beier, J. (2004) 'Knowing and Not Knowing: Style, Intention and the Translation of a Holocaust Poem', *Language and Literature* 13 (1) 25–35.

Boase-Beier, J. (2003) 'Mind Style Translated', *Style* 37 (3) 253–65.

Boase-Beier, J. (2002) 'Translating Style', in S. Csabi and J. Zerkowitz (eds) *Textual Secrets: The Message of the Medium*, Budapest: Eötvös Loránd University, 317–25.

Boase-Beier, J. and Holman, M. (eds) (1999) *The Practices of Literary Translation: Constraints and Creativity*, Manchester: St Jerome.

Booth, W. C. (1961) *The Rhetoric of Fiction*, Chicago, IL; London: University of Chicago Press.

Brittan. S. (1995) 'Language and Structure in the Poetry of Carol Ann Duffy', *Thumbscrew* 1 (Winter 1994–5) 58–64.

Burton, B. (1996) 'Through glass darkly: through dark glasses', in J. J. Weber (ed.) *The Stylistics Reader: From Roman Jakobson to the Present*, London: Arnold, 224–40.

Chesterman, A. (1997) 'Memes of Translation. The Spread of Ideas in Translation Theory' www.helsinki.fi/~chesterm/1997cMemes.html [accessed 30 April 2007].

Chesterman, A. (2000) 'Memetics and Translation Strategies' www.helsinki.fi/~chesterm/2000i Memetics.html [accessed 30 April 2007].

Crawford, M. and Chaffin, R. (1986) 'The Reader's Construction of Meaning: Cognitive Research on Gender and Comprehension' in E. A. Flynn and P. P. Schweickart (eds) *Gender and Reading*, Baltimore, MD: Johns Hopkins University Press, 3–30.

Díaz-Diocaretz, M. (1985) *Translating Poetic Discourse: Questions on Feminist Strategies in Adrienne Rich*, Amsterdam, Philadelphia: John Benjamins.

Duffy, C. A. (1993) *Mean Time*, London: Anvil Press Poetry.

Duffy, C. A. (1987) *Selling Manhattan*, London: Anvil Press Poetry.

Eagleton, M. (ed.) (1986) *Feminist Literary Theory: A Reader*, Oxford: Basil Blackwell.

Felski, R. (1989) *Beyond Feminist Aesthetics: Feminist Literature and Social Change*, London: Hutchinson Radius.

Flotow, Luise von (1997) *Translation and Gender: Translating in the 'Era of Feminism'*, Manchester: St Jerome.

Flotow, Luise von (1991) 'Feminist translation: contexts, practices and theories', *TTR* 4 (2) 69–84.

Flynn, E. A. and Schweickart, P. P. (eds) (1986) *Gender and Reading*, Baltimore, MD: Johns Hopkins University Press.

Forbes, P. (2002) 'Winning Lines' *The Guardian* 31 August 2002. http://books.guardian.co.uk/poetry/features/0,,902897,00.html [accessed 06 May 2007].

Ford, T. (2008) 'More Than "Just a Joke": The Prejudice-releasing Function of Sexist Humor', *Personality and Social Psychology Bulletin* 34 (2) 159–70.

Foucault, M. (1980) 'What is an Author?' in J. V. Harari (ed.) *Textual Strategies*, London: Methuen, 141–60.

Gumperz, J. J. and Levinson, S. C. (1996) *Rethinking Linguistic Relativity*, Cambridge: Cambridge University Press.

Jowett, B. (trans.) (1953) *The Dialogues of Plato*, Oxford: Oxford University Press.

Klein, H., Coelsch-Foisner, S. and Görtschacher, W. (1999) *Poetry Now: Contemporary British and Irish Poetry in the Making*, Tübingen: Stauffenburg Verlag.

Kramarae, C. (1981) *Women and Men Speaking: Frameworks for Analysis*, Rowley, MA; London: Newbury House Publishers.

Kramarae, C. (1980) *The Voices and Words of Women and Men*, Oxford: Pergamon.

Lakoff, R. (1975) *Language and Women's Place*, London: Harper and Row.

Lehbert, M. (trans.) (1996) *Carol Ann Duffy: Die Bauchrednerpuppe*, Salzburg: Residenz Verlag.

Locke, J. ([1690]1961) *An Essay Concerning Human Understanding*, London: Penguin.

Lotbinière-Harwood, S. de (1995) 'Geographies of Why', in S. Simon (ed.) *Culture in Transit. Translating the Literature of Quebec*, Montreal: Vehicule Press.

Miller, N. K. (1986) *The Poetics of Gender*, New York: Columbia University Press.

Mills, S. (1995a) *Feminist Stylistics*, London: Routledge.

Mills, S. (ed.) (1995b) *Language and Gender*, London: Longman.

Mills, S. (1994) *Gendering the Reader*, London: Harvester Wheatsheaf.

O'Brien, S. (1998) *The Deregulated Muse*, Newcastle: Bloodaxe.

Porter, E. (1999) 'Landscape and Language in Carol Ann Duffy's Love Poetry' *Neohelicon* 26 (1) 77–87.

Pusch, L. F. (1984) *Das Deutsche als Männersprache*, Frankfurt am Main: Suhrkamp Verlag.

Rees-Jones, D. (2001) *Carol Ann Duffy*, Tavistock: Northcote House Publishers.

Rowland, A. (2001) 'Love and Masculinity in the Poetry of Carol Ann Duffy', *English* 50, 199–218.

Samel, I. (2000) *Einführung in die feministische Sprachwissenschaft*, Berlin: Erich Schmidt Verlag.

Sapir, E. (1949) *Selected Writings of Edward Sapir in Language, Culture and Personality*, Berkeley, CA; London: University of California Press.

Schmid, S. (1999) 'Realities Within Reality: The Poetry of Carol Ann Duffy' in H. Klein, S. Coelsch-Foisner and W. Görtschacher, *Poetry Now: Contemporary British and Irish Poetry in the Making*, Tübingen: Stauffenburg Verlag, 295–306.

Schweickart, P. P. (1986) 'Reading Ourselves: Toward a Feminist Theory of Reading' in E. A. Flynn, and P. P. Schweickart, *Gender and Reading*, Baltimore, MD: Johns Hopkins University Press, 31–62.

Shiyab, S. and Lynch, M. S. (2006) 'Can Literary Style be Translated?', *Babel* 52 (3) 262–75.

Simon, S. (1996) *Gender in Translation: Cultural Identity and the Politics of Transmission*, London: Routledge.

Steiner, G. (1984) *Antigones*, Oxford: Clarendon Press.

Suleiman, S. R. (1980) 'Introduction: Varieties of Audience-oriented Criticism' in Suleiman, S. R. and I. Crosman (eds) *The Reader in the Text: Essays on Audience and Interpretation*, Princeton, NJ: Princeton University Press, 3–45.

Suleiman, S. R. and I. Crosman (eds) (1980) *The Reader in the Text: Essays on Audience and Interpretation*, Princeton, NJ: Princeton University Press.

Threadgold, T. (1997) *Feminist Poetics*, London: Routledge.

Toller, P. W., Suter, E. A. and Trautman, T. C. (2004) 'Gender Role Identity and Attitudes Toward Feminism', *Sex Roles* 51 (1/2) 85–90.

Venuti, L. (2008) *The Translator's Invisibility: A History of Translation* (2nd edition), Abingdon: Routledge.

Venuti, L. (ed.) (2004) *The Translation Studies Reader*, London: Routledge.

Venuti, L. (1995) *The Translator's Invisibility: A History of Translation*, London: Routledge.

Venuti, L. (1992) *Rethinking Translation: Discourse, Subjectivity, Ideology*, London: Routledge.

Venuti, L. (1991) 'Genealogies of Translation Theory: Schleiermacher', *TTR* 4 (2) 125–50.

Viner, K. (1999) 'Metre Maid', *The Guardian* 25 September 1999. www.guardian.co.uk/weekend/story/0,3605,268649,00.html [accessed on 06 May 2007].

Wahrig Deutsches Wörterbuch (2000) [Entries 'Marionette' and 'Freudenmädchen'], Gütersloh, München: Bertelsmann Lexikon Verlag GmbH.

Weber, J. J. (ed.) (1996) *The Stylistics Reader*, London: Arnold.

Wimsatt, W. (1954) 'The Intentional Fallacy' in Wimsatt, W. (ed.) *The Verbal Icon*, Lexington: University of Kentucky Press, 3–18.

Wimsatt, W. (ed.) (1954) *The Verbal Icon*, Lexington: University of Kentucky Press.

Winterson, J. (2005) 'It's Not Facts, it's Emotion', *The Times*, 3 September 2005.

Wojcik-Leese, E. (1999) '"Her Language is Simple": The Poetry of Carol Ann Duffy' in H. Klein, S. Coelsch-Foisner and W. Görtschacher, *Poetry Now: Contemporary British and Irish Poetry in the Making*, Tübingen: Stauffenburg Verlag, 307–16.

An Optimality Approach to the Translation of Poetry

Christine Calfoglou

Hellenic Open University, Greece

Chapter Outline

1. Introduction

Poetry has generally been treated as a most elusive form of literary expression and rewriting it, as in the act of translation, may be safely said to be just as elusive. As the Greek poet D. P. Papaditsas puts it in one of his essays, 'A poet is he who talks like an infant, that is, incomprehensibly, for those who have forgotten their original, their most real language' (1989: 26).[1] In this article I will argue that, by reflecting on what motivates language patterns in poetry and closely examining the linguistic properties of the two languages involved in a translation venture, we can record this 'incomprehensibility' in the translated text, too. In more concrete terms, I will attempt to show that what may underlie specific language forms in poetic expression and, more specifically, word order may also be made to underlie the target language options, thus somehow arbitrating the conflict between faithfulness to the source text and target text grammaticality, whenever such a conflict exists. The translation decision-making process[2] can be formalized through the adoption of a linguistic Optimality framework, which, as I will propose in what follows, may be a particularly useful tool in the hands of the translator-scholar.

In the tradition of studies exploring poetic style (see, among others, Boase-Beier 1987, 2006; Freeman 1975; Leech 1969), I begin by reflecting on what may be said to motivate word-order patterns in poetry, giving them their generic appeal. My discussion will draw on the work of two twentieth-century Greek poets, D. P. Papaditsas (1922–1987) and A. Nikolaides (1922–1996). As we will see below, their poetry, tracing its roots in surrealism, lends itself particularly to the present analysis: the orthopaedist, Papaditsas, spoke the language of an infant (see Veis 1988: 35–6) while the psychiatrist, Nikolaides, 'delved into the a-temporal, discontinuous depths of the subconscious' (Calfoglou 2000: 2). Yet, it is my contention that the overall spirit of the argument advanced may be stretched beyond the bounds of any specific poet's work to embrace poetic texts in general. In the following sections of this chapter, I will first attempt to delineate the incrementally apocalyptic elements in their poetry (see section 3: Word order and the 'incrementally apocalyptic') against the backdrop of the spatiotemporal dimension of their work (section 2: Spatiotemporal considerations) and then, in section 4, An 'optimality' translation framework, propose a translation framework that can accommodate this element, as is more specifically illustrated in Implementing the framework. My language focus will be postverbal subject sequences and adjectival postmodification.[3]

2. Spatiotemporal considerations

If the 'real', the original language spoken by poets and infants alone has slipped into oblivion, as suggested in the Papaditsas statement above, then the search for this language may be resistance to oblivion, non-lethe[4] in Nikolaides's terms, for poetry is an antidote to death' (1987: 123) and 'poets never lie in their verse' (ibid. 122). As Nikolaides again puts it, rather expressionistically, '. . . poetry may actually burrow into the burning bowels of language, where metals and structures melt, but in shocking a language through its expression, it shocks it creatively' (ibid. 111). This non-oblivion may, in turn, be reflected in the way the poem assumes its somatic presence, unveiling itself as it does so, that is in the way it extends through space – and time (see also Calfoglou 2000, 2004). And, further, this spatiotemporal dimension may be argued to be iconically reflected in the linguistic unravelling of the poem and information sequencing, seen as causally motivated by perception and experience, an instance of the 'synchrony' of language capturing the 'diachronic' element in human experience. We may then have a happy conspiracy of the information dynamics of a (poetic) text and experiential iconicity, that is an isomorphic correspondence of information linearization and perception (cf. Enkvist 1981).[5]

The relation to space is verbalized in the preface to one of Papaditsas's collections, where poems are referred to as 'an extension of the seabed towards the sky' (1997: 165). At some other point, the poet contemplates 'the inner experiencing of infinite space and eternal time, two concepts that . . . scare, annihilate and constitute us at the same time' (1989: 34). Nikolaides, on the other hand, dances a sinister dance with light, avidly conquering space in 'Light/lit low/lighting/the light-fearing/skylights//Light/from above/light underneath, light/through triple/slits . . .' (*Notes and Meanderings*, 1991: 87).[6] Papaditsas's wakefulness – 'My self who is dead and in my ear has lain awake/ For ages' (*Running Contrary Ways*, 1997: 314) – meets Nikolaides's all-devouring glance 'in the aeolic winds', in the 'olive-groves'.

What further reinforces the spatiotemporal dimension of these two sample poets' work is their strongly 'verbal' character, their 'rhematicity', defined in Athanassopoulos (2000: 301) as the strength of the language rather than of the narrative.[7] Papaditsas speaks of the poem as 'poem-opening', which, somehow in the surrealist tradition, seeks to 'track down and restore the real movement of thought' (ibid. 303, ft. 11, my translation). Through this 'poem-opening', involving a poetic reduction of phenomena, a reduction fathoming its own depths, a reality that breaks itself free of our biologically determined constraints is revealed (Papaditsas 1997: 305–6). In Nikolaides, again along the lines of surrealism, neo-lectic[8] this time, this rhematic, 'verbal' quality is testified to by the fact that, in a more aggressively Whorfean manner, Being is denied its very existence in the absence of language: 'Look at the starlit sky: planets, fixed stars, chaos. They would be nothing without their name' (1987: 101). Such statements allude to the transparency of the relationship between language and things, a transparency underlying motivated signification, that is, they are talk as iconicity. In Paul Auster's ([1985] 1990: 52) evocative words, when Adam had invented language, 'his tongue had gone straight to the quick of the world. His words had been merely appended to the things he saw, they had revealed their essences, had literally brought them to life' (see also Fischer and Nänny 1999: xv).

I would further suggest that these strongly 'verbal' properties observed in the two poets' work are given a further boost by the association between language and action, mediated by the poem itself, an association brought to the fore through Austin's (1962) *'How to do things with words'* (cf. discussion in Malmkjær 2005: 150–4). As Papaditsas puts it, 'today there are no readers of poetry, there are poets who create it (την ποιούν) and poets who receive it' (1989: 32). And, as suggested in the ancient Greek axiom he espouses in the introduction to one of his collections (ibid. 34), 'isn't both speaking an act and acting (making or doing something) a product of speech?'.[9] Nikolaides further subscribes to this idea by stating that 'When thought brings the speech of Being (είναι) to the language it does not only mean what it says (speaks) but it transforms the world much more than it interprets it, thus becoming poetic language' (1987: 37). Verbal action, then, motivating a constant search for the word ('we pine for the word', says Nikolaides 1991: 229), underlies much of the poetic work considered in this article but also, I would venture, poetic work generally. Ross (1982: 687), for one thing, argues in favour of literature as mimesis rather than as diegesis on the grounds that 'poems are not merely "about" something – rather, they "do" that thing' (see discussion in Boase-Beier 2006: 103–5).

3. Word order and the 'incrementally apocalyptic'

Let us now consider the specific ways in which this verbal action, this rhematicity is expressed linguistically. In what follows I will be focusing on relative verb-subject position, the most apocalyptic of the incrementally apocalyptic that constitutes the essence of all this talk, as well as noun-adjective sequencing, though the concept could also embrace other structures, like genitive modification, for instance. Papaditsas refers to the poem as 'a flash of lightning, which instantly and instantaneously makes the trees of the "dark forest" stand out one by one' (1989: 23) but on a micro-language level the instantaneous becomes gradual. This gradual unravelling of the poem's thread is, I believe, best to be seen in postverbal subject sequences which often denote appearance, or a coming into existence, and more often than not involve a clause-initial adverbial, locating the origins of what follows in the sequence. Consider the examples:

(1) Κι από τις πορφυρές ραγισματιές
       V   S
πετιούνται χίλια ουράνια τόξα
(ki apo tis porfires rajizmatjes
petjunte-3[10]rdperson.pl.intr. xilja-neut.nom. pl. urania-neut.nom.pl. toksa-neut.nom.pl.)

And from the scarlet fractures
(there) spring a thousand rainbows
> (Papaditsas, *The Well with the Lyres*, 1997: 15)[11]

or

(2)   V   S
Έρχονται θύελλες που δεν μπορείς να τις πλησιάσεις
(*erxonte-3rd person pl.intr. thieles-fem.nom.pl.* pu den boris na tis plisiasis)

(there) come storms that not can-you to them-approach (that you cannot approach)
> (Papaditsas, *Substances,* 1997: 155)

and

(3)   V   S
Και πανταχού *προβάλλει το σημείο*
το ίδιο πάντοτε
στίξη φαρμακερή κι αντίστιξη.
(Ke pantaxu *provali-3rd person sing.intr. to-neut.nom.sing.def. simio-neut. nom. sing.*
to idjo pantote
stiksi farmakeri ki antistiksi)

And everywhere *emerges the sign*
the same always (always identical)
point venomous and counterpoint (venomous point and counterpoint).
> (Nikolaides, *Trial and Pyre,* 1991: 12)

I would like to suggest that such postverbal subject orders may be central to poetic expression as they are more iconic experientially, 'mirroring (. . .) meaning in form' (Holman and Boase-Beier 1999: 6), that is they seem to be mimetic of an *ordo naturalis* (Enkvist 1981) and thus closer to the language of an infant, as indicated earlier in this chapter, the 'true' language of poetry. In Paul Auster's terms again, Adam's name-giving was so insightful because of his 'prelapsarian innocence' (Fischer and Nänny 2001: xv). The significance of the specific sequence seems to be nicely illustrated in the Greek poet Seferis's characterization of poetry as a kind of dance, where the previous step is never lost in the next but remains transfixed in memory to the end and intact in the poem as a whole (see Vagenas 1989: 16–17). Moreover, this element of incremental 'apocalypse' gains support from the School of Prague Functional Sentence Perspective (FSP) theory. Thus, following Firbas (1992), such presentational structures are 'basic instance level' ones in the sense that, being context-independent, they presuppose no prior knowledge and involve a 'gradual rise in CD (communicative dynamism)' (Firbas 1992: 135), that is an incremental rise in their contribution to the information content of the clause and the development of communication. Further support comes from formal linguistic analysis (see, e.g., Alexiadou 1999), which views postverbal subject sequences in Greek as performing a different informational function (that of eventive predicates) from their preverbal subject counterparts. Here is something, therefore, that needs to be taken account of in the translation process.

While all this may be most clearly the case in the instances presented earlier, where the novelty and, therefore, the increased CD of the subject noun phrase is often underscored by its indefiniteness and the low informational value of the verb by its presentational function, I would like to take this argument further to subsume definite postverbal subjects, too. For, even though they are less directly iconic, in the sense that definiteness correlates with thematicity, in other words with what is 'old' information (see again Firbas 1992), and despite the less clear subdivision of informational content in the verb-subject sequence in this case, postverbal subject sequences with a definite subject are still eventive and thus involve mounting concern over the unfolding of the action. Consider (3) mentioned earlier or, also, (4) that follows, where the 'apocalyptic' character of the postverbal subject sequence is enhanced by its post-adjectival location in the poem:

(4) Αδιάφθορη, σχιζοπεπλούσα, διαστελλογενής
    με τα σπασμόλυτα τριφυλλοχίτωνα που εντρέμαν
           V   S
    δορυφλεγής *νυχοβατούσε η Ερωφάντα.*
    (adjafthori-adj., sxizopeplusa-adj., djastelojenis-adj.
    me ta spazmolita trifiloxitona pu entreman

doriflejis-adj. *nixovatuse-3ʳᵈperson sing.intr. i-nom.fem.sing.def. erofanta-fem.nom.sing.*).

Immaculate, cleftrobed, dilatory
with her spasm-loose threefold-tunics in fibrillation
spearhot *tiptoed (the) Erofanta.*

(Nikolaides, Wordflower, 1991: 56)

Such sequences contrast interestingly with preverbal subject structures, apparently much more robustly volitional, as in:

(5) This star/survived/Pierced the stones/Went through the trees,/burnt the roof/And fell off the hands/Dead/This water/Ran off the glance/Tumbled downhill/Mirrored a tiny/Little fern ... (Papaditsas, *Substances,* 1997: 136).[12]

That subjects in poetry may be positioned clause-finally despite their definiteness, even in a language that is much less tolerant of postverbal subjects than Greek may be testified to by examples like the recurring:

(6) ... *Falls the Shadow*

in Eliot's *Hollow Men* ([1925] 1974: 81–82), presumably licensed by the location phrases that precede it in the poem.

On the other hand, to the intransitives considered so far we could add postverbal subject sequences with an object, like the one that follows:

(7) O   V   S
Μ'ευλογούν καστανιές
(*m'-acc. evlogun-3ʳᵈ person pl.trans. kastanjes-fem.nom.pl.*)

Me bless chestnuts (I'm blessed by chestnuts)

(Papaditsas, Substances, 1997: 135)

Here again, the postverbal, clause-final subject is apparently information-maximal and would thus contribute to the information flow most dynamically. And then, consider the pattern that forms by reverting to subject-verb once the 'revelation' has occurred through verb-subject:

(8) O   V   S   S   V   O
Μ'ευλογούν καστανιές, ο ήχος των νερών σκεπάζει τις ακρίδες

(m'-acc. evlogun-3ʳᵈ person pl.trans. kastanjes-fem.nom.pl., o-masc.nom.sing.def. ixos-masc.nom.sing. ton-gen.pl.def. neron-neut.gen.pl. skepazi-3ʳᵈ person sing.trans. tis-fem.acc.pl.def. akrides-fem.nom.pl.)

Me bless chestnuts, the sound of-the waters drowns the locusts (I'm blessed by chestnuts, the sound of the waters drowns the locusts)

(Papaditsas, *Substances*, 1997: 135)

I would suggest that this form of syntactic patterning, embracing transitives, is yet another forceful point to be attended to by the translator.[13]

The second sequence I will be considering is noun-adjective as against adjective-noun. Once again, I would associate the predicational features of postnominal adjectives as against the attributive features of prenominal modifiers (see Stavrou 1996, 1999) with their function as amplifiers of the rhematic forcefulness of the noun, that is as possessing increased informational content. In other words, the postnominal *point venomous* in example (3) above is more 'dynamic' informationally than *venomous point*, its prenominal counterpart.[14] With regard to the behaviour of the English preposed or postposed adjective in particular, Fischer (2001, 2006) has convincingly argued that one of the determinants of adjective position is 'the functional role the A(djective) P(hrase) plays in terms of information structure within the N(oun) P(hrase) and within the context of the discourse as a whole' (2006: 254). Thus, in periods when postnominal adjectives were far more frequent and less marked than in present-day English, adjectives containing 'given', that is thematic, information in FSP terms tended to appear prenominally, while postnominal adjectives were rhematic, that is informationally strong, and thus tended to correlate with newness, indefiniteness.[15] As an extension of the iconicity point raised earlier, once the noun has been stated and the corresponding entity has been established on the stage, postposed modification will further reinforce its presence. This may be particularly strongly felt in examples like (9) as follows, which combine a postverbal subject with a postnominal adjective:

(9)   V

Στο πρόσωπό σου *σέρνεται*
N/S Adjective
χέρι ψιθυριστό.
(sto prosopo su *sernete-3ʳᵈ person sing.intr.*

xeri-neut.nom.sing. psithiristo-neut.nom.sing.)

Upon your face *(there) creeps*
a hand whispering (a whispering hand)

(From Nikolaides, *Trial and Pyre*, 1991: 20).

Here we move from the minimally dynamic 'upon your face' to the maximally dynamic adjective amplifying the CD of the headword (cf. Firbas 1992: 84). This is also the case in

(10)   V
      και *σέρνονται* στα χείλη μας
         N/S   Genitive
      οι *σαύρες της αφής*
      (ke *sernonte-3rd person pl.intr.* sta xili mas
      i-fem.nom.pl.def. savres-fem.nom.pl. tis-fem.gen.sing.def. afis-
      fem.gen.sing.)

and *(there) creep* on our lips
the lizards of touch

(Nikolaides, *To a Belated Love*, 1991: 229),

where the amplifying function of the adjective is performed by the postmodifying genitive, which suggests that the gradual amplification idea advanced in this discussion may well go beyond the bounds of the focal structures in this article.[16]

Interestingly, verb-subject order, while by no means so uncommon in Greek as in English, is generally attested less frequently than subject-verb (see, e.g., Lascaratou 1984, 1989),[17] while postnominal adjectives, highly marked in English, may be much more common in Greek but are also licensed under certain conditions, related to noun indefiniteness mostly. Thus, the postposed adjective needs to be preceded by the definite article when the head noun is definite (see especially Stavrou 1999: 222, note 25). This could well suggest that poetry is a context strongly encouraging the use of such sequences, perhaps beyond the bounds of language specificity (cf. Ward 2002). Dillon (1980) in particular refers to instances of inversion in English literature, apparently less marked in their poetic context than their non-poetic-context counterparts.

4. An 'optimality' translation framework

In the fourth section of this chapter, I would like to introduce a framework that could smoothly accommodate interlanguage differences with regard to the sequences discussed above and facilitate translation decision-making processes. The overarching idea is that these sequences are motivated by parameters which go beyond the syntactic form of a specific language. The framework I will be talking about largely draws on Optimality Theory (e.g. Archangeli 1997, Kager 1999, McCarthy 2008, Prince and Smolensky 1993, 2004), a linguistic theory which seeks to explain universality and variance in the natural languages of the world by postulating a rich base, allowing the generation of deviant outputs to be subsequently evaluated by means of a set of constraints. The theory originated so as to capture purely linguistic facts, most saliently in the area of phonology, and to create a universal grammar possessing explanatory adequacy. Yet, it appears to me, that, as I will attempt to show below, it can be of particular relevance to the process of translating, in the sense that the rich base along with the generally rich output could accommodate the richly varied source language phenomena as well as the possibility of multiple target text outputs.

Among the tools of the theory are the generator, which 'creates a candidate set of potential outputs' (Archangeli 1997: 14) for a given language input, the evaluator, whose job is to 'select (. . .) the best (optimal) output for that input' (ibid. 14) on the basis of a 'language particular ranking of (a universal set of – my addition) constraints' (ibid. 14). The desired – grammatical – output in a specific language is secured by ranking the constraint crucial to the grammaticality of the form at issue more highly than the violable constraints giving rise to the ungrammatical form.[18, 19]

Let us now see how this output-based model operates in the translation paradigm. Suppose that what constitutes the input for the generator is the source language version, in our case the verb-subject (VS), noun-adjective sequences in L1 (Greek). Suppose, further, that for each of these input items **k** the generator generates a candidate set of outputs for the target language (English), for example, VS, SV . . . , for verb-subject. It will now be the job of the language-particular evaluator **L** to determine which is the optimal solution **k**, signalled by means of a question mark in my illustration, after considering the constraints involved. This is illustrated in Table 1, where the abstract formula is followed by an example:

Table 1 Schematic representation of the architecture of Optimality grammar, as adapted for the translation paradigm

---

GEN (Input$_k$) → {Candidate$_1$, Candidate$_2$, Candidate$_3, ...$ }
GEN (VS) → {VS, SV . . . }
EVAL$_L$ {Candidate$_1$, Candidate$_2$, Candidate$_3, ...$ } → Output$_k$
EVAL$_L$ {VS, SV . . . } → ?

(Adapted from Prince and Smolensky 1993, 2004; see also Archangeli 1997: 25)

What about the constraints, now? The constraints I propose are FAITHFUL-NESS, GRAMMATICALITY and CONSISTENCY, they are partially motivated by the theory and can be shown to capture the issues discussed in this article.[20] Let us look at each of them separately. The FAITHFULNESS constraint proposed, also dominant in Optimality theory, stipulates that *the translation output should be faithful to the source language input*.[21] This presupposes a 'conservative', 'minimalist' approach, whereby one opts for identity rather than difference whenever possible; 'be faithful if you can' or 'do only when necessary' in Prince and Smolensky's (1993) grammar description terms. As Kager (1999: 343) puts it, highlighting the spirit of the theory, 'outputs will be identical to inputs . . . except when divergence between them is forced by a high-ranking well-formedness constraint. But even then, the divergence between input and output (in terms of phonology, morphology or syntax) will be kept at a bare minimum'. In other words, 'violation must be minimal' (ibid. 343). It is for this particular reason mostly that the theory, I would argue, lends itself most readily to the translation of poetry.

According to the second constraint, GRAMMATICALITY, resembling the well-formedness constraints in Kager's quote earlier, *the translation output should conform to grammaticality criteria in the target language*. For, obviously, in translating a language we aim at an end-product which falls within the linguistic bounds of the target language system. The crucial point is that satisfying this constraint might require a breach of FAITHFULNESS. In other words, the translation output will often need to deviate from the L1 input to comply with the well-formedness constraints of the target language but then the notion of well-formedness may also need to be partially revised in the poetic context, as suggested above and illustrated in the next section.[22] This would entail a less rigid definition of the scope of GRAMMATICALITY, an issue I come back to later.

Finally, CONSISTENCY, the third constraint, decrees that *input patterns should be heeded*. If, for example, the source text follows a postmodificational pattern at some point, e.g. with adjectives systematically appearing postnominally, this may need to be carefully considered in the translation process, by producing a consistently premodificational pattern, for instance, if postnominal adjectives are disallowed. We can therefore see that this third constraint in a sense involves a FAITHFULNESS-GRAMMATICALITY interplay: If adherence to source text patterns leads to ungrammaticality, a pattern conforming to target text language standards is sought for. Though not explicitly referred to as such, CONSISTENCY gains indirect support from language-internal patterns observed in Old and Middle English. Thus, Fischer (2006: 277–8; ft. 25) refers to postposed adjectives in her corpus being motivated, among other things, by the need to also keep a morphosyntactic balance in the clause or sentence. In other words, there is a pattern in word-order decision-making, reflected in stylistic choices.

What about the ranking of the constraints? There is the rather 'obvious' answer that 'appropriation' will rank GRAMMATICALITY higher while 'foreignization', focusing on source text pattern retention despite its foreignness, will give FAITHFULNESS priority. There is then the other 'obvious' answer, namely that target text GRAMMATICALITY cannot but be what is desired most. Yet I would argue that in the case of 'expressive' language, like that of poetry, FAITHFULNESS (following the 'be faithful if you can' principle) may rank higher, as some straining of grammaticality standards is allowed. We are, in other words, hovering between the obligatory and the optional, between grammar and style, as Boase-Beier (2006) puts it. This would mean that in the Greek-English pair, for example, verb-subject sequences, generally uncommon in more mainstream uses of the language, might be optimal. It would also mean that postmodification, if possible in the target language, might be preferred in translating postposed instances over its probably less marked premodification counterpart; or, that in cases where this is entirely ruled out by structural constraints, this is at least an issue to consider.[23] And then, of course, an output that satisfies all three constraints postulated would be optimal by far, as will be illustrated in the next section.

5. Implementing the framework

So, let us see how this framework is implemented in the case of the sequences discussed earlier. Consider the line:

(11)   V   S

στο σώμα σου *βαθαίνει μια κλειστή πληγή*

(sto soma su *vatheni-3rd person sing.intr. mja-fem.nom.sing.indef. klisti-fem.nom.sing. pliji-fem.nom.sing.*)

in-the body-your *deepens one old wound*

(Nikolaides, Trial and Pyre, 1991: 14)

There seem to be three options in translating this line into English: a faithful postverbal subject sequence (11a), a partially faithful postverbal subject structure with a 'dummy' 'there' filler in preverbal subject position (11b) and an unmarked preverbal subject one (11c):

(11a) in your body deepens an old wound

(11b) in your body there deepens an old wound

(11c) an old wound deepens in your body.

How would the evaluator treat these outputs? As can be seen in Table 2 below, the first choice is optimal, since it violates neither constraint, with the second following suit, since the postverbal subject constraint is only partially violated – there is a word in subject position but this is only a dummy subject. Finally, the third choice, violating the higher-ranking faithfulness constraint, would be

Table 2 Verb-subject and subject-verb output sequences in English

	FAITHFULNESS	GRAMMATICALITY
in your body *deepens an old wound*	√	√
in your body *there deepens an old wound*	?	√
an old wound deepens in your body	*	√

disfavoured, which is in conformity with the rationale developed earlier. Note that CONSISTENCY is inoperative in this case, as it would presuppose a pattern, as will be illustrated further down. Analogous conclusions could be drawn from consideration of the target French 'de sa bouche sortaient des myriads de rats' or the target German 'aus seinem Maul entfliehen Myriaden Raten' (Nikolaides, *Notes and meanderings*, 1991: 97), as well as of 'ils s' élancent des milliers d'arcs en ciel', 'es fliegen tausende von Regenbogen', the first pair exemplifying postverbal subjects and the second postverbal subjects with some kind of a subject filler.

Similarly, a pattern like

(12) V   S
  Λάμνουν στο αίμα μας νεανικές φρεγάδες

      · · ·

  Κι από τις πορφυρές ραγισματιές
          V   S
  Πετιούνται χίλια ουράνια τόξα
  (*lamnun-3rd person pl.intr.* sto ema mas *neanikes-fem.nom.pl. fregades-fem.nom.pl.*

        · · ·

  ki apo tis porfires rajizmatjes
          V   S
  petjunte-3rd person pl.intr. xilja-neut.nom.pl. urania-neut.nom.pl. toksa-neut.nom.pl.)

  Paddle in our blood *youthful frigates*

        · · ·

  And from the scarlet fractures
  Spring thousand rainbows
                              (Papaditsas, *The Well with the Lyres*, 1997: 15),

where the postverbal subject order opens and ends the poem, would find its optimal output candidate in a consistently postverbal rendering in English, as in

(12a) *There paddle youthful frigates* in our blood

              · · ·

      And from the scarlet fractures
      There spring a thousand rainbows,

to satisfy CONSISTENCY. Conformity to consistent faithfulness is also, partly, what yields the output in

(13) ... and *there perch* by night
  inside them *crickets and silence*
  There's a grand fragrance coming from your bones.

            (Papaditsas, *In a Parenthesis,* 1997: 60)

Things are less straightforward in the case of adjectives, however. For here, as explained earlier, GRAMMATICALITY generally needs to outrank FAITH-FULNESS in the translation of postnominal structures into (Modern) English (cf. Boase-Beier 2006: 128–129). On the other hand, when translating into Greek, the translator will have to decide between a faithful prenominal render-ing, perfectly acceptable in Greek, and an incrementally amplifying postnomi-nal one, which is, however, more marked in grammaticality terms. This would not be so in the case of a more consistently postnominal adjective language like French,[24] which illustrates the fact that the relative ranking of the con-straints postulated and what is optimal in terms of violating fewer or fewer higher-ranking constraints may well vary among languages.[25] On the other hand, postulating FAITHFULNESS as a strongly competing and, as I have tried to show, independently motivated candidate, apparently transcends the bounds of language-specificity (see also note 24).

The discrimination value of the framework proposed can perhaps be best seen in the kind of decision-making involved when translating a consistently postmodificational line like

(14) ροή *τραγουδιστή* ροή *που καίει*
  (roi *tragudisti* roi *pu kei*)
  flow *gurgling* flow *that burns*

          (Papaditsas, *In a Parenthesis,* 1997: 36),

where the two middle options with a pattern, consistently pre- or post-modificational respectively in Table 3 below may be said to fare better than the other two – an example of CONSISTENCY ranking high – while the third option may be optimal in the sense that it transfers the information amplification spirit.

Finally, in translating OVS sequences it would be interesting to reflect upon the possibility of opting for a passive, which may be stylistically heavier but

Table 3 Pre- or post-modification consistency

	CONSISTENCY	FAITHFULNESS	GRAMMATICALITY
A *gurgling* flow a flow *that burns*	*	* √	√
A *gurgling* flow a *burning* flow	√	* *	√
A flow *that gurgles* a flow *that burns*	√	√ √	√
A flow *that gurgles* a *burning* flow	*	√ *	√

(NB: Grammaticality violation options have been left out)

observes the topicalized object – informationally dynamic subject/agent order, as in

(15a) I was lulled by the evening stars,
        as against the 'unfaithful'

(15b) the evening stars lulled me
        for the source text

(15)   με κοίμιζαν οι αποσπερίτες
       me kimizan i aposperites
       (me put to sleep the evening stars).

(Papaditsas, *Substances*, 1997: 135)

The main advantage of the specific attempt to formalize the translation process may, I would suggest, lie in the fact that it incorporates a robust syntactic faithfulness component,[26] which subsumes non-prototypical candidates (postposed subjects and adjectives in the case of the target language in question). The combination of grammaticality and faithfulness in the framework thus projects a conception of the former as a relativistic, graded notion, which seems to be particularly relevant to the language of poetry. This means that the translation process becomes one of gradual optimal output approximation, as the translator tries out faithfulness and/or consistency matches moving along the +/-grammaticality continuum.[27] Faithful (or consistent) options which are rather marked and therefore less clearly representative of the +grammatical end could thus gain precedence over their 'fully grammatical' counterparts. In any case, in optimizing the approximation venture, candidate outputs would have to be tested against all three constraints presented.

6. Conclusion

Suppose that, as I attempted to show above, verb-subject in poetry involves little, if any, given, presupposed knowledge in information distribution terms, as well as that, in a similar vein, this is also the case with postnominal adjectives. These sequences could then be argued to be closer to the zero point of language, allowing, in Hölderlin's words, freedom to 'spring like flowers' (based on Gadamer 1999). In experiential iconicity terms, they could be said to relate to that pre-symbolic stage where, in Simone's (1995: 158) words, 'sentence space and perceptual space have the same structure'. In the poet's terms, 'poetry is the most authentic language, the language of infancy, where the object, its expression, its name, its description, its sound, its monumental retrieval are all one' (Papaditsas 1989: 26). It may be in this sense that the 'poem-opening' iconically represents and, perhaps, also forms the real movement of thought. It may also be in this sense, among others, that poetic language marks itself out as more archetypal, more genuinely apocalyptic, guaranteeing non-oblivion, non-lethe in a world of forgetfulness, thus acting as an 'antidote to death' – for 'poetizing is remembrance' (Gadamer 1999: 159). If this is acknowledged, dealing with word order patterns in translating poetry develops a significance of its own. I hope to have shed some light on how this can inform translation practice.

7. Notes

1. All the D. P. Papaditsas and A. Nikolaides quotes included in this article are my translation.
2. Cf. Levý's (1967) seminal article in particular on a formalized presentation of translation as decision-making.
3. Needless to say, the make-up and translation of poetry also involve a number of higher order structural or other, for example, lexical-semantic considerations, not forming part of the present discussion.
4. This is how the Greek term for 'truth', 'α-λήθεια/alithja' is glossed. In a similar context, it would be interesting to consider Heidegger's 'unconcealment', suggestive of the inwardly driven conviction the poetic word carries (see Gadamer 1999: 146).
5. Enkvist stresses the fact that information dynamics is one thing, in the sense that every sentence possesses some, and what he terms 'experiential iconicism' another, in the sense that a sentence may or may not contain it. The fact that they can be seen to conspire particularly fruitfully in the data presented in this article could be interpreted as being independently motivated by the functions performed by the language of poetry.

6. Similar (space and time) distinctions are made in Cognitive Grammar. Thus, nouns and verbs, the two major grammatical categories, are defined by cognitive grammarians as 'entities . . . extending through space' and 'relations – among things (my addition) – extending through time' respectively (Tabakowska 1997: 32). Still, I will not be considering these affinities in the present discussion, though the relativistic element in my treatment of 'faithfulness' further down also borders on Cognitive Grammar (see, among others, Tabakowska 1993, Talmy 1988; see also Calfoglou 2001).

7. This definition is not to be confused with the use of 'rhematicity' in contradistinction to 'thematic-ity' in information dynamics. In this article I address both uses of the term (see section 2).

8. This is a quality less or more directly ascribed to his poetry by the poet himself and contrasts interestingly with Papaditsas's characterization of his own poetry as '*stereo*lectic', where 'stereo' equals 'solid'. The specific characterization is an allusion to the poet's 'motionless fluidity', the way he combines the Heraclitean flow with Parmenides's solid worldview.

9. '*ουχί και το λέγειν έργον εστί και το ποιείν εκ του λόγου γίνεται;*' (Clement of Alexandria)

10. Here, as well as in a number of cases that follow, the adjective, article or noun glossed may be morphologically marked as bearing either nominative or accusative case but will still be referred to as nominative due to its subject function.

11. The lines referred to in the present discussion are my (unpublished) translation of Nikolaides (1991) and Papaditsas (1997). My deepest thanks go to Maria Nikolaides, daughter of Aristotelis Nikolaides, and Anastassia Papaditsa, wife of Dimitris Papaditsas for kindly giving me permission to publish them.

12. Note that, in strictly linguistic terms, this contrast between pre- and post-verbal subject sequences may be related to transitivity issues (see note 18 below).

13. What is at work here may also be a somewhat different type of iconicity, related to the mirror image of the opening sequence in the closing one (cf. Fischer 2006).

14. Postnominal adjectives are referred to as 'assert(ing) the (perhaps temporary) possession of a property', unlike their prenominal counterparts, which denote 'a pre-existing ( ) or defining property' (Stavrou 1996: 83–4). For more on how adjectives seem to function in samples of Greek poetry see Calfoglou (2000).

15. Following Raumolin-Brunberg (1994), postmodification in Middle English is commoner when not just a single adjective is involved (see also discussion in Fischer 2006). Acquisitional translation data evidence, involving extensive adjectival postposing in translating from (L1) Greek into (L2) English when more than a single adjective is involved, as in *?? a night dim and quiet*, seems to point in a similar direction (see Calfoglou to appear).

16. In their consideration of historical changes with regard to genitive pre- and post- modification, Rosenbach *et al.* (2000) refer to the premodifier position correlating with the 'givenness' of the possessee, a property strongly associated with thematicity, which suggests that information dynamics is again at work [see also Fischer (2006); cf. Conradie (2001)].

17. But note that in her data the percentage of postverbal subjects rises substantially among intransi-tive, unaccusative structures. Still, the strong correlation between postposed subjects and indefi-niteness referred to in her work may be seen as weakened by examples like (3) above, though of course my corpus is too limited for safe conclusions to this effect to be drawn.

18. As an example of a constraint, consider Pesetsky's (1997: 157–8) TELEGRAPH, allowing the complementizer 'that' to be missing in sentences like 'I believe you are right', a constraint which ranks more highly in English than RECOVERABILITY, unlike what happens in French, where the complementizer has to be present.

19. The constraints referred to in Optimality theory 'include ones governing aspects of phonology (. . .) morphology (as well as ones determining – my addition) the correct syntactic properties of a language . . .' (Archangeli 1997: 11). It is this last aspect which is closer to the work presented in this article.

20. One important distinction between this set of constraints and other taxonomies in translation theory, for example, the Functionalists' loyalty and coherence (see Munday 2001: 73–88 for an overview), is that it is strongly focused on form-related matters. Widening its scope of reference is subject to further research.

21. More specifically, in Optimality theory 'FAITHFULNESS constraints, which say that the input and output are identical . . .' are presented as 'cut(ting) across' all domains, namely the phonological, the morphological and the syntactic (Archangeli 1997: 11).

22. This introduces the idea of constraint interaction, which deviates from the principles of Optimality theory as such. As shown in this chapter, such interaction is also to be noted in the formulation of the third constraint, namely CONSISTENCY.

23. The primacy of FAITHFULNESS may seem to suggest that differences in iconicity patterns across languages are overlooked. In other words, some languages might be less isomorphic than others, displaying less form-meaning transparency (see also discussion in Boase-Beier 2006: 103 in particular). It is in establishing such correspondences that language-internal corpus-based research may be particularly helpful.

24. cf. Buridant (2000), among others, on historical evidence regarding pre- and post-nominal adjectives in French.

25. Still, it seems that, even in English, there are a few, though restricted, instances where the post-nominal adjective with all of its predicational strength and the incremental rise in rhematicity its postnominal position entails can survive the translation (cf. Fischer 2001, 2006). Consider, for instance, Είναι η ζωή μας ένα δέντρο μέσα μας/ Μοναχικό (adjective) (Ine i zoi mas ena dentro mesa mas/monaxiko) is the life-our one tree inside-our/solitary', happily rendered as 'Our life is a tree inside us/Solitary' (Papaditsas, *Substances*, 1997: 155).

26. Needless to say, this component can only be visualized as interacting with a number of other considerations, like rhythm, style, metaphor, the overall organisation of concepts among others.

27. Although this proposal might meet with some resistance on the part of the practising poet-translator, trying to listen to the voice of the source text author and recreate it in their own words, it could, I believe, prove to be really helpful in the screening of choices in the rewriting process.

8. Bibliography

Alexiadou, A. (1999) 'On the Properties of Some Greek Word Order Patterns', in A. Alexiadou, G. Horrocks and M. Stavrou (eds) *Studies in Greek Syntax*. Dordrecht: Kluwer, 45–66.

Archangeli, D. (1997) 'Optimality Theory: An Introduction to Linguistics in the 1990s', in D. Archangeli and D. T. Langendoen (eds) *Optimality Theory*. Massachusetts; Oxford: Blackwell, 1–32.

Athanassopoulos, V. (2000) *Το Ποιητικό Τοπίο του Ελληνικού 19ου και 20ου αιώνα, Β' Τόμος* (*The Poetic Landscape of the Greek 19th and 20th century, 2nd volume*). Athens: Kastaniotis.

Auster, P. ([1985]1990) *The New York Trilogy*. London: Penguin.

Austin, J. L. (1962) *How to Do Things with Words*. Oxford, London: Oxford University Press.

Boase-Beier, J. (2006) *Stylistic Approaches to Translation*. Manchester and Kinderhook: St Jerome Publishing.

Boase-Beier, J. (1987) *Poetic Compounds: The Principles of Poetic Language in Modern English Poetry*. Tübingen: Niemeyer.

Buridant, C. (2000) *Grammaire Nouvelle de l'Ancien Français*. Paris: Sedes.

Calfoglou, C. (to appear) 'Translating "Optimally": A Proposal for the L2 Class', paper presented at the 18th Symposium on Theoretical and Applied Linguistics in Thessaloniki in May 2007. To appear in *Selected Papers from the 18th Symposium on Theoretical and Applied Linguistics*.

Calfoglou, C. (2004) 'The "Peripheral" Gains Dominance: Verb-subject Order in Poetry', in C. Dokou, E. Mitsi and B. Mitsikopoulou (eds) *The Periphery Viewing the World, Selected Papers from the Fourth International Conference of the Hellenic Association for the Study of English*. Athens: Parousia, 226–36.

Calfoglou, C. (2001) 'Γνωστική γραμματική και μετάφραση' (Cognitive grammar and translation), in F. Batsalia (ed.) *Περί Μεταφράσεως: Σύγχρονες Προσεγγίσεις* (On Translation: Current approaches). Athens: Katarti, 136–49.

Calfoglou, C. (2000) 'Translating D. P. Papaditsas and A. Nikolaides: A Linguistic Approach'. Unpublished MA Thesis, University of Athens.

Conradie, J. (2001) 'Structural Iconicity: The English s- and of-genitive', in M. Nänny and O. Fischer (eds) *The Motivated Sign. Iconicity in Language and Literature 2*. Amsterdam, Philadelphia: John Benjamins, 229–47.

Dillon, G. (1980) 'Inversions and Deletions in English Poetry', in M. Ching, M. Haley and R. Lunsford (eds) *Linguistic Perspectives on Literature*. London: Routledge, 213–33.

Eliot, T. S. ([1925]1974) *Collected Poems*. London: Faber and Faber.

Enkvist, N. E. (1981) 'Experiential Iconicism in Text Strategy'. *Text* 1 (1) 77–111.

Firbas, J. (1992) *Functional Sentence Perspective in Written and Spoken Communication*. Cambridge: Cambridge University Press.

Fischer, O. (2006) 'On the Position of Adjectives in Middle English'. *English Language and Linguistics*, 10 (2) 253–88.

Fischer, O. (2001) 'The Position of the Adjective in (Old) English from an Iconic Perspective', in M. Nänny and O. Fischer (eds) *The Motivated Sign. Iconicity in Language and Literature 2*. Amsterdam; Philadelphia: John Benjamins, 249–276.

Fischer, O. and Nänny, M. (2001) 'Iconicity as a Creative Force in Language Use', in M. Nänny and O. Fischer (eds) *Form Miming Meaning. Iconicity in language and Literature*. Amsterdam; Philadelphia: John Benjamins, xv–xxxvi.

Freeman, D. (1975) 'The Strategy of Fusion: Dylan Thomas's Syntax', in R. Fowler (ed.) *Style and Structure in Literature*. Oxford: Blackwell, 19–39.

Gadamer, H. G. (Trans. by R. Palmer) (1999) 'Thinking and Poetizing in Heidegger and in Hölderlin's "Andenken"', in J. Risser (ed.) *Heidegger toward the Turn. Essays on the Work of the 1930s*. New York: State University of New York Press, 145–62.

Holman, M. and Boase-Beier, J. (1999) 'Introduction: Writing, Rewriting and Translation. Through Constraint to Creativity', in J. Boase-Beier and M. Holman (eds) *The Practices of Literary Translation. Constraints and Creativity*. Manchester: St Jerome Publishing, 1–17.

Kager, R. (1999) *Optimality Theory*. Cambridge: Cambridge University Press.

Lascaratou, C. (1989) *A Functional Approach to Constituent Order with Particular Reference to Modern Greek. Implications for Language Learning and Language Teaching*. Parousia Journal Monograph Series, No.5, Athens.

Lascaratou, C. (1984) 'The Passive Voice in Modern Greek'. PhD Thesis, University of Reading.

Leech, G. (1969) *A Linguistic Guide to English Poetry*. London: Longman.

Levý, J. (1967) 'Translation as a Decision Process', in *To Honor Roman Jakobson*. The Hague: Mouton, II, 1171–82.

Malmkjær, K. (2005) *Linguistics and the Language of Translation*. Edinburgh: Edinburgh University Press.

McCarthy, J. (2008) *Doing Optimality Theory. Applying Theory to Data*. Massachusetts; Oxford: Blackwell Publishing.

Munday, J. (2001) *Introducing Translation Studies: Theories and Applications*. London, New York: Routledge.

Nikolaides, A. (1991) *Συγκεντρωμένα Ποιήματα* (*Collected Poems*). Athens: Plethro.

Nikolaides, A. (1987) *Ο Τρόπος της Γλώσσας και Άλλες Εγγραφές* (*The Mode of Language and Other Inscriptions*). Athens: Estia.

Papaditsas, D. P. (1997) *Ποίηση* (*Poetry*). Athens: Megas Astrolavos, Efthini.

Papaditsas, D. P. (1989) *Ως δι' Εσόπτρου* (*As through a Mirror*). Athens: Astrolavos, Efthini.

Pesetsky, D. (1997) 'Optimality Theory and Syntax: Movement and Pronunciation', in D. Archangeli and D. T. Langendoen (eds), *Optimality Theory*. Massachusetts; Oxford: Blackwell, 134–70.

Prince, A. and Smolensky, P. (2004) *Optimality Theory: Constraint Interaction in Generative Grammar*. Massachusetts; Oxford: Blackwell.

Prince, A. and Smolensky, P. (1993) *Optimality Theory: Constraint interaction in Generative Grammar*. RuCCs Technical Report #2, Rutgers University Center for Cognitive Science, Piscataway, NJ.

Raumolin-Brunberg, H. (1994) 'The Position of Adjectival Modifiers in Late Middle English Noun Phrases', in U. Fries, G. Tottie and P. Schneider (eds) *Creating and Using English Language Corpora*. Amsterdam: John Benjamins, 159–68.

Rosenbach, A., Stein D. and Vezzosi, L. (2000) 'On the History of the *s*-genitive', in R. Bermúdez-Otero, D. Denison, R. M. Hogg and C. B. McCully (eds) *Generative Theory and Corpus Studies: A Dialogue from 10 ICEHL*. Berlin: Mouton de Gruyter, 183–210.

Ross, H. (1982) 'Hologramming in a Robert Frost Poem: The Still Point', in the Linguistic Society of Korea (eds) *Linguistics in the Moving Calm*. Seoul: Hanshin Publishing, 685–91.

Simone, R. (1995) 'Iconic Aspects of Syntax: A Pragmatic Approach', in R. Simone (ed.) *Iconicity in Language*. Amsterdam; Philadelphia: John Benjamins, pp. 153–70.

Stavrou, M. (1999) 'The Position and Serialization of APs in the DP: Evidence from Greek', in A. Alexiadou, G. Horrocks and M. Stavrou (eds) *Studies in Greek Syntax*. Dordrecht: Kluwer, 201–26.

Stavrou, M. (1996) 'Adjectives in Modern Greek: An Instance of Predication, or an Old Issue Revisited'. *Journal of Linguistics*, 32, 79–112.

Tabakowska, E. (1997) 'Translating a Poem, from a Linguistic Perspective'. *Target*, 9 (1) 25–41.

Tabakowska, E. (1993) *Cognitive Linguistics and the Poetics of Translation*. Tübingen: Gunter Narr Verlag.

Talmy, L. (1988) 'The Relation of Grammar to Cognition', in B. Rudzka-Ostyn (ed.) *Topics in Cognitive Linguistics*. Amsterdam; Philadelphia: John Benjamins, 165–205.

Vagenas, N. (1989) *Ποίηση και Μετάφραση (Poetry and Translation)*. Athens: Stigmi.

Veis, Y. (1988) 'Προοπτικές Αφθαρσίας' (*Immortality Prospects*). *Tetradja Efthinis* 28 ,30–36.

Ward, R. (2002) 'The Translation of Iconicity in the Novels of Kate Atkinson'. *Norwich Papers*, 10, 101–12.

Part II
New Theoretical Horizons for New Ways of Doing Literary Translation

Re-theorizing the Literary in Literary Translation

5

Clive Scott
University of East Anglia, UK

Chapter Outline

The main purpose of the present chapter is to argue that the literary is not a stable value, that it tends to limit itself unjustifiably to a certain range of features, and that it is subject to historical erosion and conventionalization. It needs, therefore, constantly to be re-defined or re-invented. As a consequence, we should understand the ways in which literary translation is a translation *into* the literary. My particular concern is translation into performance, into the performed text, and I would like to begin this re-theorization of the literary in literary translation with Virgil, and more particularly with Virgil's *Aeneid*.

There is little point in telling us, as Geoffrey Nussbaum does, that 'to read Vergil authentically is to read him aloud' (1986: 1). We know quite a lot apparently about Virgil's dactylic hexameter, but only apparently. His quantitative metre is alien to our ear; and we do not know what relation existed in the Roman mind between syllabic quantity and word-accent, between word-accent and metrical accent, if such a thing existed. But more crucially, as with all dead languages, what is absent from this text is any sense of the vocal envelope, of the way it was recited or spoken.

Apart from Robert Fitzgerald ([1981]1992), who translates Virgil's hexameter into iambic pentameter, Anglo-American translators have either translated into prose (W. F. Jackson Knight ([1956]1958), David West ([1990]2003)) or into a verse more free-rhythmical than metrical (C. Day Lewis (1966), Robert Fagles ([2006]2007), Frederick Ahl (2007)). In other words, we move from a verse whose explanation and literary justification is inbuilt, in its metre, dactylic hexameter, to mobile heterosyllabic rhythmic structures whose rhythmicity, and perhaps literariness, is revealed principally by vocal realization. As we move from metricity to rhythmicity, the source of rhythm is less exclusively linguistic and more paralinguistic, that is, more to do with features such as tempo, loudness, tone, intonation, pausing, stress intensity; in other words, freer rhythms demand a wider range of vocal effects if they are to be properly embodied.

Here I want to make my proposition more fundamental: that all literary translation should translate from the linguistic towards the paralinguistic, from script towards dict, that is towards spoken or performed text (see Beardsley 1977). If we imagine the source text itself as recited, as a performance, we must be in a position, as translators, to answer the question: *how would you translate a performance*, that is, what means would you use? What we must also urgently affirm is this: a script and its dict may share the same text, but they will have very different modes of being and very different modes of meaning. What we begin to imagine is a set of translations which generate their own oral tradition, which are closer to each other than to the source text, and which require a re-positioning of the literary.

Why do I canvass this translational position? Because, in my view, the literariness of script is in danger of becoming a dead code, a set of inert signs. If we do not feel the need for a re-invention of the literary, it is precisely because scripts take the pressure off us, allow us into an alternative time, an eternally available time, without pressure, more dormant than latent; the dict, the performance-text, on the other hand, by very virtue of its being sounded and in-process, exists urgently in the here and now, and its actuality is loaded with both vocal and non-vocal dynamics. We identify the literary with the scriptual; that is to say that literary values exist in experience that has been alphabetized. But we know how limited and conventionalizing the alphabet is. Restoring texts to immediacy, to their apprehension in the instant, to their historicity, is, as we have said, to be ready to locate in performance literary values themselves.

Relatedly, and equally important, is the idea of translation not as the linguistic transmutation of one silent text into another, but as an enactment of the processes of reading and listening – which are themselves performance – transposed into another language; that is, reading understood not as interpretation, but as a psychophysiological response to the text. Moreover, the processes of digestion and playing over and experimenting, that reading and listening are, need to be recoverable from the translation. When I read Fagles's lines (2007: 385), from the passage in *Aeneid* Book XII (ll. 903–13), in which Turnus, in his duel with Aeneas, loses all his strength and enters a dream-like state of dulled activity, I need to be able to recover, by a process of readerly 'scansion', the possible shifts of tone and speed that indicate shifts of consciousness between narrator and Turnus, between the agents of speech and perception; I need to register the gradations of stress, the slurring together of syllables, the pauses, the changes in clarity of articulation, the notes of urgency, surprise, effort, self-satisfaction. And, consequently, I begin to look for a new system of notation, which will turn my reading into the equivalent of the Roman practice of *praelectio*, which was a preparation of text by reading to others, and in which marks were introduced into *scriptio continua*, by teachers or pupils, to indicate pauses, phrasal segmentation, long syllables, and so on, and thus help towards the most effective oral delivery of the text. But, for the Fagles lines, I need something rather different:

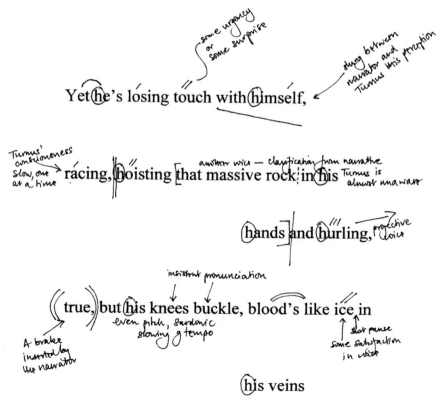

We may regret that the sounds of a text in script are 'limited to phonetic considerations which represent little more than a systematic adaptation of the Latin alphabet' (Tedlock 1977: 508), that pause, tone, loudness, tempo of delivery, and so on, are silently erased. But even *within* the limits of the script, there are ample signs that the literary has fallen victim to 'the same old alphabetic ear' (Tedlock 1977: 508). I want to consider three features, again in the light of Virgilian translations: rhythm; acousticity; punctuation.

In considering rhythm, I want to turn to prose, because prose, as we understand it, that is to say as a potentially infinite, linear, non-spoken extension of language, folded backwards and forwards across a page, is an invention of writing, that cannot find its way to the oral. As such, as the extremely scriptual, it has produced a very low sensitivity to its literariness *as a medium*, other than at the lexical, word-selective level. Penguin's other current *Aeneid* translation, beside that of Fagles, is a prose version by David West, dating back to ([1990] 2003). West defends his choice of prose in these laudable terms:

> Received wisdom, as represented by *The Proceedings of the Virgil Society* 19 (1988), 14, states that 'to translate poetry into prose is always a folly'. I believe that this view does less than justice to the range, power and music of contemporary English prose ([1990]2003: xlv).

But, looking across at Jackson Knight's Penguin Classic of ([1956]1958), also in prose, West reckons its language is dated, and agrees with Sandbach that over-preoccupation with its lexical fidelity puts 'sentence rhythm and cohesion and the emphasis that goes with form' (2003: xlv–xlvi) at risk. The argument that translations are subject to the ravages of time, in a way that source texts are not, has been part of the mythicization of 'pure' literature at translation's expense, and should be firmly rebutted. Sandbach and West's judgment, however, bears on another crucial question, namely the relation between readerly tolerance, the perception of literariness and the mode of reading. I want to take a few sentences from Jackson Knight's account (1958: 117–18) of Book IV and provide a self-consciously scanned reading of them. Dido has just fallen on her sword:

A cry rose to the palace-roof.	3+5	x / / x x / x /
Carthage was stricken by the shock	5+3	/ x x / x x x /
and Rumour ran riot in the town.	6+3	x / x x / x x x /
Lamentation and sobbing and women's wailing	4+3+5	x x / x x / x x / x / x
rang through the houses,	5	/ x x / x

and high heaven echoed with the loud mourning;	6+5	x / / x / x x x / / x
as if some enemy had broken through	6+4	x x / / x x x / x /
and all Carthage, or ancient Tyre,	4+4	x / / x x / x /
were falling, with the flames rolling madly up	3+8	x / x x x / / x / x /
over dwellings of gods and men.	4+4	x x / x x / x /
Her sister heard, and the breath left her.	4+5	x / x / x x / / x
Marring her cheeks with her finger-nails	4+5	/ x x / x x / x /
and bruising her breast with her clenched hands,	5+4	x / x x / x x / /
she dashed in frightened haste through the crowds,	6+3	x / x / x / x x /
found Dido at the very point of death,	3+7	/ / x x x / x / x /
and cried out to her	5	x / / x x

(Virgil, *Aeneid*, IV, 665–74)

[iambic: x /; anapaest: x x /; third paeon: x x / x; bacchic: x / /; ionic: x x / /; antispast: x / / x; antibacchic: / / x; I refer here to groupings of weak/unstressed (x) and strong/stressed (/) syllables using a classical quantitative terminology, that is, a terminology designed for short and long syllables, rather than weak and strong. Many might reckon this practice to be misleading, but the classical terms provide a much neater way of classifying rhythmic segments than imaginable alternatives]

This piece quite clearly does not deserve Sandbach and West's judgement. What I hear, evident in the way I have disposed the passage, and metricorhythmically analysed it, is a set of dyads, whose paired elements rock between 3 and 6 syllables, polarizing in 3+7 at the touching discovery: 'found Dido at the very point of death', but which elsewhere play with repetitions and reversals within a narrower syllabic range; the unit of 4 stabilises the passage just after the mid-point. Rhythmically, the passage is constructed on variations of measure involving adjacent stresses – the bacchic, antibacchic, ionic and antispast – and a recurrent third paeon, with leavening from iamb and anapaest.

But there are two larger points to be made. First, the translation of verse into prose is, as we have heard, much sniffed at, unless it has the express function of a crib. But, in fact, the translation of verse into prose is translation into a medium which virtualizes verse and allows verse, once folded into prose, to be folded out again, but in many re-configured forms. Prose is a medium which multiplies verse; it asks us to see the possible patterns in the carpet, to make varieties of choice, and varieties of choice about literary value. That is why prose itself needs always to be re-translated. Sadly, our sensitivity to prose's multiformity is little developed, and this we might blame on prose's inexorable linearity, which, in the mind's eye at least, levels out expressive asperity and implies a uniform mode of consumption.

The second point is equally simple: if these same lines were read less *intensively*, more *ex*tensively, more prosaically, they would have noticeably fewer stresses, so that we would be less aware of rhythmic distribution and more aware of stress highlights; thus my voice might pick out: cry – roof – Carthage – stricken – shock – Rumour – riot – Lamentation – sobbing – wailing – rang – houses – heaven – mourning – enemy – through – Carthage – Tyre – falling – flames – up – dwellings – gods – men (i.e. up to that point in the text, 24 stresses rather than 37). At the same time, a different set of reading tolerances is brought into play. A different manner of reading, we might say, presupposes a different register; or we might say that the number of possible relations between lexical register and vocal register is much greater than we think. Interestingly perhaps, C. Day Lewis says of his own translation: 'I have weeded out from the *Aeneid* some of the modernisms and colloquialisms which, though they may have served a purpose for *broadcasting*, now seem to me unacceptable in *print*' (1966: v; my emphases). Reading-mode makes its own kind of literariness, activates its own kind of literary resources and expectations.

But if we must increase our sensitivity to the relationship between reading styles and rhythms and registers, we must, at the same time, on the acoustic level, update our ears; we must assimilate into our hearing of text all the contemporary sound-worlds that new typographies, and new serial or electroacoustic musics, have added to our aural capacities. We must break out of a hearing situation in which the literary acoustic depends on our conversion of individual sounds into rhetorical devices (alliteration, assonance, rhyme); at the moment, we sacrifice our perception of particular sounds to the discovery of a structure, to a *given*, rather than created, literary resource. The trouble is that this already *given* stock of literary resources is extremely limited and holds the ear caught, for decade after decade, century after century, in the same crude auditory routine. Worse still, the translator who is not able to answer alliteration with alliteration at a particular point in the text, invokes the principle of compensation and introduces an instance of alliteration at the earliest opportunity, at some *other* textual point. This is a ludicrous policy; and instructive, in that it indicates a naïve belief in the (uninspected) literary value of a small number of devices (alliteration, assonance, rhyme), which must be salvaged at all costs from the process of translation and be allowed to maintain their monopoly. The idea that alliteration might be translated into a *different* literary effect is simply not entertained. In a similar fashion, it is felt that rhyme really ought to be translated by rhyme, even though the linguistic and cultural significance of rhyme from language to language may be completely different.

In examining translations of Virgil, therefore, I listened to Iannis Xenakis's *Persepolis* of 1971, a 56-minute, eight-track tape piece of *musique concrète*, performed through 59 loudspeakers scattered in circular arrangements throughout the audience. The methods and vocabulary of electronic music seem highly suggestive for translation: a language of engineering, editing, modulating, modifying, of mixing and re-mixing. Xenakis's *Persepolis* is accompanied in my recording by nine remixes, four by Japanese composers, two by Americans, and one apiece by a Spanish, a Polish and a German composer. During the course of this chapter, I am undertaking remixes of some of the available translations of Virgil, which themselves constitute remixes of the source text. Since I envisage these translations constructing their own oral tradition, their own family of performances, out of the Virgilian source text, I would also argue for the continual translation and re-translation of the translations themselves.

The passage I have chosen acoustically to remix is Fitzgerald's version (1992: 401) of the latter part of Turnus's physical and psychological undoing:

Justasindr EE *ms* **W** henthe n **I** ght-S **W**oonof S IEE **ρρ**
W *ai* yson ᴏᴜʀ **I** sit SEE*ms* **W** EE trΙ inv *ai*n
Tok EE**ρρ** onrunningtr **I W** ithall ᴏᴜʀ *m*Ι ght
ButinthemidStofe **FF** ort **FF***ai* ntand **FF***ai*l
Oᴜ rtongueis **ρρ**o **W**erle SS **FF** *ai*miliar Strength
W illnotholdu **ρρ** ᴏᴜrbodynota SS ᴏᴜ nd
Or **W** ord **W**illcome juStSo **W** ithTurnu Snoᴜ **W** [1]

Here represented is a kind of pathology of listening. When sounds in language are heard acousmatically, that is to say, without reference to a source, to the word which makes them and by which they acquire their raison d'être, then they become part of the pathology of listening and hearing, equivalent in the ear to the pathology of speaking (glossolalia, echolalia, Tourette's syndrome). This is to place the literary squarely in the activation of poorly controlled associations and subconscious pulsions. These are not sounds artificially isolated for the purposes of identifying pattern, structure, acoustic hierarchy; these are sounds isolated by a kind of psycho-phonetic attentiveness, aural neurosis, as audiences of modern music might be prompted to listen to a particular arrangement of separated timbres, or the vocal range of a particular instrument, or to a melody as a discontinuous string of notes. Translation, let us not forget, is a recording of a reading, of a listening, which has within it the invitation to further elaborations, the invitation to further translations. It reminds the reader and listener that their own isolating mechanisms will work differently, separating out different sounds and combinations. We too easily forget that listening itself is a process of improvisation.

In this text I have highlighted some of the strings of voiceless consonants: we are in the wadded atmosphere of dream, of the voice that cannot enter the throat, cannot find its vibrations; and the isolation of sounds acts out the disintegration of Turnus's belief in himself and in his bodily capacities. I have used variations between roman and italic, between bold and unbold, between different fonts – Broadway, Wide Latin, Bauhaus 93, Franklin Gothic Medium Condensed, Bernard MT Condensed – to try to capture the different ways in which these sounds might materialise themselves in the voice, or in different voices. The visual is a new kind of acoustics, in the sense that a typeface may project its own paralanguage of, say, tone, or loudness, or enunciation. And where I have not isolated sounds but rather kept to the default setting of Times New Roman, I have fallen into *scriptio continua*, as a reminder that, in text-presentational terms, Virgil predates the kind of textual Virgil *we* are familiar with.

Next, I make an interlinear addition of the Latin text:

Justasindr EE *ms* **W** henthe n **i** ght-**S W**oonof **S** IEE **pp**
AC VELUT IN SOMNIS, OCULOS UBI LANGUIDA PRESSIT
W *ai* yson our **i** sit SEE*ms* **W** EE tr**i** inv *ai*n
NOCTE QUIES, NEQUIQUAM AVIDOS EXTENDERE CURSUS
Tok EE**pp** onrunningtr **i W** ithall our *mi* ght
VELLE VIDEMUR ET IN MEDIIS CONATIBUS AEGRI
Butinthe*mid*Stofe **FF** ort **FF***ai* ntand **FF***ai*l
SUCCIDIMUS; NON LINGUA VALET, NON CORPORE NOTAE
Ou rtongueis **pp**o **W**erle **SS FF** a*mi*liar Strength
SUFFICIUNT VIRES NEC VOX AUT VERBA SEQUUNTUR:
W illnotholdu **pp** ourbodynota **SS** ou nd

Or **W** ord **W**illco*me* juStSo **W** ithTurnu Snou **W**
SIC TURNO, [. . .]

By this device I seek to do two things; first to both highlight and scumble chronology: if *scriptio continua* allows the English translation intermittently to predate the familiar Virgil, the interlinear translation makes Virgil now a version of Fitzgerald, now the other way round. This would square with the Borgesian view of translation, where translations may from time to time turn the tables on their originals.[2] At the end of the passage, Virgil outpaces Fitzgerald, waits for him to catch up; so we feel something, too, of Virgil's economy, his narrative impatience. Secondly, it helps me to imagine the relevance to translation of the electro-acoustic notion of 'morphing'. In a recent radio programme (*Discovering Music*, R3, 17/02/08), the composer Jonathan Harvey, in conversation with Alwynne Pritchard, described how, in his work 'Mortuos plango, vivos voco', a tolling church-bell morphs into a boy's singing voice and vice versa; at the same time, one might add, the medieval church morphs into an electro-acoustic studio. At the moment, our view of translation is too much governed by the *jump* rather than the *morph*; bilingual dictionaries, the notions of equivalence, of transferring text from one synchronic language-system to another, of updating or modernizing, are all governed by the jump, by this sudden, peremptory, hygienic process of substitution. Jump-thinking subscribes to a view of time and space which nullifies time and space as a gradualism of lived experience. The past, for example, is something that one leaps back to, as if time were constantly being left behind. The morph, on the other hand, thrives on a Bergsonian view (1984: 495–500), in which, on the contrary, time always catches up with us; the past is merely a coexistent part of an accumulated present, the snowball in the snowman. But we can only express Virgil's being contemporary with us if we equally express the cumulative and assimilative process itself. And this argues for a practice of translation in which the source text expands, to absorb all that has accrued to it in the unfolding of time, a translation practice that is temporally and spatially ragged, heterochronic and multidimensional, and never done with reconfiguring the distance between source and target.

My interlinear presentation is designed to suggest not only a notion of indivisible coexistence, but also two languages measuring up what kind of morphing is necessary to get from one to the other. The so-called homophonic translation of Catullus by Celia and Louis Zukofsky (1969) gives us this sense more immediately: consider these three lines of their translation of poem VIII, with Catullus inserted interlinearly:

> Billowed in tumultuous joys and affianced,
> IBI ILLA MULTA TUM IOCOSA FIEBANT,
> why you would but will it and your girl would have it.
> QUAE TU VOLEBAS NEC PUELLA NOLEBAT.
> Full, sure, very candid the sun's rays glowed solace.
> FULSERE VERE CANDIDI TIBI SOLES.[3] (ll. 6–8)

The Zukofskys show us how the translator can begin to work towards the signifier of the source text, rather than towards its signified, and in so doing multiply the Englishes present in the text, in terms both of history and register. We begin to see what series of permutations, perceptual as much as acoustic, across time and space, might be necessary for, say, Virgil's 'FULSERE VERE' to become 'Full, sure, very'. The distance between languages is the distance that the translator must be seen to travel, along dusty roads, with manifold byways and detours and guidebooks. And the literariness of translation is as much in the sense of journey, in this sense of languages trying to arrive in new places, new homes, as it is in achieved fluency.

In his preface to *Vergil's Metre* (1986: v), Nussbaum breezily affirms: 'In some ways, learning to read Latin hexameters should be easier than Greek. The script and punctuation are familiar [. . .]'. But what punctuation does Nussbaum mean? Malcolm Parkes (1992: 13) tells us that the earliest surviving codices belong to the fifth and sixth centuries AD, including Turcius Rufius Asterius's copy of Virgil, which Asterius punctuated – as a reader of course, not as a scribe – when he was consul in 494. The punctuation we now have in Virgilian texts is in no sense Virgilian, but is an accommodation to modern linguistic expectations, developed across the years by editors.

Punctuation 'is a phenomenon of written language' (Parkes 1992: 1). The development of the written language is, however, in part, a development from the written as transcription of the spoken to the written as a source of both vocal and non-vocal information; the written word becomes peculiarly poised between a text which is performable by the voice (i.e. with signs to guide that performance) and a text whose signs tells us about performance inscribed *in* the text, which may have more to do with the psyche of the writer and reader than with the vocal organs of a potential speaker. Vocality may be a demonstration of the expressive resources of the voice, but vocality may also be an embodiment of what are essentially non-vocal events. Correspondingly, punctuation has enlarged its range, to include alongside the grammatico-syntactical and respiro-intonational functions, the task of representing response, thought, subdiscursive pulsions, and so on – in short, punctuation has at its disposal the ability to register the temperamental and psychic landscape of the writer and reader, over and above the service it could render to a text's purely linguistic constitution. We might say, too, that the visual and the vocal have combined to deepen the vocal, to give it a conceptual dimension that it has not much enjoyed hitherto.

Let us return to the passage describing Turnus's being overcome by a corrosive weakness, at the end of Book 12. This is a re-disposition of West's prose version (2003: 289), which I have tinkered with, changing words or syntax here and there; I am, after all, translating West:

But he had no sense
             of running
                of going
                of lifting
                        of
moving; the huge rock.
His knees gave way. His
       blood grew chill
and froze – and the rock rolled
away   under its own momentum . . .
                 over the open ground . . . between them.
But it did not go/the whole way
it did not/strike
                       its target
Just   as when we   sleep
       when in the weariness of night
              rest
              lies
              heavy on our eyes:
we dream, we,, are,,, trying   desperately
to run further and we are not succeeding
till   we fall   exhausted
             in the muddle of our efforts.
The tongue   useless
The strength (we know we have) fails the body.
               no voice
no words to obey our will –
this is how it was
          with   Turnus.

My translation of West combines punctuation, in elasticated form, with paginal space, as two systems of communication, each concerned to explore the continuum between specific vocal effects and the multiple ways in which a mind inhabits a text as it reads, the ways in which inner duration expresses itself in changes of perceptual pace and perceptual focus, as a voco-psychic and voco-affective dynamics. What the page maps out in its two non-verbal languages is both a vocal adventure *outside* the text, in performance, and, at the same time, a sub-vocal, or voco-visual adventure *in* the text, in which voice is, as it were, conceptualized, and in which we hear the mental processes behind voice: doubt, anticipation, digestion, puzzlement, movedness, associative reverberation.

If remixing and morphing have been our metaphor for translation to date, I want now, as a coda, to turn to another metaphor, a culinary one: translation is a recipe in which the source text is the main ingredient, the meat. Other ingredients, the translator's ways of reading and hearing the source text, are designed to infuse the meat with particular flavours and accompaniments. At this point, too, we move forward in history, to Apollinaire, to his poem 'Zone' from *Alcools* (1913). If, in my translation, 'Zone' is my meat, then my other ingredients are perambulatory writing,[4] Situationism (1957–72),[5] and street photography. In this short glimpse of a work-in-progress, I want to shift more firmly from the oral to the visual as another locus of the literary, remembering, however, that the visual will ever remain an inner resonance of the oral.

We think of Situationist psychogeography as the psychological climates and affective ambiences generated by different urban spaces, from which the drifting walker can, as it were, take passing nourishment. As Apollinaire, in 'Zone', strolls through Paris, towards the early morning in Auteuil, I imagine him responding to the changing psychogeographic atmospheres with different feelings, actions, memories. I express these different psychogeographic atmospheres in different fonts:

ZONE

$ $ $ ⏃ ∘ ⨎ ∼ ⊺ ∼ ⨎ ⋯ ╲ ⨎ ∼ ⊺ ⇌ ⌒ $ ⸓ ⨎ ḣừừừŷầừʌ
╲ ⨎ ḣ ⨎ $ ȳừȳḣ $ ⏥ ḣ ⨎ $ ⌒ ∘ ꝁ $ ⌋
⨎ ╲ ∼ ⨎ ḣ ╲ ⸓ ḣ ⨎ ╲ ⸓ ḣừỳừʌᾱⱦʌ ⨎ ╲
⨎ ḣ ╲ ḣ ⨎ ╲ ⨎ ╲ ⸓ ∼ ɔ̄ḣầừầừừʌừœⱦʌʌⱦ
⸓ ╱ ╱ ⨎ ⋯ ⏥ ᵕ ⇌ ꝁ ⋯ ⌒ ⨎ ⸓ ╱ ⇌ Ǫ̇ [Bookshelf Symbol 7]
ɔ́ʤɔ́ḣɔ́ɔ̄ɔ́ɔ̄ɔ̄Ǧɔ̄Ǧɔ́ɔ̄ʌŜ ⇌ ⨎ừɔ̀ⱦɔ̀Ṗɔ́ɔ̀ⱦṄɔ̄
ḣɔ́ɔ̀X̄ ⨎ ╲ ḣ ⏥ $ ḣừⱦầừ ḣʌừừⱦừʌɔ̀
$ m X̄ ⨎ ⨎ ✳ ⸓ m ╱ ┐ ⌋ ╲ ┐ ⱦ
♥ ⌋ ╲ⱦᵕ ♥ ⇌ ╲ ꝁ ✓ ⱦǦ3ḣ ∼ ḣ
⋯ ⨎ ∼ ⌒ ⌋
∼ Ǧ ⌒ V̄œ́ɔ́
⨎ ⋯ ⏥ ╲ ᵕ Ǧ ⋯
ⱦ ⋯ ∼ ⌋ X̄
ⱦ ⌒ ⱦ ⇌ ⨎ ᵕ
ḣ ⋯ ⇌

Yes,
In the end
You're tired of
This antiquated world
[Papyrus]

Shepherdess O Eiffel Tower
The flock of bridges bleat
This morning

You've done with living
In antiquity
Greek and Roman

φηγλφυ χλυψγγβ./   :κκ η/4λκλ;
Σψμβολ [Symbol]
.,φκνφκηκιρι31λρλ:κλ;λ;φγθμ;1 ōρτ
νδωφυδνηδψγ   εμξ;πολ   δμφ
.θ   μν,κνσ/κσ;λ21εφΔM≅![πρμφΣA
MNΞMΣMδ;δνκ3o31≅;ε

HERE EVEN THE MOTOR-CARS
[WIDE LATIN}
LOOK OUT OF DATE[6]

There are two things I would like the reader to notice in this rendering of the poem's opening lines: first, these fonts are different languages, with different expressive ranges: some remind us of architectures, some of art-styles, some of behavioural characteristics, some of bodies in different states of compression, expansion, elongation. All fonts enjoy their own specific temperaments. It is for this reason that I have named them in the text. These are languages we still do not know, but when we do, their manipulation can become a true source of the literary. Secondly, when I say that fonts are languages, I also mean that quite literally: we have on our computers repositories of symbols which may be alternative alphabets, or may remind us of lost hieroglyphic languages. I have opened the poem with a language on the point of shifting from the hieroglyphic to the alphabetic; and, a few lines further on, I have indulged in a pseudo-Greek, the kind of Greek that a modern computer would want to write if the Symbol font was chosen and fingers were left to play randomly over the keyboard. This is the computer equivalent of Surrealistic automatic writing.

But in tracing this sequence of different psychological climates across Paris, I want also to refer to the Situationists' love of alternative map-making, maps devoted precisely to drifting and psychogeographic experience. These maps register the pathways of a kind of insubordinate walking, which subverts canonical maps and encourages experimental behaviour. Best known of these maps are perhaps those of Guy Debord and Asger Jorn, *The Naked City* (1957) and its predecessor the *Guide psychogéographique de Paris* (1956), whose subtitle – *Discours sur les passions d'amour* – not only alludes to Madeleine de

Scudéry's *Carte du Tendre* (1656) but is also particularly apt for Apollinaire's amatory preoccupations. My presentation of maps of the brand-new street whose name the poet has forgotten ('Zone', ll. 15–24)[7] –

```
                                   PESME
                              A    A
                              C    SPANKING NEWAND
                              S    Y
                              E    O
                              E    N
                              M    T          C
                              A    HYGIENE-CLEANTHE
                              N    E          A
                              E    E          R
              T               S    Y          I
         H              O     E          O
         E              H     F     NUSEHTFO
    THIS MORNING I SAW A STREET
              A                     O          G
              N                     M          N
              A                     M          I
              G                     O                  N
              E                     N          E
              R                     D          V
    SHORTHANDTYPISTSPASSBYFOURTIMESADAY
    T                          Y               Y
    H                          M               A
    E                          O               D
    W                          R               R
    O                          N               U
    R                          I               T
    K                     NGTOSA
    ERSTHE ELEGANT
```

– takes two forms which are designed to create connections between psychic mapping and the Apollinairian calligram, whether printed or handwritten. They are also designed to show how new experience, new itineraries of psychic or affective adventure, might re-write language and suggest new syntaxes. But I also want the printed and the handwritten to play against each other in two related senses: first, I want to suggest that with the technologically and industrially advanced new street, with its regimentation of managers, workers and shorthand typists, the individual soul, the eccentric and idiosyncratic, still

have freedom to express themselves; and secondly, at another level, I want to suggest that if the first map has much in common with Futurist views of street-life as a complex dynamic of lines of force, in the second, Apollinaire is able to re-affirm his belief in the continuing centrality of the intimate lyric voice (1991: 971).

Finally, I want to argue that the spirit of documentary photography – the spirit of the conditioned, the transfixing, the confrontational – dominates in *Alcools* (1913), even though the street-photographic, that celebration of coincidence, distraction, transformation, which comes into its own in Apollinaire's second collection of poems, *Calligrammes* (1918), tries from time to time to assert itself. In 'Zone', for example, the street-photographic tries, initially, to establish itself as the spirit of the new; but it is restrained, then suppressed, by the documentary. I have chosen two passages to exemplify, first, this eruption of the street-photographic, and then its suffocation by the documentary, the one being the passage about which we have already been speaking, the brand-new street (ll. 15–24), the other the passage about Jewish emigrants (ll. 121–34).[8]

In order to express the documentary spirit in the emigrant passage, I wanted a verse-form which would enact the repetitive cycles of aspiration and resignation, which would capture the mirage of change that masks debilitating routine, but which, at the same time, would distil a predicament, and block further metamorphosis. I chose the terza rima sonnet. I wanted terza rima to embody mindless reiteration, as it is does in Hugo von Hofmannsthal's 'Ballade des äusseren Lebens'. I wanted the final couplet to act not as a moment of invocation, stocktaking, exhortation, as it does in Shelley's 'Ode to the West Wind', but rather as a movement of entropic congealment. And I was reminded that Robert Frost's terza rima sonnet 'Acquainted with the Night' draws on the motions of perambulation. This is what emerged:

> Believer-emigrants; you watch them; tears well
> Up. They pray. The women suckle their young. At Saint-Lazare,
> The station hall is seasoned with their smell.
>
> They, like the Magi, are following their star,
> Looking to earn some silver in the Argentine
> And then come back to where they are.
>
> You transport your heart, a family transports its eiderdown,
> Bright red. Our dreams, that eiderdown, are all untruths.
> Some stay, in shabby digs in town,
>
> The rue des Rosiers or des Écouffes.
> Often, at evening, I've seen them in the street.
> Like chess pieces they seldom move.
>
> They're mostly Jews. Their wives wear wigs.
> And, pallid, in the backs of shops, they sit.

I begin to imagine 'Zone' as a cycle of poems in the way that other poems in *Alcools* are: 'La Chanson du Mal-Aimé', for example, or 'Le Brasier', or 'Les Fiançailles'.

What I am trying to do, in these acts of translation and re-translation, is to relocate a work's literariness; to shift the literary from textual features and devices which are no longer relevant to the target text or which have lost all literary efficacy by their conventionalization, to features which express our active engagement with the text. Inasmuch as translation is an account, an autobiography if you will, of a reading and listening process, then the literary should be installed more in this readerly procedure than in the text itself, and this requires me to give more literary weight to performance values, to the paralinguistic and typographical, whether that performance be *of* the text or *in* the text. And what is the literary? The literary lies in the excess of the signifier over the signified, and that excess is created by literature's maximisation of the materiality and conceptuality of language, so that both the body and the psyche of the reader are maximally involved. And this excess may derive, in a performance-based text, from vocal complexity, from the dynamics of acoustic fields, from the languages of punctuational and diacritical marks, of fonts and of paginal disposition.

Notes

1. The 'plain' version of Fitzgerald's text is as follows:

   Just as in dreams when the night-swoon of sleep
   Weighs on our eyes, it seems we try in vain
   To keep on running, try with all our might,
   But in the midst of effort faint and fail;
   Our tongue is powerless, familiar strength
   Will not hold up our body, not a sound
   Or word will come: just so with Turnus now.

2. This is an idea that Borges returns to with some consistency, for example: 'To assume that every recombination of elements is necessarily inferior to its original form is to assume that draft nine is necessarily inferior to draft H – for there can only be drafts' (2001a: 69); 'The Cervantes text and the Menard text are verbally identical, but the second is almost infinitely richer' (2001b: 40).

3. Francis Cornish's literal, prose translation of these lines gives: 'There and then were given us those joys, so many, so merry, which you desired nor did my lady not desire. Bright for you, truly, shone the days' (1988: 11).

4. For reflections on the discourses of urban perambulation, see Certeau (1984: 91–110) and Solnit (2002: 171–246).

5. For accounts of Situationism, see Plant (1992), Sadler (1998), McDonough (2002) and Ford (2005).

6. The French text of these opening lines runs:

   A la fin tu es las de ce monde ancien
   Bergère ô tour Eiffel le troupeau des ponts bêle ce matin
   Tu en as assez de vivre dans l'antiquité grecque et romaine
   Ici meme les automobiles ont l'air d'être anciennes

7. The French text runs:

> J'ai vu ce matin une jolie rue dont j'ai oublié le nom
>
> Neuve et propre du soleil elle était le clairon
>
> Les directeurs les ouvriers et les belles steno-dactylographes
>
> Du lundi matin au samedi soir quatre fois par jour y passent
>
> Le matin par trois fois la sirène y gémit
>
> Une cloche rageuse y aboie vers midi
>
> Les inscriptions des enseignes et des murailles
>
> Les plaques les avis à la façon des perroquets criaillent
>
> J'aime la grâce de cette rue industrielle
>
> Située à Paris entre la rue Aumont-Thiéville et l'avenue des Ternes

8. The French text runs:

> Tu regardes les yeux pleins de larmes ces pauvres émigrants
>
> Ils croient en Dieu ils prient les femmes allaitent des enfants
>
> Ils emplissent de leur odeur le hall de la gare Saint-Lazare
>
> Ils ont foi dans leur étoile comme les rois-mages
>
> Ils espèrent gagner de l'argent dans l'Argentine
>
> Et revenir dans leur pays après avoir fait fortune
>
> Une famille transporte un édredon rouge comme vous transportez votre cœur
>
> Cet édredon et nos rêves sont aussi irréels
>
> Quelques-uns de ces émigrants restent ici et se logent
>
> Rue des Rosiers ou rue des Écouffes dans des bouges
>
> Je les ai vus souvent le soir ils prennent l'air dans la rue
>
> Et se déplacent rarement comme les pièces aux échecs
>
> Il y a surtout des Juifs leurs femmes portent perruque
>
> Elles restent assises exsangues au fond des boutiques

Bibliography

Ahl, Frederick (trans. and ed.) (2007) *Virgil: 'Aeneid'*, intro. by Elaine Fantham. Oxford: Oxford University Press.

Apollinaire, Guillaume (1991) *Œuvres en prose complètes II*, Pierre Caizergues and Michel Décaudin (eds) Paris: Gallimard.

Beardsley, Monroe C. (1977) 'Aspects of Orality: A Short Commentary'. *New Literary History*, 8, 521–30.

Bergson, Henri (1984) *Œuvres*, 4th ed., André Robinet and Henri Gouhier (eds) Paris: Presses Universitaires de France.

Borges, Jorge Luis (2001a) 'The Homeric Versions', in *The Total Library: Non-Fiction 1922–1986*, Eliot Weinberger (ed. and trans.) Esther Allen and Suzanne Jill Levine (trans.). London: Penguin, 69–74.

Borges, Jorge Luis (2001b) 'Pierre Menard, Author of the *Quixote*', in *Fictions*, Andrew Hurley (trans.). London: Penguin, 33–43.

Certeau, Michel de (1984) *The Practice of Everyday Life*, Steven Rendall (trans.). Berkeley, CA: University of California Press.

Cornish, Francis Warre, Postgate, J. P., and Mackail, J. W. (trans.) (1988) *Catullus, Tibullus, Pervigilium Veneris*, 2nd ed. revised by G. P. Goold. Cambridge, MA: Harvard University Press; London: William Heinemann.

Day Lewis, Cecil (trans.) (1966) *The Eclogues, Georgics and Aeneid of Virgil*. London: Oxford University Press.

Fagles, Robert (trans.) ([2006]2007) *Virgil: 'The Aeneid'*, Bernard Knox and Michael Putnam (eds). London: Penguin.

Fitzgerald, Robert (trans.) ([1981]1992) *Virgil: 'The Aeneid'*, Philip Hardie (ed.). New York: Everyman's Library.

Ford, Simon (2005) *The Situationist International: A User's Guide*. London: Black Dog Publishing.

Jackson Knight, W.F. (trans. and ed.) ([1956]1958) *Virgil: 'The Aeneid'*. Harmondsworth: Penguin.

McDonough, Tom (ed.) (2002) *Guy Debord and the Situationist International: Texts and Documents*. Cambridge, MA: MIT Press.

Nussbaum, G. B. (1986) *Vergil's Metre: A Practical Guide for Reading Latin Hexameter Poetry*. Bristol: Bristol Classical Press.

Parkes, M. B. (1992) *Pause and Effect: An Introduction to the History of Punctuation in the West*. Aldershot: Scolar Press.

Plant, Sadie (1992) *The Most Radical Gesture: The Situationist International in a Postmodern Age*. London: Routledge.

Sadler, Simon (1998) *The Situationist City*. Cambridge, MA: MIT Press.

Solnit, Rebecca (2002) *Wanderlust: A History of Walking*. London: Verso.

Tedlock, Dennis (1977) 'Toward an Oral Poetics'. *New Literary History*, 8, 507–19.

West, David (trans. and ed.) ([1990]2003) *Virgil: 'The Aeneid'*. London: Penguin Books.

Zukofsky, Celia and Louis (trans.) (1969) *Catullus (Gai Valeri Catulli Veronensis Liber)*. London: Cape Goliard Press.

6

In the Furrows of Translation

Agnieszka Pantuchowicz

Warsaw School of Social Psychology, Poland

This chapter originated in an interest in how the category of gender does (and does not) function in Polish translations of gender-conscious women's texts. I will ground my arguments on my readings of a few fragments of texts from Sarah Waters' *The Night Watch* (2007) and *Affinity* (2000), and from Jeanette Winterson's *Written on the Body* (1996). I will attempt to theorize the tendency to neutralize the potentially *distractive* gender issues in the translation practices of different Polish translators of these texts. Building on the work of Sherry Simon (1996), Luise von Flotow (1997) and Lawrence Venuti (2000), I will argue that some kind of blindness to the relevance of theory, even when culturally informed, may, and often does, result in a reduction of the literary and cultural significance of a given text. Another important result of this blindness is an inherent domestication and familiarization of those aspects of the translated texts which might challenge, or perhaps only question, the unnoticed, seemingly irreducible, non-literary premises inbuilt within the furrows of translators' practices or even training. What I want to show in this chapter are not so much mistranslations occurring in the texts, but rather a certain tendency toward making choices dictated to the translator not so much by the translated text itself, but by the confining strength of the ideological furrows which limit particularity for the sake of universality. The analysed brief fragments of texts and their translations into Polish hint at the ideological work of what can be generally called 'universal humanism,' to whose universalizing power the final part of the paper is devoted. This power is also, as it were, translational, as what is at stake is what Slavoj Žižek (Cf. Žižek 1997: 82) sees as the power to reorganize, or translate, collections into sets, particulars into functional systems in which differences are either effectively void, or marginal.

Jeanette Winterson's *Written on the Body*, constructed as a meditation on the losses and gains of love, was much criticized for its plot construction, though simultaneously applauded for the gender indeterminacy of its first person singular narrative protagonist (Cf. entry *Winterson, Jeanette* in Smith [not dated] and Moore 1995. Numerous reviews in this vein can be found at *amazon.com* and *amazon.co.uk*). Winterson's text perfectly resists any attempt at singular interpretation, or domestication, or any reduction to the socially acceptable grounds and borders of the dominant discourse of sexuality and gender role divisions. Any insightful reading of the text makes it possible to ascribe the narration either to a butch lesbian identity or to a masculine one, thus blurring the borders of socially identifiable stances. For this reason it seems obvious that any interpreter, or translator, of the text should be at least minimally gender-conscious, that is to say, realizing the problems and questions arising from that undecidability. Ignoring the gender complications constructed by the text in fact does not even deconstruct it, but translates it into a discourse alien to its original conception and thus annihilates its potential of really making a difference.

The Polish translator of Winterson's book, Hanna Mizerska, precedes her translation with a brief introduction which she begins with a general statement on the novel:

> The work of Jeanette Winterson represents the current of feminism and postmodernism. The reality which she creates is scattered and unhomogeneous, the experience fragmentary, and the identities of the characters escape a univocal definition.[1] (Winterson 1999: 7)

Further on she informs the reader that the author of the story 'questions the very distinction between the masculine and the feminine, and consciously does not fix the sex/gender of the narrator' (Winterson 1999: 7). As the translator claims, Winterson's aim is a universalization of experience, a usurpation which already in the beginning seems to be telling the reader that the genderization of the narrator is not really necessary, as universal truths are expressible only from the perspective of a uniform, orthodox teller. The translator presents her assumptions as dictated by the demands of the Polish grammatical system in which the hiding of the sex of the narrator [...] is possible in the first person singular of the present tense, while the use of the past tense ascribes gender to all verbs' (Winterson 1999: 7) – (e.g. the first person present tense singular of the verb *to be* is gender neutral *jestem*, while in the past tense it is necessary to gender it either as masculine or feminine – *byłam/byłem*). Any other way of gendering the text, like for example the introduction of the androgynous 'third sex' (which is grammatically possible in Polish), she deems an artificial device. Hence, according to Mizerska, to 'sex the narrator was a necessary compromise' (Winterson 1999: 7). She also informs the reader that in the first version of the translation she opted for a masculine narrator because 'most of the experiences described in the novel concern man, regardless of the sex' (Winterson 1999: 7), adding that a number of the situations in the novel are 'typically masculine,' like the fight of the rival for the lover. She also writes that the 'spice of the erotic terminology' better fits a masculine narrator. These claims, implicitly dictated by the predicament of the inevitable unfaithfulness of the translator, in fact translate gender into an irrelevant aspect of any kind of writing. To support the choice of a feminine-gendered narrator, Mizerska refers to the scene in the novel in which urinals are blown up and, quite significantly, to the demonstration supporting new matriarchy in which, as she phrases it, 'a masculine participant of the action would have been a dissonance' (Winterson 1999: 8). Moreover, the subtle shades of feeling are seen as alien to the masculine. The final decision as to the choice of the feminine narrator is that the author of the book herself 'consequently did not agree to a male narrator' (Winterson 1999: 8), as the translator put it in her foreword. Hanna Mizerska perceives her choice of the narrator as an inevitable compromise which, however, does not diminish the artistic value of the novel. She concludes that 'for the reader plunging into Winterson's world the sex of the narrator is of secondary significance' (Winterson 1999: 8), which conclusion, for the reader of the English text, might come as a kind of surprise.

Though the argument concerning the Polish grammar seems to be even-handed, yet there are some possibilities of meeting the problem. Instead of sticking to the temporality of the events of the story, one could use the grammatical present tense first person narrative which, as in English, can also refer to the past without necessitating the choice of gender. This could be supplemented with variants of indirect speech and the use of passive voice, thus staging the presented world in all its relevant aspects.

The first occurrence of the first person singular in the text is not problematic, as the category of gender does not interfere:

> I am thinking of a certain September: . . . (Winterson 1996: 9)

> Wracam myślami do pewnego września [I'm returning with my thoughts to a certain September]. . . . (Winterson 1999: 9)

Yet on the same, first page an immediate gendering of the protagonist takes place:

> I did worship them [words] but now I am alone on a rock hewn out of my own body. (Winterson 1996: 9)

> Sama je kiedyś czciłam, ale teraz jestem sama na skale wyciosanej z mego ciała [I worshipped them myself, but now I am alone on a rock hewn out of my body]. (Winterson 1999: 9)

The verb 'czciłam' [I worshipped – first person feminine gender in Polish] gives the reader no choice as to the gender of the speaking persona. The adjective 'sama' [alone – feminine gender in Polish] reiterates the speaker's femininity. An alternative translation could read:

> Pamiętam moje uznanie dla tych słów [I remember my admiration for these words].

> or

> Uwielbienie dla tych słów też nie było mi kiedyś obce [The worship for these words was once not strange to me].

The ungendering in the above sentences has been achieved simply by the avoidance of the usage of gender-marked past tense verbs.

Moreover, the act of being engaged is rendered as being exclusively heterosexual in Mizerska's translation, with the implication that for a woman, if such engagement is lacking, she suffers from painful distraction:

> But I am not engaged I am deeply distracted. (Winterson 1996:10)

Mizerska's translation is quite literal, and the gendering is hidden in the '-a' ending of the adjective 'zaręczona':

> Ale ja nie jestem zaręczona, jestem w głębokiej rozterce [But I am not engaged I am deeply distracted]. (Winterson 1999:10)

The ungendering effect can be achieved quite easily through the avoidance of the gender-marked adjective:

> Nic nie wiem o zaręczynach, jestem w głębokiej rozterce [I don't know anything about any engagement I am deeply distracted]

or simply

> Zaręczyn nie było jestem w głębokiej rozterce [There was no engagement I am deeply distracted].

Also in the case of the verb 'to do' the gendering in the Polish translation is totally unnecessary, as in the forms of grammatical future tense in Polish there is always a choice of the gender neutral infinitive 'będę robić'. For instance, instead of translating the sentence:

> They did it, my parents did it, now I will do it . . . (Winterson 1996: 10)

as

> Robili to oni, robili moi rodzice, teraz ja to będę robiła . . . (Winterson 1999: 10)

one could easily solve the problem by choosing the ungendered 'robić' instead of the feminine gendered 'robiła'.

Along with the practices of the seemingly necessary genderization, in the same fragment we are confronted with instances of estheticization and a kind of moralization:

> It's all right, millions of bottoms have sat here before me. (Winterson 1996: 10)
>
> W porządku. Miliony siedziały w nim przede mną [It's all right. Millions have sat here before me.] (Winterson 1999: 10)
>
> . . . my grandma . . . in white muslin straining a little at the life beneath. (Winterson 1996: 10)
>
> . . . moi dziadkowie . . . ona w białym muślinie zgrabnie opinającym ukryte pod spodem nowe życie [my grandparents . . . she in white muslin nicely holding on to the new life hidden beneath]. (Winterson, 1999, p.10)

In the first of the cases just described, individuals become a multitude of universalized, 'bottomless' creatures while in the second case 'straining' is transformed into seductive eroticization in which 'muslin' seductively half-exposes the thus aestheticized body of the life beneath.

The discussed examples from the translation of Winterson's novel delineate the governing principles of the translational project which, at least declaratively, was supposed to possess the rhetorical power of the original text. Going after the furrows of the generally accepted norms and patterns, this particular kind of translation mode narrows the rhetorical registers of the text, thus wasting the chance for the creation of a plurality of new, even if utopian, readerships.

Yet another example comes from Sarah Waters' *The Night Watch*. Unlike her earlier books, which are verifiably set in the Victorian era, this novel deals with the realities of the 1940s. However, the book's title may be also read as a reference to the well-known seventeenth-century painting by Rembrandt. The Polish translation of the novel (by Magdalena Gawlik-Małkowska) is titled *Pod osłoną nocy* (Waters 2007b) which, back-translated, means 'under the cover of the night.' The Polish title not only completely excludes any reference to a dutiful service elaborately depicted in the novel, but also to the possibility of any association with Rembrandt's masterpiece. The latter association is relevant, and I will have a closer look at its interpretive potential somehow disabled by the Polish version of the novel's title. The construction of the novel interestingly reflects the complicated history of the painting which does not quite depict what is suggested by the title attributed to it at the turn of the eighteenth and nineteenth centuries. As Walter Wallace noticed in *The World of Rembrandt*

> . . . this celebrated work will always be known by an incorrect title, and since those who have not seen it continue to believe, quite logically, that it is a nocturne Company of Captain Frans Banning Cocq and Lieutenant Willem van Ruytenhurch, and not until late in the 18th Century did it acquire the name by which it is now known. Unfortunately, both 'Night' and 'Watch' are wrong. The civic guards who are depicted had, by the time Rembrandt painted them, become quite pacific; it was no longer necessary for them to defend the ramparts of Amsterdam or to go out on watches by night or by day. Their meetings had been diverted chiefly to social or sporting purposes; if they may be said to have any particular destination in the painting, it is perhaps to march into the fields for a shooting contest or to take part in a parade. (Wallace 1968: 107)

This turn from a dutiful kind of activity to pleasurable sport is accompanied by the equally significant turn from darkness to brightness reflected in the actual rediscovery of light in the 'physical' history of the painting:

> 'Night' is even less apt than 'Watch.' When the critics and the public attached that word to the painting, the canvas had become so darkened by dirt and layers of varnish that it was difficult to tell whether the illumination Rembrandt had provided in it came from the sun or moon. Not until after the end of World War II was the painting fully restored so that the viewer could get an idea of the brightness it had when it left Rembrandt's hand more than 300 years before. (Wallace 1968: 107)

This story of making brightness visible is reflected in the reversed order of the narrative of Waters' novel which follows the pattern of the rediscovery of the original painting, of the removal of the layers of the varnish. The novel also shows the work of the recovery of the marginal figures which disappeared from the painting due to the adaptation of its size to the interiors in which it was displayed. Waters' social image offers a recovery not of those cut out from Rembrandt's picture, but an enlargement of the margin with the figures of women for whom there was no space in the traditional social imagery. Here, in Waters' novel, women become central figures who actually, unlike in Rembrandt, do the watching during the war. These interpretative traces are lost in the Polish translation of the book. Though a title, one might say, is only a road sign for the reader, its mistranslation in the case of *The Night Watch* hints at a securely covered space in which uncertainties are but peripheral contingencies.

The final examples I would like to look at are two cracks in the Polish translation of Waters' *Affinity* (2000). Translated by Magdalena-Gawlik-Małkowska (Waters 2004), literally and quite tellingly, as 'Non-banal bond' or 'bondage' (*Niebanalna więź*), the Polish version of the book reduces the complex notion of affinity (of souls, spirits, bodies, flesh, kinship . . .) into a Harlequin-like relationship in which seeking another person is glossed into 'looking for' (Waters 2000: 275). One of the crucial statements in the book: 'You were seeking me, your own *affinity*' (Waters 2000: 275), becomes trivialized into what in a back-translation may read: 'Did you feel the bond between us?' The Polish text thus fails to cross, and reinforces the boundaries between, as Lawrence Venuti writes, 'domestic audiences and hierarchies in which they are positioned' (Venuti 2000: 477). The lowering of rhetorical registers results in a failure of a potentially formative (in the sense of social and political creation) force of the translated text. However utopian the translational intention to communicate the foreign text may seem (cf. Venuti 2000: 485), translation should at least attempt at 'divorcing itself from the unrealizable ideals of universal humanism,' as Sherry Simon (Simon 1996: 166) puts it in her *Gender in Translation*. This universal humanism, assumed as fact by the analysed translations, in fact banalizes and trivializes certain complexities so as to communicate to the readers what is, anyway, obvious. In order to be in any way 'enriching' the movement of ideas, translation, as Simon notices, 'must work today through new logics of communication, through new configurations of commonality' (Simon 1996: 66). What the discussed translations evade and avoid is exactly the commonality of difference and the inevitable partiality of the cultural transmission (cf. Simon 1996: 166) which, though partial, can at least partially inform the reader about that difference.

Perhaps the paradox of a universal-humanist approach to translation is its blindness to difference as something which does not partake in translation and which should, by any means, remain invisible. It is sameness which, rather than difference, evaluates translation while difference is perceived as a violation of the originality of the text. Mark Currie notices that

> difference is often misrepresented either as an entirely structuralist issue, or more specifically, as a Saussurean invention. But to represent difference in this way is to ignore the much broader context, and longer history, from which it derives its unusually complex meanings and uses. (Currie 2004: 7)

Structuralism looms large in the construction of the universal-humanist furrows of any articulation, translation included. The furrows guard the silent presence of the articulated from any threat of violence from the outside, from the threat of difference whose uncultivated 'thereness' is but an irrelevant background of the present. The presence of the articulated must remain silent, because in this way it silences the remorse of violence, the voice of violated difference which any act of articulation or translation suppresses.

Articulation and translation meet in a certain violence, a violence which, for Cixous, is a mark of love, a bite (*mordre*) hidden in the remorse (*remords*) which results from the betrayal always inherent in 'translation from the language of the other' (Cixous 2003: 11). Translation and articulation trigger violence. This Derridean claim, articulated long ago in *Writing and Difference*, seems to be positing difference as a 'victim' of the desire to articulate, to pronounce distinctly, but also to particularize. This violence, however, is simultaneously protective, it protects a certain silence of peace (Derrida 1978: 148).

Discourse is inevitably inhabited by violence, perhaps by an arche-violence, which 'appears with *articulation*' because it is 'tied to phenomenality itself, and to the possibility of language' (Derrida 1978: 125). Hence the necessity of an economy of violence, which is also an economy of war: 'violence against violence, light against light' (Derrida 1978: 117). Such an 'economy of war' is inescapable, because inscription infinitely articulates a horizon of silence, a horizon of what Derrida elsewhere called 'paradise.' Though possibly a place free from the violence of translation, such a paradise is not what Derrida would embrace, as there would be no space to respond to responsibility (Cf. Szydłowska 2003: 171, notes from Derrida's Seminar at Ecoles des Hautes Etudes en Sciences Sociales, Paris, 13 March 2002).

Paradise is inarticulate, an unthinkable pure non-violence brought to being through a violence which can also never be pure: 'Pure violence, a relationship between beings without face, is not yet violence, it is pure nonviolence. And inversely: pure nonviolence, the nonrelation of the same to the other . . . is pure violence' (Derrida 1978: 146–7). Discourse can thus be viewed as an articulatory violence committed on the silence of an inarticulate paradise, perhaps also that of universal humanism. What this violence is calling to is some provisional kind of being, a 'being there' whose full articulation is unthinkable: 'the violence of writing, the violence of founding, of in-stating, of producing, of judging or knowing is a violence that both manifests and dissimulates itself, a space of necessary equivocation' (Grosz 1999: 12).

Roman Jakobson's well-known definition of literature/literariness which he saw as 'organized violence committed on ordinary speech' (Jakobson 1960: 353) is a call to preserve the silence of paradise by way of violating the language which violates. More accurately, however, Jakobson's idea is a certain repetition of, or from, Victor Frankenstein's creation – an attempt at putting in motion a violated, estranged language which signifies nothing but itself, and which stands in opposition to the paradisal innocence of ordinary speech which figures as both norm and nature. As a distorted version of ordinary language, Jakobson's literature is, ideally, abruptly torn off from the contexts of communication, it is a monstrous figure stitched out of the already dead words which can now become subject to an analytic insight, to an anatomical study of the stitches and devices that had put it together, and thus deprived of difference by way of being translated back into the norm of the categories of universal humanism. Jakobson's literature, or literariness, dwells within the sphere of an unprotected difference, a violated body of writing, an estranged 'hideous progeny' with which Mary Shelley ends her introduction to the re-edition of

Frankenstein. Barbara Johnson's suspicion that 'there may perhaps be meaningful parallels between Victor's creation of his monster and Mary's creation of her book' (Johnson 1987: 150) seems to be also a suspicion that writing itself might be monstrous.

What is also monstrous from the perspective of universal humanism is the idea of untranslatability, the idea which veils the monstrosity of any text, of any writing, positing it as something which is never different from itself. If Saussure simply hid writing in a special compartment for teratological cases (Saussure 1966: 22), the monstrous untranslatable figures in translation theory as a result of a weakness of the translation process which leaves it (the untranslatable) behind as waste. This waste figures as something irrecoverably lost in translation by way of becoming excluded from the newly created text not as difference, but as an identifiable object which the text cannot embrace. A significant aspect of Victor Frankenstein's creation is, in this respect, the fact that it is made up of waste, of parts of dead bodies which the scientist as it were resurrects, thus bringing to life something which all human creation refuses to see, a certain *refuse/al* of difference, embodied within the stitched body of the monster. If waste, as Zygmunt Bauman (Cf. Bauman 2004: 47), claims, is the dark and shameful secret of all production then what Mary Shelley puts in motion in her text is an uncanny revelation that waste is a constitutive part of any presence in the world, be it of monsters, or of books for that matter.

It is also a matter of living. What Frankenstein achieves is not so much a creation of a new life, but a stoppage of decomposition, of the process which inscribes difference into living, and thus questions the stability of any living authenticity of identity. Built up of 'parts from charnel-houses and cemeteries', the creature is a carrier of decomposition and decay and thus also a reminder of the future putrefaction which inscribes regression within the otherwise progressive idea of change, constitutive of the teleological promise of some finality. Perhaps the reason why the creature can be read as monstrous is that it radicalizes Darwin's evolutionism, its historicity which limits itself to seeing change as progress, and is as it were blind to seeing change as decay. In Darwin, as Collingwood argues in his *The Idea of Nature*,

> . . . life was conceived as like mind and unlike matter in developing itself through the historic process, and orientating itself through this process not at random but in a determinate direction, towards the production of organisms more fitted to survive in the given environment, whatever that might be. (Collingwood 1960: 135)

This view of nature, or life-force, as producer which gives forth, or perhaps articulates, the fittest, has been readily embraced by the discourses of economy which saw economic growth as a natural continuation of the production of life. Matter seems to be figuring there, but its maternity is 'unlike mind,' and though it somehow precedes the formation of the species, it does not take part in the process of production which is given over to the thus spiritualized life-force. This separation of mind from matter gives rise to a life which lives only in its own context, the matter which is a waste of sorts. The coming out from the matter, coming to life, is silently defined by the ability to *use* the environment, the use thus becoming a bio-economic principle of life. Collingwood repeatedly metaphorizes matter 'as the stage on which life plays its part,' thus as it were trying to separate matter from life by way of reducing it to a context which can be used, though only given that it does not play a part in the dramatic activity of living. Interestingly, he criticizes Bergson's idea of *élan* which conflates matter and life exactly as 'a monstrous and intolerable paradox' (Collingwood 1960: 139), as a monstrosity which, as in *Frankenstein*, gives a living form to death, to the absolute difference of the dead matter. Hence Collingwood's translation of natural science into history, his strong claim that 'natural science as a form of thought exists and always has existed in a context of history, and depends on historical thought for its existence' (Collingwood 1960: 177). Nature can thus only be understood through commemoration, through the selective process of writing down some historical facts, to the inevitable exclusion of the non-facts, of what Evelyn Fox Keller calls a 'mercilessly recalcitrant diversity of nature' (Keller 1989: 44).

Though history as the model for scientific investigations seems to be a descriptive kind of enterprise, an attempt to transcribe nature in the form of knowledgeable language, in Bauman's view it is projective and realizes itself in 'a positional war against nature' (Bauman 2004: 42). History shapes the world from the position of a sculptor who, like Michelangelo, sees the finished product through the already useless fragments of a yet shapeless block of marble, through waste whose separation and destruction has become the secret of modern creativity (Cf. Bauman 2004: 39). The 'positional war against nature' is also a war against difference and diversity, a war whose trenches are architecturally erected whitened sepulchres which commemorate life. 'The tomb is appealing,' writes Peggy Phelan, 'precisely because it is static and still, unlike the decomposing body it covers. If death were guaranteed stillness, perhaps it would be less dreadful. Architecture offers us this monumental stillness and helps transform dying into death' (Phelan 1997: 83). Death is culturally preferable to dying due to its singularity which limits life and thus transforms it into an equally singular event which is both natural and historical. Dying, on the other hand, is a tacit figure of waste which we hide under the sequestered territories of cemeteries which harbour the memory of life rather than the decomposition of the flesh.

What the culture of universal humanism seems to be quite systematically repressing to the point of oblivion is, let me repeat, decomposition, the decay which silently accompanies all kinds of progress and development, the promises of some future accomplishments. Biodegradability is culturally welcome only as a process which has been already delegated to the spheres of waste and refuge. The culturally valuable things are only those which 'rest' in culture not as rest, but as unchangeable presences which must remain resting in peace, undisturbed by the decomposing, perhaps also deconstructing, elements. One of the ways of growing to be more hospitable to difference is, as Derrida phrases it, 'to oppose a certain resistance to living biodegradability,' and thus to become more sensitive to the living decomposition which provides a soil for culture, which 'nourishes, enriches, irrigates, even fecundates' (Derrida 1989: 824).

Resistance to living biodegradably has been, to a large extent, marked by a certain anxiety of excess which, for a translator, might be a distant relative of Harold Bloom's authorial anxiety of influence. The gesture which always accompanies this resistance is the desire to familiarize, to assimilate within the horizon of the already familiar. This relationship, or perhaps tension, between familiarity and otherness is not simply coextensive, and it always entails domination and subordination, as Richard J. Bernstein notices (cf. Bernstein 1992: 180). Otherness, of course, can always be translated into sameness, subordinated to the familiar and thus become a norm. The example, cited earlier, of Jakobson's definition of literariness is exemplary here. The Formalists' idea of 'defamiliarization' as the result of an act of violence committed on the otherwise ordinary and familiar use of language is in fact a normalizing, classificatory gesture which posits literariness within the scope of a grammar, within a systematic order of things which, in this way, fully subordinates the Other. Since order and peace usually go hand in hand as desirable, Jakobson's 'organized violence' is clearly systematic. What reverberates in it is the ethical-political question of control over surplus, over the excess of difference which this kind of violence transforms into the subaltern. This subaltern not only cannot speak, as Gayatri Spivak (Cf. Spivak 1988: 271–313) puts it, but sometimes quite openly is made speechless by the discourses running along the furrows of universal humanism. Universal humanism also dictates the strategy of translation, frequently not even noticing its voice in any articulation which, inevitably, confronts us with the untranslatable. Translation, Derrida once wrote, 'translates always and only the untranslatable' (Derrida 2000b: 17). Marta Segarra comments on this statement and translates it into terms seemingly unrelated to translation. The mere focus on 'normal' translation suggests that there is also something which might seem to be an 'abnormal' translation:

> To translate normally means to choose between options that mutually exclude: it means, therefore, to betray the homonymic richness of the original text, as the traditional formula traduttore, tradittore states. But if there is a translation that refers to the untranslatable, carrying it without appropriating it, one that rejects the other text's devoration, having nonetheless the remorse of the inevitable betrayal, this translation would be the other name of love and friendship, of the loving and respectful relationship with the other. (Segarra 2007: 99)

Perhaps the key word here is appropriation, making proper and owning the proper, mastering. Since property and mastery are at stake, Mizerska's statement, cited near the beginning of this paper, that 'most of the experiences described in the novel concern man, regardless of the sex' (Winterson 1999: 7) can be aptly recalled and equally aptly refer not only to Winterson's *Written on the Body*.

This kind of appropriation qua internalization can be found, for instance, in Goethe's glorification of German culture as a kind of global enterprise which already in the romantic era managed to accommodate all the others. For Goethe the power of language is exactly the power to devour: 'The force of a language is not to reject the foreign, but to devour it' (quoted after Berman 1992: p. 12, no reference provided). The foreign is thus not rejected as foreign, but as it were accommodated by the body of the state without any care about what is left after this peculiar digestive process. In this way the appropriation of the foreign is envisioned as complete, as full, and the language, in this case German, the richest of languages which, in addition to being itself, also contains other foreign languages: 'Independently of our own productions,' writes Goethe,

> we have already achieved a high degree of culture (*Bildung*) thanks to the full appropriation of what is foreign to us. Soon other nations will learn German, because they will realize that in this way they can to a large extent save themselves the apprenticeship of almost all other languages. Indeed, from what languages do we not possess the best works

in the most eminent translations? (quoted after Berman 1992: 11–12, no reference provided).

The 'full appropriation' of the foreign is, in the same paragraph, reduced to 'almost all' languages and some 'best works' whose choice, eminently translated, make the German language a desirable source of other cultures. The devouring of the Other through translation is, in Goethe's view, a seeming offer to share it with others, with other cultures, given that those cultures will learn German with all its hidden treasury of the well translated Other, a universal human language in which, ideally, no translation processes will be involved. The paradox hidden within this project is that through the acquisition of such a superlanguage, one's native language becomes, in fact, redundant because it is through the German language that the appropriation of what is Other, not German, is also achieved. In this way, any kind of relationship with the untranslatable becomes zeroed along with the possibility of Segarra's translational 'carrying' without appropriation, an activity which also demands some care for the Other.

Learning Goethe's universal German with its inbuilt humanistic values is the only effort which is demanded from its prospective practitioners. What universal humanism seems to be also strongly marginalizing is exactly the act of carrying, the fact that translation is a performance, a careful and caring carrying of the Other. Perhaps an alternative evaluation of translation could be its carefulness, rather than quality, measured in terms of an adequacy in which foreignness is welcome as an absent presence marked by the fact that something has been translated. In an essay devoted to performativity and 'bad translation,' Alfian Sa'at (cf. Sa'at 2006) suggests that what in the light of appropriative translation seems to be 'bad', to be something obstructing the smooth and seamless passage from original to copy, can also be seen as a performative indication of transitions which cannot be appropriated by the translated text. This transition, this passage, is the effort of movement in which we are suspended between there and here, between departure and destination. A 'bad' translation is always already an unfinished one, a translation in progress whose provisional status is comparable to the travail of travel, to the effort of movement opposed to the peaceful homely place of destination governed by the economy of travel in which the 'law of the home (*oikonomia*)', like Lacan's law of the Father, establishes the 'sexual division of labour: the domestic(ated) woman, Penelope, maintains the property of the home against would-be usurpers while her husband wanders about' (Abbeele 1992: xxv).

Translation can thus be seen as a return home enriched by the appropriated Other or as a travelling which refuses to be governed by the economy and the law of the home, as it is the practice of travelling, the travel itself, which may 'displace the home or prevent any return to it, thus undermining the institution of that economy and allowing an infinite or unbounded travel' (Abbeele 1992: xxv). If Goethe's German home of culture seems to be one from which no travel is necessary any longer because it has been already well supplied and no travail of translation is needed, the masculine wandering about becomes as it were an inappropriate kind of labour, an activity which threatens the law of home with the indeterminacy of appropriation, with its re-opening to what remains of the Other. With the return of Odysseus, Penelope's textual work of weaving loses its sense and the usurpers must die. From the perspective of the now seemingly safe home of man, of universal humanism, attempts at opening that home to other(s) is perceived as a betrayal, as the stereotypically feminine 'dislike' for solid stability and faithfulness. Sa'at's bad translation, or Segarra's implied abnormal one, seem only to be possible in spaces which are located away from home. They would then open up other spaces in which translating is, as I have already said, both careful and caring for the Other, an activity which is hospitable without forcing the Other into what is mine.

An enforced hospitality is an oxymoronic construct which implies both subjection and hospitality which, far from being freely given, is demanded. The problem with unenforced hospitality is that it hosts an insoluble antinomy between what Jacques Derrida calls

> the law of unlimited hospitality (to give the new arrival all of one's home and oneself, our own, without asking a name or compensation . . .), and on the other hand, the laws (in the plural), those rights and duties that are always conditioned and conditional, as they are defined by the family, civil society, and the State. (Derrida 2000b: 65)

Hospitality, not only in translation, is thus bound to be not so much bad as, by way of litotes, no good, an errant kind of event, or performance which puts the home of universal humanism on the road and thus translating it, hospitably, into one more stranger among ourselves, the foreigner within us, 'that "improper" facet of our impossible "own and proper"' (Kristeva 1991: 910).

Note

1   All translations from Polish into English as well as back-translations are mine.

Bibliography

Abbeele, G. van den (1992) *Travel as Metaphor: from Montaigne to Rousseau*. Minneapolis, MN: University of Minnesota Press.

Bauman, Z. (2004) *Życie na przemiał* [*Wasted Lives: Modernity and Its Outcasts*. Cambridge: Polity 2004] (Polish translation by Tomasz Kunz). Kraków: Wydawnictwo Literackie.

Berman, Antoine (1992) *Experience of the Foreign: Culture and Translation in Romantic Germany* (trans. S. Heyvaert). New York: State University of New York Press.

Bernstein, R. J. (1992) *The New Constellation: The Ethical-Political Horizons of Modernity/Postmodernity*. Cambridge MA: MIT Press.

Cixous, H. (2003), *L'amour du loup et autres remords*. Paris: Galilee.

Collingwood, R. G. (1960), *The Idea of Nature*. New York: Oxford University Press.

Currie, M. (2004), *Difference*. New York: Routledge.

Derrida, J. (1978), *Writing and Difference* (trans. A. Bass). Chicago, IL: University of Chicago Press.

Derrida, J. (1989) 'Biodegradables: Seven Diary Fragments' (trans. P. Kamuf). *Critical Inquiry* 15, 812–73.

Derrida, J. (2000a) 'H.C. pour la vie, c'est a dire . . ', in M. Calle-Gruber (ed.), *Helene Cixous, croisees d'une oeuvre*. Paris: Galilee.

Derrida, J. (2000b) *Of Hospitality* (trans. R. Bowlby). Stanford, CA: Stanford University Press.

Flotow Luise von (1997) *Translation and Gender: Translating in the 'Era of Feminism'*, Ottawa, ON: University of Ottawa Press.

Fox Keller, E. (1989) 'The Gender/Science System: or, Is Sex to Gender as Nature Is to Science?', in N. Tauna (ed.), *Feminism and Science*. Bloomington, IN: Indiana University Press, 33–44.

Grosz, E. (1999) 'The Time of Violence; Deconstruction and Value'. *College Literature* 26, 8–18.

Jakobson R. (1960), 'Concluding Statement: Linguistics and Poetics', in T. E. Sebeok (ed.) *Style in Language*. Cambridge MA: M. I. T. Press, 350–75.

Johnson, B. (1987) 'My monster/My Self', in *A World of Difference*. Baltimore, MD: Johns Hopkins University Press 1987, 144–54.

Kristeva, Julia (1991) *Strangers to Ourselves* (trans. L. S. Roudiez). New York: Columbia University Press.

Moore, L. (1995) 'Teledildonics: Virtual Lesbians in the Fiction of Jeannette Winterson', in Elizabeth Grosz and Elspeth Probyn (eds) *Sexy bodies: The Strange Carnalities of Feminism*. New York: Routledge, 104–127.

Phelan, P. (1997) *Mourning Sex. Performing Public Memories*. New York: Routledge.

Sa'at, A. (2006) 'Out of Synch: On Bad Translation as Performance', in J. Lindsay (ed.), *Between Tongues: Translation And/Of/In Performance in Asia*. Singapore : Singapore University Press, 272–301.

Saussure, F. de (1966) *Course in General Linguistics* (trans. W. Baskin). New York: McGraw-Hill.

Segarra, M. (2007) 'Friendship, Betrayal, and Translation: Cixous and Derrida', *Mosaic* 40, 91–102.

Simon, S. (1996) *Gender in Translation. Cultural Identity and the Politics of Transmission*. New York: Routledge.

Smith, P. J. (not dated) *Encyclopedia of Gay, Lesbian, Bisexual, Transgender and Queer Culture*, www.glbtq.com/literature/winterson_j.html [accessed 21 March 2009].

Spivak, G. C. (1988) 'Can the Subaltern Speak?', in C. Nelson and L. Grossberg (eds) *Marxism and the Interpretation of Culture*. Champaign, IL: University of Illinois Press, 271–313.

Szydłowska, V. (2003) *Nihilizm i dekonstrukcja*. Warszawa: IFiS.

Venuti, L. (2000) 'Translation, Community, Utopia', in L. Venuti (ed.) *The Translation Studies Reader*. New York: Routledge, 468–88.

Wallace, W. (1968) *The World of Rembrandt: 1606–1669*. New York: Time Life Books. 1968, 107–11.

Waters, S. (2007a) *The Night Watch*. London: Virago.

Waters, S. (2007b) *Pod osłoną nocy* (trans. M. Gawlik-Małkowska). Poznań: Prószyński i S-ka.

Waters, S. (2004) *Niebanalna więź* (trans. M. Gawlik-Małkowska). Poznań: Prószyński i S-ka.

Waters, S. (2000) *Affinity*. London: Virago.

Winterson, J. (1999) *Zapisane na ciele* (trans. H. Mizerska). Warszaw: Rebis.

Winterson, J. (1996) *Written on the Body*. London: Vintage Books.

Žižek, S. (1997) *The Plague of Fantasies*. London: Verso.

Part III
Behind the TT: Translational Priorities and Asymmetrical Relationships of Power

The Taming of the Eastern European Beast? A Case Study of the Translation of a Polish Novel into English

Paulina Gąsior
University of Wroclaw, Poland

Chapter Outline

1. East is beast?

This chapter explores the processes involved in the translation and publication of a Polish contemporary novel in the United Kingdom. It focuses on translation as the final product offered to the British readers, its poetics and politics treated as an index of the cultural and social relationship not only between the United Kingdom and Poland, but also between Western and Eastern Europe.

There is an ongoing debate in Translation Studies regarding issues of power, asymmetries and linguistic imbalance that operate in translation. Yet both the theoretical propositions and case studies have tended to be limited to the post-colonial context and entrapped within the opposition of the colonized and the colonizers. Cultural relations within Europe itself, particularly between the East, the countries scarred by the Soviet occupation, and the capitalist West still demand attention.

Davies (1997), in his essay 'West Best, East Beast' points out that the origins of the intellectual construct known as 'Eastern Europe' can be traced back to the Enlightenment, when the West was equated with light, progress and culture, while the East of Europe was associated with half-barbarian lands plunged in intellectual darkness. Even nowadays in the political and economic EU discourse, the notion of Europe seems to be split between the 'EU 15' and 'new accession states'. The dichotomy between the West, (Western) European Union and the Eastern European countries is still persistent both in front page European politics and in common beliefs. The inner divisions and hierarchies within Europe are a legacy of the cold war and communism, and Eastern European countries, including Poland, continue to be constructed as the Other, despite significant changes in the political and economic arena. The common use of the phrase 'the other Europe' is meaningful in this respect and the contexts in which it is used are multiple (see *Cinema of the other Europe: the industry and artistry of East Central European film* (Iordanova 2003), *The Other Europe: Eastern Europe to 1945* (Walters 1988) or the Penguin series 'Writers from the Other Europe' edited by Philip Roth). In an important collection *Central Europe: Core or Periphery?* (Lord 2000) Croatian writer, Slavenka Drakulić criticizes the Western Europe (and the EU) for excluding Eastern Europe as the 'other Europe' and in this way limiting the notion of the European identity.

2. Discourse, imitation and migration

It may be argued that the production of knowledge about Eastern Europe and its culture takes place through and within a specific *discourse* (Foucault 1972) generated by the West and that certain preconceptions (see previous discussion) have persisted as a part of this discourse for centuries.

As Hall (2003: 56) points out, discourses construct 'subject positions' from which they become meaningful. Eastern Europe has located itself/has been located in the *peripheral* position of a 'minor culture' and in a sense it relies on the 'gaze' of the West. Eastern Europe resides in the 'periphery', that is, behind the curtain, which is no longer iron, but is still comprised of many deeply rooted images, stereotypes and beliefs. Yet, I would argue that in the case of Poland, this peripheral position is gradually shifting through two processes: *imitation* and *migration*.

After the fall of the communist regime in 1989, Poland underwent a crucial political transformation and with the first free elections in nearly 50 years, made its way towards a democratic and independent state. During this period, when communism was gradually being replaced with capitalism, Poland found itself, as sociologists term it, in a 'cultural void', described as a general feeling of disorientation, helplessness and lack of values (Reykowski 1993). This void has been filled, to a large extent, by Western, and primarily Anglo-American, values and cultural patterns. Poland and Eastern Europe began to look up to the West and *imitate* – therefore becoming some of the major recipients and importers of the Western culture. The changes of the Polish language are an example of the process of imitation. The large number of borrowings from English and its systematic increase shows how great was the impact of British and American culture. By 1961 around 700 loanwords were registered as existing in Polish while a book on English loans in Polish published in 1994 gathers around 1600 borrowings (Mańczak-Wohlfeld 1994). The influx of English borrowings stems both from the need to fill semantic gaps (for example in technology) and from the fascination that the Anglo-American culture awakens, particularly among young people.

Another example is the enormous inflow of books translated from English. After 1989 there was a sharp rise in the number of translations published in Poland, accompanied by a fall in the publication of Polish books (Adamiec, Kołodziejczyk 2001). In the 1990s the Polish book market absorbed a large number of translations of Western literature, especially popular and commercial books: horror, science fiction, thrillers, erotic fiction, love stories and so forth. As data shows, most translations are from English: in the decade between 1989 and 1999 the number of translations from British originals increased 6 times, and from American originals 11 times.

Thus, in a sense, by becoming a recipient and imitator, Poland subjected itself to the rules of the dominant discourse and put itself into a peripheral or minor position.

One more important factor is the migration of Polish people to the United Kingdom, that is, the movement from the periphery to the centre, which still raises anxiety in the Western world. Malena (2003; quoted in Cronin 2006: 45) talks about migration by means of a translation metaphor: 'Migrants are translated beings in countless ways. They remove themselves from their familiar source environment and move towards a target culture which can be totally unknown or more or less familiar (...)'. Similarly, Polish people, who thronged to Britain after Poland joined the EU in 2004, 'translated themselves' from their native culture to the culture which, they believe, offers better opportunities. The reasons for migration vary, but underlying the motivation of labourers, students, young scientists etc. is the conviction that Western culture is more 'central', 'major' and consequently – superior. And the question that arises is the cultural implications of these 'translation' processes that take place both in Eastern and Western Europe. Of particular interest to me are the ways in which the East is received, read and interpreted, in other words – how does the West, or Britain, 'translate' Eastern Europe and specifically Poland?

My chapter specifically focuses on the issues of translation and processes involved in the publication of a Polish novel in Britain and the ways in which the dominant discourse may govern the production of meanings conveyed by the translation as a product.

According to some translation academics, such as Lawrence Venuti, power relations are inextricable from the translation process. According to him, translation in the context of inequality (economic, cultural, linguistic) from a minor culture/language to a major culture/language involves assimilation or adjustment and is a form of violence performed on the 'weaker' party (Venuti 1995, 1998). Assuming there is an asymmetry between Poland as an Eastern European country, and Great Britain as one of the strongest countries of Western Europe, I would like to explore how power operates at the level of literary translation by carrying out a particular case study of the translation of a Polish contemporary novel *Dom dzienny, dom nocny* by Olga Tokarczuk (1998) into English (*House of Day, House of Night* (2002), published by Granta). This will show whether, because of translation choices and publication strategies, the novel has been subject to 'domestication' and 'ethnocentric violence' (in Venuti's terms) – in other words, whether the Eastern European 'beast' has been tamed. I will also look at the cultural images of 'Polishness' that emerge out of the translation and potential stereotyping practices that construct Poland as the Other. In order to support my analysis a brief survey was carried out to find out what ideas the British have about Polish women and what associations are brought up by the cover photo. I also contacted the publisher, as well as the translator herself on some specific issues related to translation strategies.

3. The construction of the product

i. Selecting the novel for translation

The Polish novel, *Dom dzienny, dom nocny,* is the fourth novel by Olga Tokarczuk. Tokarczuk is one of the most critically acclaimed contemporary Polish writers. She is a trained psychologist, a devotee of Jung and is noted for the mythical and feminist tones in her writing. She published three novels and then drifted away from the genre towards collections of short stories, novellas or essayistic sketches. *Dom dzienny, dom nocny* was first published in Poland in 1998 by a small publishing house, Ruta, in Wałbrzych. It was nominated for the prestigious literary award Nike in 1999 and since then the writer and her novels have been gaining growing attention from critics and popularity among readers. Set in the Lower Silesia region (Dolny Śląsk), near the Polish-Czech and Polish-German borders, the novel is composed as a diary. It consists of fragments that combine stories, scraps of memories and dream visions from various periods of the past – the ancient past, and the Middle Ages – and from contemporary times. The novel also embraces philosophical remarks on various features of time, being, death, the past, memory and the present, dream and reality. The English translation was published in 2002 by Granta. In 2004 the novel was short-listed for the International IMPAC Dublin Literary Award.

There are two aspects that need to be considered from the point of view of the presence of this novel outside its original – Polish and Eastern European – context. First of all, it is the 'Polishness', the regionalism, Polish history and politics present in the novel which constitute a challenge for both the translator and the target language readers. The novel is topographically rooted in the towns of Lower Silesia (Dolny Śląsk), a region marked by the two World Wars and other historical events, border shifts (between Poland, Germany and Czech Republic), as well as the political transformation of the 1990s.

In a sense, Tokarczuk's fiction attempts to come to terms with the past and history, but it also contains meanings that go beyond a local specificity and allow for a universal interpretation, not limited by cultural and national differences – it tells private stories by means of a mythical narration known to English language readers, primarily through Latin American prose.

Still, it is not an easy read for the target readership – a postmodern form, with mythical and philosophical content, playing out against complex issues related to Central European history. According to one of the editors of Granta, Liz Jobey, the target audience was expected to be composed of demanding readers, who like good quality fiction, both written in English and in translation (Jobey, pers. comm., April 2007).

ii. Translation strategies

Despite the existence of certain asymmetries and a power imbalance between the Western Europe (Great Britain) and Eastern Europe (Poland), the choice of the text is far from 'ethnocentric'. Even though the novel has a central status in the Polish literary canon, due to its content and form it does not easily lend itself to a domesticating strategy and assimilation to the target culture's aesthetic values. It is likely to have a peripheral or marginal position in the target literary system and thus the choice of such a text for translation conforms to Venuti's resistant or minoritising translation (Venuti, 1995, 1998). The translation strategies employed in *House of Day, House of Night* by Lloyd-Jones, in general do not reflect Venuti's thesis about the 'ethnocentric violence' that resides in acts of translation into English – a global hegemonic language. In fact, the translation choices are far from cultural appropriation and they barely make an effort to meet the needs of a target reader and facilitate the reception of the book. Even though the translator does not usually retain the original Polish terms (e.g. in case of culture-specific items, like dishes or specialties like *pierogi*, *oscypek*), she rarely resorts to overt cultural substitution, which is the most distinctive indication of a domesticating method. The only exception is for the term *pierogi* (a Polish specialty mentioned several times in the novel) which became *piroshki* (which sounds Eastern European, but refers to something else, i.e. Russian meat pies) and are replaced with the international term *meatballs* just once in the novel. Another item (*oscypek*) was rendered as 'Tatra Highland sheep's milk cheese' where the translator offered an explanation rather than a substitution. Also, Lloyd-Jones often provides commentaries, which are aimed at familiarizing British readers with the cultural and social aspects of the source culture, rather than sparing them a foreign encounter (i.e., by employing an omission). For instance, the fact that someone crossed out the price 30 gr and wrote 10,000 zł on a book cover would have been meaningless for the British reader, if it weren't for the translator's comment explaining inflation during the period of communism: 'someone had crossed out "30 groshys" and written 10,000 zlotys, a reminder of the era of rapid inflation' (Tokarczuk 2002: 51). Moreover, there are many instances of procedures which leave the foreign reader defamiliarized (to use a Formalist term) and do not minimize the effect of foreignness, for example, retaining original names (Krysia Popłoch, Jasiek Bobol, Paschalis, Kummernis, Wrocław, Bógdał) and the obscure orthography (Polish diacritical marks, such as ą, ę, ó, ż, ź, ń, ć, ś, ł).

However, there is a major shift in the macrostructure of the novel, namely the omission of a particular chapter, entitled 'Listy' ('Letters'). This chapter is a metalinguistic treaty on words that are 'unfair probably because they originate from an unequally and sloppily divided world' [my translation] (Tokarczuk 1998: 104). To show this inequality in language, the narrator comments on the morphology and etymology of several Polish words. She observes the lack of the feminine equivalent of the word *męstwo* – *bravery*, which in the Polish language shares the same root with *mężczyzna* (*a man*) and *męski* (*masculine*). She wonders about the ways of naming this particular virtue in a woman, without 'erasing' her sex. Similarly, the narrator bemoans the associations brought up by feminine counterparts for *mędrzec* (*a sage* or *a wise man*) and *starzec* (*an old man*). The masculine words evoke dignity, solemnity and knowledge, while the feminine ones (*staruszka, starucha*) are merely associated with old age or, at most, with witchcraft – 'as if an old woman could not be wise' points out the narrator (Tokarczuk 1998: 104).

The reason why this chapter has been left out in the translation is presumably its linguistic untranslatability, which relates to the specificity of the Polish lexical items discussed in the aforementioned fragment of the novel. Lloyd-Jones told me explicitly that the cut was made for purely linguistic reasons – because there are no equivalents in the English language that would carry the same connotations, both positive and negative. Moreover they were agreed with the author (Lloyd-Jones, pers. comm., August 2007).

However, it may be argued that the decision by the translator (working together with the editor) to omit the chapter, although not ideological, may have significantly influenced the reception of the novel in the target audience. As several Polish literary critics pointed out (Lengren 1999; Nowacki 1999), these metalinguistic comments are a proof of Tokarczuk's feminism and they largely determined the perception of her work as an instance of 'feminist literature'. In comparison, a major review in *The Observer* (Marsden 2002) that appeared after the publication of the translation fails to comment on this particular aspect of the novel or on Tokarczuk's status as a feminist writer.

The absence of the chapter in the translation deprives the novel and its target readers of a vast range of meanings and overlooks its feminist aspects. The framework of the narrator's discussion on sexism in language casts a different light on many stories and female characters in *House of Day, House of Night*. Without this context, the ordinary women in the novel, like Krysia, a bank clerk who falls in love with a voice that declares love to her, or Marta, an elderly wig-maker, appear more banal. It is Marta, always shown as performing ordinary tasks – cooking, shopping, chopping cabbage – who is the female *sage* of the novel, whose stories are a source of wisdom and philosophical depth. Also, the decision made by the translator and publisher goes against the theory and practice of feminist translation widely discussed in the work by Sherry Simon (1996). Simon discusses well-known projects undertaken by feminist translators such as Barbara Godard (the translation of Nicole Bossard's *L'Amér*) or Suzanne Jill Levine (the translation of Guillermo Cabrera Infante's *Tres tristes tigres*). These examples prove that linguistic untranslatability can be overcome by wordplay, puns, the creation of neologisms, new forms and other self-effacing strategies, even if they involve manipulation.

The omission of the chapter also raises the issue of cultural representation, to which I shall return later.

iii. The metatextual framework of *House of Day, House of Night*

In the following section of this chapter I discuss several 'paratexts' (to use Genette's term) closely related to the novel itself: the 'Translator's note' preceding the novel, the publisher's advertising comments on the back of the cover and the review from *The Observer*. According to Genette, paratexts are devices that surround the book and mediate between the book (the publisher) and the reader, affecting its reception (Genette 1997). Thus, the purpose of this analysis is to lay bare the cultural images that may be hidden in the paratexts, the ways in which they may affect the understanding of the novel in the target culture, and whether they correspond to the preconceptions and social constructs of 'Eastern Europeanness' that prevail in the British society.

a. The Blurb

The publisher's commentary that has been added as part of the cover gives an extremely cursory outline of the historical and cultural background of *House of Day, House of Night*. After a short introduction intended to familiarize the readers with the places where the novel is set, the publisher stresses the universal content of the book – the experiences and stories of the characters. The role of the blurb on the back cover is naturally to encourage the British audience to reach for the book. The strategy of the publisher is to arouse interest in Polish fiction by emphasizing the mysteriousness of the novel's world and its enigmatic and quirky characters. The blurb enumerates the novel's heroes, so that it turns into a gallery of unusual, half-real, half-imaginary portraits:

> A farmer is tormented by a mournful bird inside him that struggles to be free; a bank clerk sets out to find the owner of the voice that declares love to her in her dreams; the gentle classics scholar grapples with his monthly metamorphosis into a werewolf; and a monk comes to terms with his own sexual ambiguity (Tokarczuk 2002)

The publisher's blurb on the cover reveals a tendency to foreground those aspects of *House of Day, House of Night,* that are universal and that go beyond cultural specificity. The publisher presents Tokarczuk as an 'exciting new voice for British readers', which suggests that he also expects the target audience to be tempted by the novelty and freshness that foreign and, to some extent, exotic writing may evoke.

b. The Translator's Note

The 'Translator's note' preceding the novel, on the other hand, is completely different in character. The short note by Lloyd-Jones is a brief introduction to the complex history of Dolny Śląsk, the region where the novel is set. The translator acts as a spokesperson for Polish history and culture on a foreign territory. She realizes that the numerous references to the history of Silesia found in Tokarczuk's novel (names of towns and villages, stories of their founders, local legends etc.) could obscure the reader's understanding of the book. Thus, she decides to familiarize the British audience with the heritage of the region by providing a brief historical note:

> The book is set in south-west Poland, in the region known as Silesia. This was part of the German Reich until 1945, when at the Yalta and Potsdam conferences the Allies agreed to move the borders of Poland westwards. Many Polish citizens were transported from the land lost to the east (annexed by the USSR) and resettled in formerly German territory to the west, where they were given the homes and property of the evacuated Germans (Tokarczuk 2002)

However, there is another aspect of the translator's note that I wish to consider. The information Lloyd-Jones provides, to some extent, steers readers' attention toward one particular aspect of the novel – namely its historical dimension. By presenting encyclopaedic facts, it foregrounds history as a prevailing theme and encourages readers to look at the fate of the characters through the filter of the historical heritage of Dolny Śląsk rather than see their complex identities and inner selves.

The translator's note also contains a playful and humorous remark about the culinary recipes that occur throughout *House of Day, House of Night*: 'Readers are advised that some of the recipes in this book should carry the health warning, "Don't try this at home!"' (Lloyd-Jones 2002). It visibly contrasts with the encyclopedic historical information and now the translator's note acquires a personal and warm tone. Not only does the translator become a visible medium between the author of the original and a target reader, but she also enters into a friendly and familiar dialogue with the new audience. On the other hand, the 'health warning' makes the recipes (and the culture they stem from) appear dangerous and seem to heighten the 'Otherness' because of their exoticism and foreignness.

c. The Review

Finally, I would like to comment on the review of *House of Day, House of Night*, published by *The Observer* (Marsden 2002). At the beginning the author makes a remark that the Polish people are a nation that can boast of two living Nobel laureates: Wisława Szymborska and Czesław Miłosz (the article was written in 2002, Czesław Miłosz passed away in 2004). He also lists other writers, such as Zbigniew Herbert, Sławomir Mrożek, Ryszard Kapuściński and Paweł Huelle. He adds Olga Tokarczuk to the list and points out that she deserves a place among these writers. What they all seem to share, according to the critic, is the fact that they all draw on 'collective faith and an irony that often seems the only sane approach to the cruel joke of Polish history' (Marsden 2002).

Unlike the Polish critics (see Lengren 1999; Nowacki 1999) who comment extensively on such issues as the feminism in the novel, postmodern structure, magic realism, sexuality and self-identification, Marsden concentrates primarily on the historical background of *House of Day, House of Night*. He views the novel as a collection of stories and myths from the life of the local community set against the backdrop of the wider history and historical changes, border shifts and relocations that took place in the multicultural region of Dolny Śląsk. For example, as one of the many recurring motifs of the book, he mentions the motif of absent Germans who fled to the new Germany. Marsden appreciates other aspects and dimensions of the novel, such as the mingling of the imaginary and the real, dreams and reality, and past and present. Yet the vision of Polish literature he creates is a vision of a literature which is immersed in history and obsessively attempts to come to terms with the past. To some extent, he may have been led to such a vision by Lloyd-Jones's preface, which in a way stresses what she thinks is important in the novel. Both the preface and the review help create the readers' 'horizon of expectation' (Jauss 1982: 24). The target culture readers are likely to interpret and judge the work based on the set of expectations and assumptions suggested by the translator's introduction and the review.

It may be argued that this preoccupation with the past and the historical heritage is a construct that prevails among British readers of Polish fiction and that reading Polish fiction through a historical lens is a dominating reception paradigm. An example I would like to quote is from the Lonely Planet Guide – one of the major guidebooks on Poland. The introductory section, 'Destination Poland', presents Poland as a country burdened with the past and history:

> Overrun countless times by marauding aggressors, subjugated to over-bearing foreign rule for centuries, and now told their beloved vodka can be made from anything the Polish nation has endured more than most. Yet Poland, a country crushed flat so many times it has become inde-structible, is shaking off the last vestiges of forced slumber and rushing with great abandon into a modern 21st century. (Bedford et al. 2008: 16)

Another example is the opening sentence of *The Guardian's* travel section, devoted to Poland, which states: 'Poland certainly has a troubled past' (Guardian Travel 2008).

I posit that the paratexts discussed above foreground some aspects of the novel, especially the historical dimension of *House of Day, House of Night*. On the other hand, the feminist overtones lurking in the narratorial fragments of Tokarczuk's book have been ignored, which deprives the novel of the mean-ings related to gender inequality and sexist language.

d. The Design of the Book Cover

According to Genette (1997) book covers, as types of 'paratexts', are usually the first manifestations of books which may steer readers to particular read-ings of a literary work. Also, in an article on the bindings of translations, Harvey (2003) posits that book covers (including cover photos) may be sites for presenting certain ideological positions. In this part of the chapter I discuss whether the cover of the translation conveys any covert messages and whether it is a vehicle for cultural images connected with the concept of being Polish and Eastern European. The discussion also touches upon the potential ways in which the cover design may affect readers' perception of the novel or antici-pate their interpretation of the novel.

First of all, let us look at some design-aspects of the original covers of *Dom dzienny, dom nocny*. The cover of the novel's first edition, published by the Ruta publishing house in Wałbrzych in 1998 is unadorned and uses black, white and grey as the only tones. The cover features a surreal pencil drawing showing two old fashioned chairs (incomplete) and an indistinct image of what may be the frame of a mirror or a painting with stairs and a human silhouette. The entire image is vague and the outlines and boundaries of the objects are blurred.

The cover plays on the opposition of day and night, light and darkness, and thus makes a close link to the title. The cover can be regarded both as an illustration and as a metaphor for the philosophical content of the novel that functions as a superstructure built on top of its plots, that is, the stories of various characters. The numerous digressions and narratorial commentaries touch upon a variety of themes and particularly upon the borderline phenomena – imagination and the real, dream and reality, life and death, fact and myth, past and present, as well as inner life and social circumstances. The surreal picture on the original cover reflects the mysteries and uncertainties that life encompasses and that are inextricable from the lots of the characters of *House of Day, House of Night*.

The cover of further editions, published by Wydawnictwo Literackie, is similar in style. It features a surreal image of what appears to be both a house and a teapot. The shapes are fluid, the image is blurry and the house-teapot appears to be surrounded by fog or smoke. The dominating colours are rather dark and gloomy – grey, purple and black – which evoke associations with twilight. As in the case of the first edition, the cover plays on the darkness and light (night and day) opposition – behind the doors of the teapot house there is a beam of light contrasting with the bleak imagery. This dichotomy is an illustration of the novel's constant shifting between the mysteries of life and death, day and night, affirmation of life and its absurd and gloomy side.

The cover of the English translation shows a photograph of a woman standing by the window of an old house and preparing a meal in a rather out-dated pot. The colour spectrum of the photograph involves grey, black, dark purple and olive green, which make the picture seem slightly old-fashioned and remote.

I would thus argue that the cover of the translation is not nearly as closely linked to the content of the book as the original Polish covers. The message that is conveyed to the target readers about the novel by means of the cover is that it is 'different', 'non-West European' and perhaps 'exotic' or 'unfamiliar'.

The cover-image of the translated novel becomes, then, a vehicle for a process of cultural representation, as it promotes a certain understanding of Polish 'femininity' and of the prevailing paradigm of gender roles in Eastern Europe. This paradigm may be based on stereotypical constructs, which envisage women's role as primarily domestic – limited to household chores and childbearing.

This assumption stems from the two disparate, not to say opposite, semantic fields that are built around the images on the original Polish editions and on the cover of the translation. Both the two Polish covers and the English cover make a link with the title and draw on the concept and imagery of a *house* – the teapot house, the chairs as house requisites and a kitchen space. Yet, I posit that the original covers treat the idea of the house metaphorically – just as in the novel, the house can evoke a variety of meanings: the house stands for life, body, death, eternity, and the space where past and present coexist – it is the centre of the universe and of Tokarczuk's philosophy. These metaphorical senses are achieved also due to the surreal style of the cover drawings and to the use of colours. In contrast, the *house* on the English cover is much more literal – it brings up a concept of 'domesticity' – it is a space of domestic life, and household chores. However, the colours of the photograph make it seem a little distant and enigmatic.

4. Survey findings

In order to test these assumptions a brief survey was carried out, and the target respondents were 20 British people from various age groups, both men and women. The aim of the questionnaire was to find out whether there exist any stereotypes about Polish women and gender roles among the Western (British) society, and also whether the front cover image can be perceived as part of a social knowledge about Eastern Europe and women in particular. This kind of survey could be usefully incorporated into studies of reader response.

The respondents were 20 British people – 10 men and 10 women. Among them was one person under 25, 6 people aged 25–34, 4 people aged 35–44, 3 people aged 45–55 and 6 people over 55. They were asked about the role of women in contemporary Poland regarding household roles, employment, educational attainment and participation in political life. The majority of respondents (65%) believed that Polish society is 'male' and envisage women primarily in household roles, which are 'all-encompassing and very traditional and burdening'. The British imagined that there is a 'strong maternal and domestic role surrounding women, more so than in Britain'. They see Polish women as taking the main role at home – they do the household chores (housekeeping, cleaning, cooking), as well as rear the children. As far as employment is concerned, 6 respondents (30%) believed that women are 'still not very visible in the employment sector' because of the domestic responsibilities or imagine that they perform non-professional or low-skill jobs.

The respondents were also asked about their reaction to the cover and the keywords recurring in the description of the cover are the following: *domestic, tradition, hardship, pre-feminist, male-dominated society, peasant, rustic, rural, old-fashioned, hard work.*

To sum up, the image on the cover certainly is a vehicle for cultural representation and the photograph produces certain meanings (a mental construct which can be condensed in the phrase 'The Polish woman is primarily a housewife'), which may affect the expectations of target readers towards the novel. These meanings promulgate a fairly limited vision of what it is to be a Polish woman, but, as the survey proves, they are also a reflection of existing (and stereotypical) target culture knowledge about Polish women.

5. Concluding remarks

To conclude, there is certainly a significant cultural asymmetry between Polish culture as a 'minority culture' and British culture which makes its global, hegemonic presence felt throughout the world – largely by means of language. Primarily because of this cultural gap and long lived and deeply rooted preconceptions (the image of the East as a beast), the translation of *Dom dzienny, dom nocny* was a challenge for the translator and is also a challenging encounter for British readers. Whether this imbalance however, significantly affects the overall translation strategy and the overall presentation of the book on the target culture book market, remains a dubious issue.

As the analysis of translation strategies demonstrates, the translation method is not a proof of an 'ethnocentric violence', which, as Venuti (1995, 1998) argues is present in acts of translation into English as a hegemonic language. In fact, Lloyd-Jones's translation choices do not involve frequent cultural substitution or overt appropriation – strategies which are an obvious indication of domestication. On the contrary – the reader of *House of Day, House of Night* may find procedures which escalate the effect of 'foreignness' and leave the reader defamiliarized (e.g. the retention of original names and Polish orthography).

This chapter has also investigated the meanings constructed by the metatexts surrounding the novel, such as the translator's note, the publisher's 'blurb', reviews in the British press (e.g. in *The Observer*) or the photograph on the cover. Nor do we find distinct examples of domestication here. Strategies such as the visibility of the translator as a medium, her tone towards target readers and her defamiliarizing remarks, as well as the blurb encouraging new readers to find interest in a fresh and exotic writing, enable us to place *House of Day, House of Night* near the foreignizing polarity.

However, I discussed certain choices undertaken on the level of translation, publication and circulation of the novel, which may have affected the perception of the book in the target culture, especially the translator's note, the review and the design of the book cover. These aspects of the translation and reception of *House of Day, House of Night*, became, in my view, a vehicle for cultural representation. By foregrounding specific dimensions of the novel (particularly the historical background of *House of Day, House of Night*), and ignoring other ones (the feminist content of the novel and the fragments pertaining to sexism in the Polish language), the translation promulgates an image of the Polish which is partly based on stereotypical constructs, and which is a reflection of what the British imagine Polish culture to be. The major images of 'Polishness' which I see as part of a much larger *discursive formation* were the following:

1) the image of the Polish people as a nation burdened by the past and historical issues, entangled in its own memory. This preconception enables the 'future-oriented' Western Europe to see Eastern Europe (and Poland), which looks back into the past, as the Other. This imagery is particularly visible in the way the novel was reviewed by the critics, who emphasized the historical backdrop against which the fates of the characters are enacted.

2) the image of a Polish woman as a housewife as envisaged by the British respondents. The survey confirmed the hypothesis that the prevailing associations related to being a woman in Poland make up a construct of 'housewife' who performs traditional gender roles in a male dominated society. It could be argued that the idea of gender imbalance in Poland (and perhaps Eastern Europe) that pervades in Western Europe is one of the preconceptions that create a cultural gap between the two 'Europes'.

The cultural space where Western Europe and Eastern Europe meet is definitely an interesting one, where new and unusual values may occur. Even though Venuti's thesis about the implications of translation in the context of cultural, economic or political imbalance may not seem to hold true in this particular case, there is still room for further research into other cultural phenomena that arise out of the East-West dichotomy. This case study provides a curious insight into the relations between the two 'Europes'. As the Poles (and in fact many other Eastern Europeans) increasingly 'translate themselves' into the Western lifestyle, the parallel process has become an object of interest: how the British, in response to the influx of Polish people, translate the Poles and Polish culture. This chapter has attempted to provide some answers to this question and to analyse the potential stereotyping practices that are at work where the British and the Polish cultures meet.

6. Bibliography

Adamiec, W., Kołodziejczyk, B. (2001) *Rynek książki w Polsce* [Book market in Poland], in Elektroniczny Biuletyn Informacyjny Bibliotekarzy. Available online at: http://ebib.oss.wroc.pl/2001/28/adamiec. html [Accessed on 7 June 2009].

Bedford, N., Fallon, S., Wilson, N., McAdam, M., Richards, T. (2008) *Poland*. Poland Travel Guide. Footscray: Lonely Planet Publication.

Cronin, M. (2006) *Translation and Identity*. London; New York: Routledge.

Davies, N. (1997) 'West Best, East Beast'. *Oxford Today*, 9 (2) 29–31.

Foucault, M. (1972) *The Archeology of Knowledge*. London: Tavistock.

Genette, G. (1997) *Paratexts: Thresholds of Interpretation*. Trans. by Jane E. Lewin. Cambridge: Cambridge University Press.

Guardian Travel (2008) 'Poland. Essential Information'. Available online at: http://travel.guardian.co.uk/ countries/information/0,8766,420785,00.html [Accessed on 15 June 2009].

Hall, S. (2003) 'The Work of Representation', in S. Hall (ed.) *Representation. Cultural Representations and Signifying Practices,* London: Sage Publications.

Harvey, K. (2003) 'Events and Horizons. Reading Ideology in the Bindings of Translations', in M. C. Pérez (ed.) *Apropos of Ideology: Translation Studies on Ideology, Ideologies in Translation Studiem*. Manchester: St Jerome, 43–69.

Iordanova, D. (2003) *Cinema of the Other Europe: The Industry and Artistry of East Central European Film*. London; New York: Wallflower Press.

Jauss, H. R. (1982) *Toward an Aesthetic of Reception*. Brighton: Harvester Press.

Jobey, L. (2007) Personal communication, 13 April 2007.

Lengren, M. (1999) 'Książka – dom' ['A book – a house']. *Twórczość*, 11, 127–29.

Lloyd-Jones, A. (2007) Personal communication, 28 August 2007.

Lloyd-Jones, A. (2002) 'Translator's Note', in O.Tokarczuk *House of Day, House of Night*. Trans. A. Lloyd-Jones. London: Granta.

Lord, C. (2000) *Central Europe: Core or Periphery?*. Copenhagen Business School Press.

Malena, A. (2003) 'Presentation', *TTR*, 16 (2) 9–13.

Mańczak-Wohlfeld, E. (1994) *Angielskie elementy leksykalne w języku polskim* [English lexical items in the Polish language]. Kraków.

Marsden, P. (2002) 'Poles Apart'. *The Observer*, 29 October 2002 Available online at: http://books. guardian.co.uk/impac/story/0,14959,1285756,00.html [Accessed 16 June 2009].

Nowacki, D. (1999) 'Jest o czym mówić' ['There is a Lot to Talk About']. *FA-art*, 1, 43–5.

Reykowski, J. (1993) *Wartości i postawy Polaków a zmiany systemowe* [The values and attitudes of the Polish people and the change of system]. Warszawa: Wydawnictwo Instytutu Psychologii PAN.

Simon, S. (1996) *Gender in Translation: Cultural Identity and the Politics of Transmission*. London; New York: Routledge.

Tokarczuk, O. (1998) *Dom dzienny, dom nocny*. Wałbrzych: Ruta.

Tokarczuk, O. (2002) *House of Day, House of Night*. Trans. A. Lloyd-Jones. London: Granta.

Venuti, L. (1995) *The Translator's Invisibility: A History of Translation*. London; New York: Routledge.

Venuti, L. (1998) *The Scandals of Translation: Towards an Ethics of Difference*. London; New York: Routledge.

Walters, E. G. (1988) *The Other Europe: Eastern Europe to 1945*. New York: Syracuse University Press.

Network & Cooperation in Translating Taiwanese Literature into English*

Szu-Wen Cindy Kung
University of Newcastle, UK

1. Introduction

Translation as a means to enable cross-cultural communication has become one of the most important cultural strategies in presenting Taiwan to the outside world. The activity of translating Taiwanese literature has been carried out over the last three decades. When a dominant culture is translated into a less-dominant one, translation can exert a powerful influence on the target culture (Robinson 1997). Contrary to this, when a minority culture is translated into a majority culture, translation functions as an agent introducing the literature of the lesser-known culture to the target one (Jones 2000). Translation from a minority culture into a dominant one can be identified as being of two types. When the translation activity is initiated by the target culture, it is an act of cultural importation. On the other hand, if the source culture initiates the translation activity, it is an act of cultural exportation (Liu 2006: 493). The translation of Taiwanese literature falls into this latter category. However, since the Anglo-American culture still remains dominant in comparison to other cultures, any translation activity initiated by the source culture is never an easy task.

Furthermore, recent scholarship in Translation Studies has begun to view translation as a meaningful social action conducted by a wide range of agents in addition to the translator (Buzelin 2005: 191–200). The translation agents, their individual social impact, and their relations can be influential upon the creation of the final translation product. Against this background, this chapter aims at exploring the translation agents' and network's influence on the translation production of lesser-known literatures in the dominant culture. That is, it will examine to what extent the translation agents' and network's agency can enhance the visibility of lesser-known literature in the major culture. Moreover, how the agents' and network's agency is reflected in the final production of translations is also explored. A case study of the translation of Taiwanese novels in the United States post 1980s is examined in order to answer this question. Two types of translational activity in translating Taiwanese novels in the United States will be identified and compared: the translator-led network and the subvention network. Two sociological theories: actor-network theory and Bourdieu's concepts of capital are important to the discussion.

2. Method

In terms of the research methods adopted, the data collected is mainly gathered from the survey of 'paratexts' and 'extratexts'. These concepts are directly linked to Gérard Genette's term 'paratext', which refers to all the materials surrounding a text. These could include materials outside a text, such as interviews and letters. The former is called 'peritext' and the latter is called 'epitext' by Genette (1987: 7–11). In this chapter, the term 'paratext' refers to the surface fragments that cover all the textual material that introduces a text proper, such as the cover, author's name, title, blurb, table of contents, preface, introduction, publishers; literally all the material that surrounds the text and forms a book; and 'extratext' refers to material outside the book, such as letters, interviews, book reviews, which in all consist of the intertextuality of any text (Kovala 1996: 120). It is argued that paratexts and extratexts are the discourse formed around a translated text, which may indicate collective trends and intentions

(Toury 1995: 65). Through the examination of paratexts and extratexts, two types of translation networks: translator-led and subvention networks are identified. The translator-led network and its translation activity are firstly discussed. Subsequently the emphasis is placed upon the subvention network; in so doing, the translation series: *Modern Chinese Literature from Taiwan* published by Columbia University Press, which is sponsored by the Chiang Ching-kuo Foundation for International Scholarly Exchange (here onwards referred to as CCKF) in Taiwan, is the core of the study. The analysis of the selected translated novels and the study of the translation agents involved in the production of this translation series via interviews are used to support the discussion.

This chapter is organized into the following components: first, the theoretical framework in question, derived from actor-network theory and Bourdieu's concepts, is discussed. This is followed by a brief history of translated Taiwanese literature. Then, a case study is provided to explore the impact of the agency of the dynamic agents and their network on translation production in the United States. The final part considers the possible implications of this study.

3. Theoretical framework

i. Bourdieu's theory of practice

In recent Translation Studies, more and more scholars have begun to see that translation is the result of a series of practices conducted by social agents, which suggests that translation is bound up with social contexts (Wolf 2002: 34). A number of scholars have already applied Bourdieu's theory of capital and social constructivism in translation and interpreting research. In particular, Bourdieu's approach is useful in its attempt to grasp the meaning of social agents' behaviour and social practice (Gouanvic 2005: 147–148; Inghilleri 2005: 126). Bourdieu sees social life as realized in social practice through the interaction and relationship between agents and the social structure, not only conceptualizing the meaning of action, but also making clear the constructed nature of the relationship between the individual social agent and the objective social structure (Gouanvic 2005: 148).

Bourdieu's theory of cultural action synthesizes both the institution and its agent, and can be used to examine the translation agents and their relation with and within their social environment (Buzelin 2005: 191; Gouanvic 2005: 148–50). The interest shown by the discipline of Translation Studies in Bourdieu's work is partially due to the change of research focus from a concentration on purely textual products to seeing translation as social, cultural and political acts closely connected to local and global relations of power and control (Cronin 2003). As Hermans points out, the inclusion of a sociological model, such as that developed by Bourdieu, can help researchers to conceptualize the autonomy and the heteronomy of translation practice, whilst the model can also provide researchers with a means to consider translation in terms of its social and intellectual space (Hermans 1999: 138). In this vein, it is argued that Bourdieu's theory can serve as a distinguishable agent-/sociologically-oriented approach to conceptualize and understand translation as a meaningful social action.

Bourdieu's concepts of 'habitus', 'capital' and 'field', in particular, provide a framework for translation scholars to discuss translation more closely in its social context. These concepts can be used to understand social action in relational terms, which arise from the intersection between agents' dispositions, or their 'habitus', which is shaped by their social trajectory and their position within fields (Bourdieu 1983: 311). 'Habitus' and 'field' have been particularly applied to studying translation agents and the meaning behind their actions during the process of translation production (Buzelin 2005: 193; Inghilleri 2005: 126; Simeoni 1998). Bourdieu defines 'habitus' as 'a transposable disposition acquired by the socialized agent which invests in practice the organizing principles that are socially constructed in the course of a situated and dated experience' (Bourdieu 1983: 311–20). On the other hand, 'field' is conceived of as a social area within which agents struggle and manoeuvre over specific resources and access to them. The individual agent and institution occupy specific social positions, and a series of power relations and struggles can take place within the field (Jenkins 1992: 84).

Bourdieu's concept of capital is not confined to the traditional sense of economic capital, and is not related to the idea of exploitation in the sense of extracting surplus value. Capital in the Bourdieusian sense is accumulated labour, as can be demonstrated in its materialized or embodied form (Bourdieu 1986: 241). Bourdieu distinguishes between four types of capital, so that, apart from the material form of economic capital, there are also 'immaterial' and 'non-economic' forms, that is, cultural, social and symbolic forms of capital (Bourdieu 1990: 128; Browitt 2004: 2–6). Economic capital may include money, commodities, means of material production, and other material assets (Smart 2000: 278–9). Cultural capital refers to the educational background or professional position of the social agent, which consists of the agents' knowledge and ability; agents can use their cultural capital to generate privilege, products, income or wealth. Social capital means that the social agent has a network of valued relations with significant individuals and institutions; social capital is inherent in social relationships and notions of obligation or trust are contained within them. Symbolic capital can be defined as the social agent's prestige or social honour; for Bourdieu, it is probably the most valuable form of accumulation within society (Smart 2000: 280–1; Wolf 2002: 37).

Capital, in all its forms, can therefore be equated with power or anything that 'can be used to influence the behaviour of others or to aid in achieving desired goals' (Smart 2000: 279). Not only is the concept of capital important in exploring the power of individual agents and institutions of society as a whole, it is also a useful concept to employ when examining the impact of agents on the translation production process. The particular focus of this chapter, therefore, is on the social impact of agents on the translation production process, using the concept of capital as an aid to this exploration.

ii. Actor-network theory

Bourdieu claims that social life can be illustrated by studying the practices of social agents and by relating these practices to the agents' position and influence in society as well as to their trajectory. However, as far as translation research is concerned, Bourdieu's theory is not entirely satisfactory in terms of investigating the links which connect people together. In particular, it is difficult to apply his concepts to an agency which consists of multiple agents or teamwork. In other words, one of the shortcomings of using the Bourdieusian approach in Translation Studies is that it tends to reduce the agent to the translator, and only considers agency from an individualistic perspective (Buzelin 2005: 215). This missing link can be supplied by Latour's actor-network theory, which has been applied in Translation Studies only very recently (Abdallah 2005; Buzelin 2005; Jones 2009).

Latour's theory has already been applied in other fields to investigate production and power, for example in investigating marketing departments, financial markets and legal courts (Buzelin 2005: 194). Actor-network theory provides a theoretical model to examine how a network of contacts links different actors and produces a project (Latour 1987). Latour's network theory allows researchers to observe an ongoing process of how each of the influential factors is connected and thus forms a network while an artefact is being produced. Latour believes that rather than focusing on the analysis of the final product, it is more essential to explore the logic of innovation in order to understand the logic of society (Buzelin 2005: 196). That is to say, Latour mainly aims at analysing the 'process' rather than the 'product' in order to reveal the dynamic nature of the final work. To this end, the idea of how products or artefacts are produced, manipulated, and transformed can be brought forward (Buzelin 2005: 196).

Within an actor-network, it is not only human actors who can induce an action, but all other influencing factors regarded as artefacts or non-human actors can also become a possible 'actant' to cause an action (Buzelin 2005: 194; Latour 1997). In short, both influential human and non-human actors can induce an action and, in a particular network, existing actors can invite new actors into it (Jones 2009: 304). The overall goal of actor-network theory is to comprehend the nature of networks, how they are formed and appropriated, and how different actors connect and negotiate with each other. By studying a network, one can understand the complexity underlying network formation and the elements circulating within it (Buzelin 2005: 198). It is argued that actor-network theory enables researchers to explore the bigger picture of social practices and interaction.

4. Translational activity of Taiwanese literature

Before turning to the main discussion, which will apply Bourdieu's concept of capital and Latour's actor-network theory, this section will briefly examine translational activity in Taiwanese literature over the course of three decades. The purpose is to provide an overall picture of the kinds of activities which are the research focus of this paper. Generally speaking, the translation of Taiwanese literature has been initiated by source culture actors. Various efforts have been made to translate and publish this literature since the late 1950s. The translational activities which took place from the 1950s through to the 1970s, however, were only a handful and mainly carried out by local publishers in Taipei. As such, these activities did not actually attract any attention from outside the domestic realm, at least not in the United States (Hsia 1971: ii–iii). Since the 1970s the translation of Taiwanese literature has started to grow, mostly in the form of translations for anthologies. Some of these anthologies were only published in Taiwan, but a number of them began to be published in the United States, mainly by university presses. Some important examples are: *An Anthology of Contemporary Chinese Literature: Taiwan, 1949–1974* (2 vols.) edited by Chi and published in 1976; *The Unbroken Chain: An Anthology of*

Taiwan fiction since 1926 edited by Lau and published in 1983; *Bamboo Shoots After the Rain: Contemporary Stories by Women Writers of Taiwan* edited by Carver and Chang and published in 1990. However, although the amount of translated Taiwanese literature certainly began to increase through these anthologies, they were mainly circulated in scholarly circles rather than within the milieu of the general reading public (Chang 2000).

Over the course of the next 30 years, source culture agents continued to place more and more effort in their work to translate Taiwanese literature. Among these there were three major translation teams which began to create a real impact with their translations of Taiwanese literature. The first one was, and is still, centred on *The Chinese PEN*, a journal established in 1972 in Taipei, Taiwan, which translated a great deal of Taiwanese literature over the years. This journal is the oldest of these translation teams and has translated more than 800 works of Taiwanese literature, mostly short stories and poems. The second of the teams is involved with *Taiwan Literature: English Translation Series*, another journal established in 1996 in the United States. The third team works with *Modern Chinese Literature from Taiwan*, a translation series established in 1998 in the United States (Pino 2006: 158). The number of trans-lations published by these three main teams make up more than half of all translated Taiwanese literature (Pino 2006: 159).

The translations published by the first two teams have mostly been received as academic material and subscribed to by libraries (Chang 2000). The third team is the only one attempting to work on translating Taiwanese literature in book form, including novels or literary works by individual writers from Taiwan, and aiming to sell the translations to more general readers in the pub-lic sphere of society (Wang 2007). Before the establishment of this translation series, single writers or complete literary works were rarely translated indi-vidually and published in the United States. For instance, between 1977 and 1997, only about 16 literary works by individual writers were translated into English and published in the United States.

5. Networks in the translation of Taiwanese literature

This section aims to explore the translation agents' and network's influence on the translation production of lesser-known literature in a dominant culture, in particular, the translation of Taiwanese novels, or more generally, translations of Taiwanese literary material in book form, in the United States or within the Anglo-American culture. It is worth noting that this chapter primarily uses the terms 'agent(s)' and 'actor(s)' or 'translation agents/actors' to refer to the professionals, including people and organizations, involved in the translation production process. In particular, the term 'translation agents/actors' alludes to professionals involved in the translation production of the translation series: *Modern Chinese Literature from Taiwan*, including translators, editorial board members, Columbia University Press and the sponsoring organization, CCKF. As already mentioned, since the Anglo-American culture remains dominant in comparison to other cultures, any translation activity initiated by the source culture is never an easy task.

iii. Translations in the United States

By and large, translated foreign literature has a small market and low reception in the United States. This issue has been raised by Venuti, who points out that very few translations are published in English. For example, in 1990 American publishers brought out 46,743 books, of which merely 1380 were translations, that is, around 3 per cent (Venuti 2008: 11). According to *Publishers Weekly*, in 2001 of the total number of translations worldwide only 6 per cent were translated into English, and this figure was still considered to be a generous estimate. On the other hand, the number of translations from English contrasted strongly with this situation, with, for example, 50 per cent of all translations worldwide in 2001 being from English into other languages (Wimmer 2001). As Venuti points out, 'English has been the most translated language worldwide, but it isn't much translated into' (Venuti 2008: 14). These facts signal a very narrow market for translations in America.

The low reception and limited readership result in modest profit margins, which mean that there is even less encouragement for a publisher to translate and publish foreign literature. The profit-oriented trade publisher lacks interest in little-known foreign authors whose work cannot stimulate profitable sales figures. In a similar fashion, university presses are cautious of the non-profitable market of translation (Wimmer 2001). This situation demonstrates the difficulty faced by translation agents and networks in attempting to translate and publish Taiwanese novels.

iv. Translator-led network in translating Taiwanese novels

In this type of network, the translation of Taiwanese novels is generally initiated or led by the translators themselves, who are often the experts in Sinology, for example, Howard Goldblatt and John Balcom. Goldblatt is currently a research professor of Chinese at the University of Notre Dame in the United States and has taught modern Chinese literature and culture for more than a quarter of a century; he is also the foremost translator of modern and contemporary Chinese literature in the West (Wang 1998). On the other hand, John Balcom is an associate professor in the Graduate School of Translation and Interpretation at the Monterey Institute of International Studies and has translated many works of Chinese literature from Taiwan and China into English (Li 2001). The text selection and translation, in both cases, are mainly based on personal interest or enthusiasm for the original work. For example, Goldblatt, who has translated over 30 novels from both Taiwan and China, points out in an interview that he selects and translates the works based on two factors: the work that he likes and the books recommended by acquaintances for translation or co-translation. Above all, the work has to be of interest to him (Goldblatt 2007). In terms of a text selection mainly based on the personal interest of the individual translators, however, the novels or authors translated can be more limited in a translator-led network because only works that are of interest to such translators would be selected and translated.

Apart from carrying out the text selection and translation, translators have to contact publishers that may be interested in publishing a specific translation. According to translators' statements in news articles or interviews, this process can require much effort, in addition to being very time-consuming; it is quite common for translators to have to translate a few chapters, or even the entire book, as a sample before approaching a publisher. Publishers reject translators' requests either when they are not interested in the sample translations or when they do not see the profit-making potential in these translations, which means that the translators' time and effort may have been spent in vain (Balcom 2007; Goldblatt 2007; Yen 2003).

In a translator-led translation network, therefore, it is mainly the translator initiating the activity. However, the influence of the target culture agent, that is, the publishing company, especially with regard to its profit-making orientation, is at a maximum. Although there is nothing in theory to prevent translated Taiwanese novels being published in the American target culture, nevertheless a translator-led network is more strongly subject to the agent situated within the target culture, particularly in cases when a lesser-known literature is translated into the dominant culture (Even-Zohar [1978]2000). In other words, the power-locus of translator-led/-initiated translation activity in translating Taiwanese novels sides more towards the target culture agent, in particular the publisher, for whom the most important purpose of a given translation is that it should achieve commercial value – that it should be marketable. Without the participation of other agents from the source culture, the effect of enhancing the visibility of translated Taiwanese literature in the United States via the translator-led network may only be minimal and not completely effective.

v. Subvention network in translating Taiwanese novels

This section proceeds to the focus of this article: the subvention network of the translation series *Modern Chinese Literature from Taiwan* published in the United States. As mentioned earlier, this translation series team, established in 1998, is the only team attempting to work on the translation of Taiwanese literature in the form of single-author books and aiming to sell such translations to the general reader (Wang 2007). The establishment of the translation series subsidized by CCKF has improved the situation of translated Taiwanese novels in the United States. The term 'subvention' used in this study refers to fact that the network that carries out this translation series is subsidized by CCKF[1]. It is worth noting that, firstly, earlier translations of Taiwanese literature, including literary works of an individual writer that were translated and published in the United States, were not published with the help of subvention. Secondly, the majority of material presented in this section is primarily from interviews with the main actors, which form a valuable, but not the sole source of information. A survey of extratexts and paratexts also provides a source of information in this study. It is also worth noting that the formation of this network was initiated by the source culture agent and involved more agents situated in both source culture and target culture. The agents studied in this network are the translators, editorial board members, the publisher and the sponsoring organization.

The network formation began in 1998. As one of the most important organizations making an effort to support the efforts of scholars researching aspects of Taiwanese life and culture, particularly in America (Brown 2004: 2), CCKF decided to distribute a budget to launch and support a translation series of Taiwanese literature into English in order to promote the literary voice of Taiwan. The coordinator of this project, also an editorial board member of the translation series, Der-wei David Wang, who was teaching in Columbia University at that time, points out in a personal interview that he was invited by CCKF to preside over the translation series project. Since he is from Taiwan and therefore appreciates the abundant repertoire of contemporary Taiwanese literature, he agreed to take responsibility for running the translation series project (Wang 2007).

After the decision was made to establish the translation series, it was important to have a publisher in America who could publish the translations. According to Wang, Mrs. Crewe, the associate director and editorial director responsible for the Asian Humanities section of the Columbia University Press, agreed to Professor Wang's request to join this translation project (Wang 2007). The decision of Columbia University Press to participate in the translation project and establish a series for literature from Taiwan was not straightforward. The different forms of 'capital' of the agents, to use Bourdieu's term, that is, Wang's social and cultural capital, and CCKF's financial capital, were important to the decision of the press to go ahead with the project.

Once the translation project had been mooted, Wang expressed the idea of establishing the translation series to Crewe. Wang stated that, apart from teaching at Columbia University, he had also served on the publication committee of Columbia University Press for a number of years, and that it placed trust in his judgment (Wang 2007). In addition, in e-mail correspondence with me, Crewe corroborated the fact that Wang was able to secure important funding for the series from CCKF (Crewe 2007).

The discussion so far shows the social power of Wang and CCKF. It appears that social relationships, or social capital, to use Bourdieu's term, and economic capital are important forms of social power which enable the translation actor to invite or recruit other actors to join the network. Wang's cultural capital and social capital, that is, his professional experience and working relationship with Columbia University Press, as well as his connecting role between both the press and CCKF, ensured the press's participation in this translation project. The financial capital of CCKF further reinforced the willingness of Columbia University Press to publish the translation series. For the university press, profit may not have been a priority, yet seeking financial support from other organizations is crucial to the business of university presses (Givler 2002: 112). It can be argued that in the early stage of network formation, social capital and economic capital are two crucial resources or forms of power that increase the actor's social agency 'to influence the behaviours of others or to aid in achieving desired goals' (Smart 2000: 279).

Wang's social capital further enabled him to recruit more people, or agents, with different types of social power to form the network. The interview with Wang and several different articles indicate that other professionals joined the editorial board at his invitation. For example, the fact that he already had a good personal relationship with Pang-yuan Chi, an important figure in promoting the translation of Taiwanese literature over the last three decades in Taiwan, meant that he could invite her to join the editorial board. In addition, the Sinologist Göran Malmqvist, based in Sweden, who has translated various volumes of Chinese literature from different epochs, was invited to join the team. Wang claimed that Malmqvist's cultural capital, the academic reputation of his involvement with Chinese literature, could enhance the credibility of the series.

The editorial board mainly worked on the early stages of the translation production process, that is, on the text selection and seeking suitable translators. In terms of text selection, the editorial board members claim that under CCKF's sponsorship they were given complete freedom to select texts for translation (Wang 2007). That is to say, in this case, the actors from the editorial board, especially the actors originating from the source culture, are the key players in taking charge of the selection of texts for translation. One of the most important criteria directing the selection process is to consider the wider possibilities of the literary works, so that they may include more diversified samples of the writers and literary genres current in Taiwanese literature (Wang 2007). With CCFK's economic capital giving important backing to the project, the text selection in the subvention network is primarily subject to the decisions of the source culture players, and hence is more independent of the constraints or demands of actors from the target culture, such as the publisher, as seen in the translator-led network.

Once the texts were selected, the editorial board members then recruited or invited suitable translators to take part in the project. Similar forces play a part as in the formation of an editorial board: the agents' social capital is an important aspect in decisions as to which translators may be invited to translate. For example, the personal interview with Goldblatt, with whom Wang was acquainted before the establishment of the series, showed that Goldblatt was invited by Wang to translate (Goldblatt 2007). Similarly, Chi invited other translators to participate, based on her personal relations with the translators

(Du 2007; Liu 2007; Wu 2007). It can, therefore, be argued that the agents of the editorial board held great influence in enabling the formation of this sub-vention network. In addition, some of the translators who participated in the translation project were known and experienced. Both the editorial board and the publisher believed that the participation of these translators may have also enhanced the credibility or reputation of the series (Goldblatt 2007; Wang 2007).

The formation process of the network, including the recruitment of editorial board members and the translators, implies the importance of agents' social power or 'capital'. The concept of 'capital' in Bourdieu's theory can be equated with power or viewed as 'the set of actually usable resources and power' (Smart 2000: 278). The power possessed by the translation actors in question should not be understood as the power to exert control over other people. Rather, their social power should be seen as a quality of social relationships that can cause others to act or participate in the network (Smart 2000: 282). In this regard, this network is connected in a more associated way; each actor can become the 'actant', inducing the action by drawing on their social power.

Since the translation series was supported by a secure fund and established as a plan to promote contemporary Taiwanese literature, the publication of the translated Taiwanese novel has become steady and consistent since the launch of the translation project in 1998. The press has been continually publishing one to two translations with quality book presentations annually or biannually (Columbia University Press Website). In other words, Taiwanese literature has a more stable and better opportunity of being published and received in the United States. The higher frequency of publishing indicates a greater probability for the works to draw the target culture's attention.

For instance, *Three-Legged Horse (San Jiao Ma)* by Ching-wen Cheng, has not only been reviewed by several major publications, such as the *New York Times Book Review*, *Publishers Weekly* and the *Kirkus Review* but also won the 1999 Kiriyama Book Prize (Cheng 1999); *Notes of a Desolate Man (Huang-jen Shou-ji)* was reviewed by the *San Francisco Chronicle*, as a Best Book by the *Los Angeles Times Book Reviews*, as a Notable Book by the *New York Times Book Reviews*, and, in addition, won the National Translation Award of the American Association of Literary Translators (Chang 2000; Columbia University Press Website). *Frontier Taiwan: An Anthology of Modern Chinese Poetry* has been reviewed as a Best Book by the *Los Angeles Times Book Reviews*; *Indigenous Writers of Taiwan: An Anthologies of Stories, Essays and Poems* has won the 2006 Northern California Book Award for Translation (Balcom 2007).

Some of these publications receive over a hundred new books awaiting review each issue. In other words, it is not easy to be selected and reviewed by these publications. Therefore, one can see the examples given above as a fairly fruitful result produced by the translation network. It suggests a certain breakthrough for the translation exportation activity of modern Taiwanese literature in America.

This case study of the subvention network and its translation agents reveals translation as a result of social causation involving a mediated process among various actors. It shows that translation production is a process of conversation, influence, and cooperation or complicity (Jones 2009: 304; Pym 2007: 724–6). The financial capital of CCKF is crucial to the network formation, yet without the social and cultural capital of other agents, such as the editorial board members, it might not be easy to locate either translators or a publisher.

Applying Bourdieu's theory and Actor-Network terminology, it can be seen that the effectiveness of this network is mainly underpinned by incorporating individual social power into it, or to use Bourdieu's terms, capital of various forms. In other words, the network could not have yielded fruitful results without the influence of any one of the main agents; however, an individual agent's capital can only be brought into full play by working together within the network. As Jones points out, 'who holds more or less power within the network is less important than whether the network forms and performs efficiently and effectively' (Jones 2009: 320).

6. Conclusion

This chapter set out to explore to what extent the translation agents' and network's agency could enhance the visibility of lesser-known literature in major cultures. It can be argued that a subvention network formed by different agents sitting in both source and target cultures and possessing individual social power can be more effective in translating and exporting lesser-known literature, particularly in terms of the text selection and the possibility of publication than a translator-led network.

Furthermore, the case study suggests that literary translation has become a useful tool for identity recognition and cultural transmission, especially when a culture that is perceived as weak or small attempts to export its literature to the dominant culture (Cronin 2003; Even-Zohar [1978] 2000; Tymoczko 1999; Venuti 2008). Translation has the potential to enable the internationalization of the internal literary and cultural experience by translating literature into the global language – English (Jones and Arsenijević 2005: 87). That is to say, translation can be a manipulative tool used by the translation agents situated in the source culture to translate its literature into the major language, which may create a channel through which other cultures may be reached (Zauberga 2000: 51).

Finally, the article shows that when a lesser-known culture wishes to translate its literature and promote its image more systematically and effectively in the dominant culture, sufficient financial support, overseas connections, good interpersonal relations as well as cooperation are particularly important to achieving the objective. It can be argued that multiple agents and the translation network working cooperatively in the globalized era may typically 'extend domestic structures of literary power into the international arena' (Jones and Arsenijević 2005: 87).

7. Notes

[*] An earlier version of this text has been published as 'Translation agents and networks, with reference to the translation of contemporary Taiwanese novels' in A. Pym and A. Perekrestenko (eds) (2009) Translation Research Project 2. Tarragona: Intercultural Studies Group. 123–38.

1. CCKF was established in 1989 and headquartered in Taipei. It has four regional review committees in America, Europe, and Asia Pacific. Currently, it has two international centres for sinological research: the CCKF centre for Chinese Cultural and Institutional History at Columbia University; and the CCKF International Sinological Centre at Charles University in Prague (Chiang Ching-kuo Foundation for International Scholarly Exchange). CCKF's aims are first, to award grants to institutions and individuals conducting research and academic projects and second, to promote a broader understanding of Taiwan (Chiang Ching-kuo Foundation for International Scholarly Exchange 2007).

8. Bibliography

Abdallah, K. (2005) 'Actor-network Theory as a Tool in Defining Translation Quality'. Paper presented at the Translating and Interpreting as a Social Practice, University of Graz, Austria.

Balcom, J. (2001) 'Translator's Introduction', in *Wintry Night*. New York: Columbia University Press.

Balcom, J. (2001) Email correspondence.

Bourdieu, P. (1990) 'Social Space and Symbolic Power' (M. Adamson, trans.), in *In Other Words: Essays Towards a Reflexive Sociology*. Cambridge: Polity Press.

Bourdieu, P. (1986) 'The Forms of Capital', in J. Richardson (eds) *The Handbook of Theory: Research for the Sociology of Education*. New York: Greenwood Press.

Bourdieu, P. (1983) 'The Field of Cultural Production, or the Economic World Reversed', *Poetics*, 12 (4/5) 311–56.

Browitt, J. (2004) 'Pierre Bourdieu: Home Sociologicus', in J. Browitt and B. Nelson (eds), *Practicing Theory: Pierre Bourdieu and the Field of Cultural Production*. Newark, DE: University of Delaware Press, 1–12.

Brown, D. (2004) 'Organizations That Support Taiwan Studies: A Select Overview', *Issues and Studies*, 40 (3/4) 281–314.

Buzelin, H. (2005) 'Unexpected Allies: How Latour's Network Theory Could Complement Bourdieusian Analyses in Translation Studies'. *The Translator*, 11 (2) 193–218.

Chang, C-f. [Zhang, Q-f] (2000) 'Taiwan Literature: The Next Export Success Story?' *Taiwan Panorama*. www.sinorama.com.tw/en/show_issue.php?id=2000128912006e.txt&table=2&h1=Art%20 and%20Culture&h2=Literature [accessed on 20 May 2007].

Cheng, C-w. [Zheng, Q-w] (1999) *Three-Legged Horse [San Jiao Ma]*. New York: Columbia University Press.

Chiang, Ching-kuo Foundation for International Scholarly Exchange. www.cckf.org.tw/e-organization. html [accessed on 16 January 2008].

Columbia University Press. http://cup.columbia.edu/app [accessed on 10 March 2007].

Crewe, J. (2007) Email correspondence.

Cronin, M. (2003) *Translation and Globalization*. London and New York: Routledge.

Du, N. (2007) Personal Interview in June 2007.

Even-Zohar, I. ([1978]2000) 'The Position of Translated Literature Within the Literary Polysystem', in L. Venuti (eds) *The Translation Studies Reader*. London and New York: Routledge, 192–7.

Genette, G (1987) *Seuils*. Paris: Seuil.

Givler, P. (2002) 'University Press Publishing in the United States', in R. Abel and L. Newlin (eds), *Scholarly Publishing: Books, Journals, Publishers and Libraries in 20th Century*. New York: Wiley, 107–20.

Goldblatt, H. (2007) Personal interview on 1 March 2007.

Gouanvic, J. (2005) 'A Bourdieusian Theory of Translation, or the Coincidence of Practical Instances: Field, "Habitus", Capital and "Illusio"', *The Translator*, 11 (2) 147–66.

Hermans, Theo. (1999) *Translation in Systems: Descriptive and System-oriented Approaches Explained*. Manchester: St Jerome Publishing.

Hervey, S. and Higgins, I. (1992) *Thinking Translation: A Course in Translation Method: French to English*. London: Routledge.

Hsia, C-t. (1971) 'Preface', in C-t. Hsia (eds), *Twentieth-century Chinese Stories*. New York: Columbia University Press.

Hsiao, L-h. (2000) *A Thousand Moons on a Thousand Rivers* (M. Wu, trans.). New York: Columbia University Press.

Inghilleri, M. (2005) 'The Sociology of Bourdieu and the Construction of the "Object" in Translation and Interpreting Studies', *The Translator*, 11 (2) 125–45.

Jenkins, R. (1992) *Pierre Bourdieu*. London: Routledge.

Jones, F. (2009) 'Embassy Networks: Translating Post-war Bosnian Poetry into English', in J. Milton and P. Bandia (eds) *Agents of Translation*. Amsterdam: John Benjamins Publishing Company, 301–25.

Jones, F. (2000) 'The Poet and the Ambassador: Communicating Mak Dizdar's "Stone Sleeper", *Translation and Literature*, 9 (1) 65–87.

Jones, F. and Arsenijević, D. (2005) '(Re)constructing Bosnia: Ideologies and Agents in Poetry Translation', in J. House, R. Martin Ruano and N. Baumgarten (eds), *Translation and the Construction of Identity*. Cornwall International Association for Translation and Intercultural Studies, 68–95.

Kovala, U. (1996) 'Translations, Paratextual Mediation, and Ideological Closure', *Target*, 8 (1) 119–47.

Latour, B. (1997) 'On Actor-network Theory: A Few Clarifications', http://amsterdam.nettime.org/Lists-Archives/nettime-1-9801/msg00019.html [accessed on 12 April 2006].

Latour, B. (1987) *Science in Action*. Cambridge, MA: Harvard University Press.

Li, C. [Li Q.] (2001) *Wintry Night [Han Ye]*. New York: Columbia University Press.

Liu, K. (2006) 'Translation and Cultural Exportation: A Case Study of Huang Chun-ming's Short Stories', in T. Hermans (eds) *Translating Others Vol. 2*. Manchester: St Jerome Publishing, 493–510.

Liu, T. (2007) Personal interview in April 2007.

Pino, A. (2006) 'An Overview of History and Situation of Taiwan Literature in Germany, USA and France', *Chung-Wai Literary Monthly*, 34 (10) 155–65.

Pym, A. (2007) 'Cross-cultural Networking: Translators in French-German Network of *petites revues* at the End of the Nineteenth Century', *Meta*, 52 (4) 724–42.

Robinson, D. (1997) *Translation and Empire: Postcolonial Theories Explained*. Manchester: St Jerome Publishing.

Simeoni, D. (1998) 'The Pivotal Status of the Translator's Habitus', *Target*, 10 (1) 1–39.

Smart, A. (2000) 'Gifts, Bribes, and Guanxi: A Reconsideration of Bourdieu's Social Capital', in D. Robbins (eds) *Pierre Bourdieu*. London: SAGE Publications.

Toury, G. (1995) *Descriptive Translation Studies and Beyond*. Amsterdam: John Benjamins.

Tymoczko, M (1999) *Translation in a Postcolonial Context: Early Irish Literature in English Translation*. Manchester: St Jerome Publishing Company.

Venuti, L. (2008) *The Translator's Invisibility: A History of Translation*. London: Routledge.

Wang, C-h. (1998) *Rose, Rose, I Love You [Mei-gui Mei-gui Wo Ai Ni]*(H. Goldblatt, trans.). New York: Columbia University Press.

Wang, D-w. (2007) Personal interview on 20 February 2007.

Wimmer, N. (2001) 'The U.S. Translation Blues'. *Publishers Weekly*. www.publishersweekly.com/article/CA83242.html [accessed on 15 April 2007].

Wolf, M. (2002) 'Translation Activity Between Culture, Society and the Individual Towards a Sociology of Translation', *CTIS Occasional Papers*, (2) 33–43.

Wu, M. (2007) Personal interview in June 2007.

Yen, C-y. [Yan, J-y]. (2003) 'The Publication and Marketing of Chinese Language Literature', *Publishing Circle*, 66, 20–22.

Zauberga, I. (2000) 'Rethinking Power Relations in Translation', *Across Languages and Cultures*, 1 (1) 49–56.

Rendering Female Speech as a Male or Female Translator: Constructed Femininity in the Japanese Translations of *Pride and Prejudice* and *Bridget Jones's Diary*

9

Hiroko Furukawa
University of East Anglia, UK

Chapter Outline

1. Introduction

When translating a literary text into Japanese, one of the most significant transformation tasks for translators is to decide how feminine or masculine to make a specific character in the text. This is because of a characteristic feature of the Japanese language, namely the explicit marking of femininity and masculinity. Japanese is a gender-based language. Japanese speakers indicate the level of their masculinity or femininity by using different language markers such as sentence-final particles. The particles are 'gender markers indexing femininity and masculinity' (Inoue 2006: 2). For example, when a translator renders into Japanese a very simple utterance from a character, such as 'I'll tell you,' a translator has at least five choices: '*iu wa* [*iu* {tell} + particle]' (strongly feminine), '*iu no*' (moderately feminine), '*iu ze*' (strongly masculine), '*iu yo*' (moderately masculine), and '*iu*' (neutral). They have to choose from a wide variety of choices depending on the speaker's perceived level of femininity or masculinity. Hence, it is essential for the translator to infer the characters' femininity or masculinity from descriptions in the original and construct their personality appropriately in the target language. That is, the translator's choice of language largely affects the image of the characters, who tend to be more clearly feminized or masculinized in Japanese translation than they are in the original (see also Furukawa 2009).

Feminist theory became a central concern for many Western theorists in Translation Studies in the 1990s. The movement was actively seen especially in Canada, and scholars started to see Translation Studies from the perspective of gender studies. One of the pivotal interests of feminist translation practice is to raise awareness of links between social stereotypes and linguistic forms (Flotow 1997: 14). In the radical approach to feminist translation, language is considered not only a 'man-made artefact' (Flotow 1997: 8) but also a reflection of male-dominated ideas. Therefore, by making the feminine visible in language, it is aimed to make social exploitation of women visible (Godard 1990: 90). For example, in an English translation of the French lesbian writer Michèle Causse, de Lotbinière-Harwood emboldens 'e' to make the foregrounding of the feminine in Causse's writing visible. In the French original, Causse feminizes some words by using new spellings such as 'nulle' ('nul') (Simon 1996: 21). In the English translation, the author's grammatical construction is recreated by the emboldened 'e'.

Due to the 'gender-marking' aspect of the Japanese language, gender issues are inevitable when considering Translation Studies in Japanese. However, the links between gender issues and Japanese translation have so far been written about relatively little compared to the situation in European countries and North America. There are two reasons for this silence. First, there is a general lack of awareness within Japan of feminist theory. In actual fact, there are very few Japanese translations of feminist theory. For instance, translations of prominent books on gender and language such as Robin Lakoff's *Language and Woman's Place* (1975), or Dale Spender's *Man Made Language* (1980) have long been out of print. Also, Simone de Beauvoir's epoch-making *Le Deuxième Sexe* [*The Second Sex*] (1949) is not available in Japanese[1]. Secondly, translation is usually regarded as a practical task and Translation Studies as an academic discipline has not attained a proper status in Asian countries (Hung and Wakabayashi 2005: 2). As a result, there are limited numbers of scholars in Japan who explore the intersection of gender and translation. This academic tendency stands in the way of developing people's awareness of translation as a shaper of gender ideology.

There are distinctive disparities between how Japanese men and women speak. When standard Japanese was established, the concept of the language was 'men's' standard language. The Japanese government adopted the language of middle-class educated males in Tokyo as the standard Japanese language at the turn of the twentieth century (Nakamura 2007: 43–5). Women's language is a version of standard Japanese which emphasizes femininity (Nakamura 2007: 35). That is, standard Japanese is for men, and women's language is considered marginal. Women's language is labelled as showing certain feminine manners such as being polite, formal, sympathetic, soft-spoken, indirect, hesitant, and non-assertive (Inoue 2006: 2, Okamoto 1995: 307). These characteristics create 'an image of powerlessness, social sensitivity, and femininity' (Okamoto 1995: 307).

Even today, while men are rarely taught to use men's language in formal situations, women are still repeatedly taught to speak like 'women' through their upbringing (Tanaka 2004: 26). There are many books available that instruct women how to speak in the correct way. A female writer points out in her bestselling book that if women do not use polite language properly, they will be considered ill-mannered and inappropriately brought-up women. This book, titled *Kashikoi Hito ni Narinasai: Utsukushiku Ikitai Anata ni* [*Be a Wise Woman: To You Who Want to Live Beautifully*] (Tanaka 1986), was reprinted 73 times between 1986 and 1995. The big success of this book shows the popularity of how-to-speak books for women (Okamoto 2004: 42).

With reference to Japanese, Smith argues that even women in a high position or in power are influenced by childhood training because of their 'verbal interactions with subordinates' (1992a: 61–2). In Ohara's linguistic analysis (2004: 224), bilingual women used higher voice pitch when they spoke in Japanese than in English. A high voice pitch is regarded as an aspect of Japanese women's language, and Ohara's findings demonstrate that female Japanese speakers are under cultural constraints of expected femininity in Japanese society. The existence of a clear definition of women's language might affect women's behaviour or way of thinking. However, the differences have not been discussed enough in Japan; as Reynolds (1993: 4) states, 'although Japanese people speak with a language which has clear differences between the sexes, they rarely discuss the differences.'

The sensitivity to gender difference and social roles is clearly also a crucial consideration in translation into Japanese, especially of key works of foreign literature. Therefore, this chapter will explore differences of femininity in the Japanese translations of a classic and a contemporary novel to show how translators' language choice impacts upon characterization. First, I compare three different translations of *Pride and Prejudice* (*PP*), which are currently on the market in Japan: Akira Tomita's version (*PP1*, first published in 1950), Yoshio Nakano's version (*PP2*, first published in 1963) and Kōji Nakano's version (*PP3*, first published in 2003). Each translator's perception of *PP* can be seen in the afterword of their translations. The translator of *PP1*, Akira Tomita considers *PP* to be an educational novel and 'the best social novel in the world' (Tomita 1950: 279). *PP2* is translated by an authority in translations of English and American literature, and the translator Yoshio Nakano categorizes *PP* as an entertainment novel, by praising Austen's sense of humour. Yoshio Nakano provides an explanatory note that his version is not a perfect literally translation. In the latest version *PP3*, which is aimed at a new translation, the translator Kōji Nakano also emphasizes Austen's sharp wit.

In this study, I focus on women's language. *PP* is a romantic novel first published in 1813. The central concern is Elizabeth's marriage to Mr Darcy. Despite the dominance of female characters and the target audience, all of the versions were translated by men. Thus, the motive of this comparison is to investigate how a male translator's perspective might influence the translation. In relation to this point, there is a hypothesis that 'a male translator tends to use Japanese women's language too much when he renders female characters' speech in a novel and the tendency makes the characters' speaking style unnatural. This is because the male translator has a stereotypical image of women's speech patterns' (Yamamoto 2000). However, so far there has been no analysis to support this hypothesis empirically. Hence, this project also tests this hypothesis by using some data from texts translated by the two genders.

Secondly, I analyse the Japanese translation of *Bridget Jones's Diary* (*BJD*) to examine how Japanese women's language functions as an ideology in society. *BJD*'s eponymous protagonist is a single woman in her 30s who lives and works in London. Her speech style is modern and colloquial. Classics tend to use language which is different from contemporary lived experience. In the Japanese literary world, however, an exaggerated female figure can be seen even in contemporary novels such as *BJD*. The difference between literary language, so-called authentic women's language, and real-life language is notable and the gap can reinforce gender ideology. *BJD* shows how translation is used to emphasize stereotypes that no longer exist in the target culture.

2. Elizabeth's femininity as constructed by language

According to West and Zimmerman, gender is 'a routine, methodical, and recurring accomplishment' (1987: 126). Gender is not something given but developed through nurture, hence gender is 'done' by individuals; an exemplar of this can be seen in Japanese translations. The notion 'doing gender' (West 1987: 125) can be related to Butler's view on gender. Butler indicates that gender reality is constructed 'through sustained social performances' (2006: 192). Performability is, therefore, at the heart of gender acquisition. If 'doing gender' is a skill which individuals acquire, their social situation and education could affect the construction of femininity or masculinity. As West and Zimmerman (1987: 126) discuss, even if 'doing gender' is the activity of an individual, social situations make them 'do' it.[2] Female characters' constructed femininity in Japanese translation show Japanese readers how to 'do gender.' This convention can also be seen in newspapers, magazines and television programmes (Nakamura 2007: 81). The representation of females in the media or popular culture is constructed in accordance with the social norms in the Japanese literary system, and the dominant models encourage Japanese women to 'do gender.' Translation has a bigger impact on the Japanese book market than in the UK and the United States[3] and plays an important role with respect to the way women are represented in literature.

For that reason, I focus on a specific analysis of how Elizabeth 'does gender' in the three Japanese translations of *PP*. First, different versions of Elizabeth's femininity in *PP1*, *PP2* and *PP3* will be compared. Then, I investigate how male interpretation affects the target text and verifies Yamamoto's hypothesis indicated in the Introduction.

i. Different versions of Elizabeth in *PP1*, *PP2* and *PP3*

On the subject of Elizabeth's femininity in the Japanese translations, there are three remarkable features: the highest degree of politeness, strongly feminine sentence-final forms, and indirect expressions. The use of feminine sentence-final particles is the quintessential feature of women's language as indicated above. In the Japanese language, women are considered to be inferior to men, and are supposed to use polite forms to men, but not vice versa. Consequently, women are forced to use polite forms. This linguistic superior or inferior relationship is related to women's social powerlessness in society (Smith 1992a: 540; 1992b: 59). Also, indirect expressions are used to avoid indicating the object straightforwardly. This use is a part of politeness, as well as non-assertiveness and hesitation (Inoue 2006: 2, Okamoto 1995: 307). These features can be seen in the renditions of the following phrase. The original sentence is 'You do not know what he really is . . . ' (356), ('you' meaning 'father' here). In this scene, Elizabeth is talking about Mr Darcy with her father. The translations of these phrases are as follows:

PP1 (vol.2, 257):

お父さま	は、	ほんとうの	あの方	を	御存じないんです	わ
[otōsama	ha	hontōno	**anokata**	wo	**gozonjinaindesu**	**wa**]
Father (very polite)	particle	real	the person (indirect)	particle	do not know (very polite)	particle (strongly feminine)

PP2 (574–575):

お父様	は、	まだ	ほんとの	あの方	を	ご存じないんです	のよ
[otōsama	ha	mada	hontono	**anokata**	wo	**gozonjinaindesu**	**noyo**]
Father (very polite)	particle	yet	real	the person (indirect)	particle	do not know (very polite)	particle (strongly feminine

PP3 (vol.2, 285):

彼	が	どういう人間か、	お父さま	は	ご存じないのです
[Kare	ga	dōiu ningen ka,	**otōsama**	ha	**gozonjinainodesu**]
he (direct)	particle	what he is	father (very polite)	particle	do not know (very polite)

In terms of the highest degree of politeness, the three translators choose the Japanese word 'otōsama [father]' お父さま (PP1 and PP3), お父様 (PP2) to address her father in this line. The word 'otōsama' is the refined version of the more usual form 'otōsan [father]' (*Shinmeikai Japanese Dictionary* 2005: 192). 'Sama' is a suffix that demonstrates the highest respect for the hearer. It sounds over formal when it is directed at the speaker's own family member. In contrast, when another suffix '*san*' is added after the person's name, it sounds friendly although it also expresses respect for him or her (*Shinmeikai Japanese Dictionary* 2005: 581, 586).

There is another characteristic related to the highest degree of politeness which can be seen here. The translations of the phrase 'do not know' also contain the highest degree of politeness. There are at least three options to express the meaning 'do not know': a neutral and general form '*shiranainodesu*' 知らないのです, a more polite and humble form '*zonjinainodesu*' 存じないのです or '*zonjinaindesu*' 存じないんです, and the most polite and humble forms '*gozonjinainodesu*' ご(or 御) 存じないのです or '*gozonjinaindesu*' ご(or 御) 存じないんです. Elizabeth in all three translations uses the highest degree to show her respect to her father. Humble forms are used to indicate that the speaker's own status is lower than that of the hearer. Therefore, Elizabeth's use also makes her lower status clear by this language choice.

Considering the writing systems, there are two writing systems: Chinese characters and *hiragana* characters. To express '*otōsama* [father],' *PP1* and *PP3* use *hiragana* characters さま for '*sama*,' and *PP2* employs a Chinese character 様: お父さま (*PP1* and *PP3*), お父様 (*PP2*). Also, *PP1* uses a Chinese character for '*go*': the first sound of the verb, '*gozonjinaindesu* [do not know]' 御存じないんです. Whereas, *PP2* and *PP3* use *hiragana* character: '*gozonjinaindesu*' ご存じないんです (*PP2*), and '*gozonjinainodesu*' ご存じないのです (*PP3*).

Although the diversity does not make any difference with respect to meaning, another gendering aspect can be implied through the different writing systems. That is because they denote the long history of gender-marking in Japanese. Chinese characters are ideograms which were originally used to express Chinese, and were introduced into Japan from China in the third century. *Hiragana* characters were coined from the sound of Chinese characters (*New Encyclopædia Britannica* 2002: 501, 708, *Shinmeikai Japanese Dictionary* 2005: 310, 1274). Chinese characters used to be exclusively used by men for public and official documents since the introduction of those characters, and women were not supposed to learn them. On the other hand, *hiragana* characters were for private and unofficial documents, and mainly used by women. Japanese people spoke in Japanese at that time, but when men wrote official documents, they translated into Chinese and used Chinese characters. Chinese characters were called '*mana*' (literally 'true names' in English) and *hiragana* characters were '*kana*' (literally 'temporary names') and this fact implies the particular function of these two types of characters in the society. Symbolically enough, Chinese characters were also called '*otoko-de*' (literally 'men's hand' in English) and *hiragana* characters were 'onna-de' ('women's hand'). If women were able to read Chinese characters, they were regarded as 'unfeminine' (Chino 2003: 22–25, Endo 1997: 16–26). Nowadays, Japanese people of both genders usually combine these two types of characters and another one: *katakana*[4], and there is no longer a significant discrepancy in written system in terms of gender. However, for historical reasons, the use of hiragana characters in *PP1* and *PP3* may give a feminine impression on some readers.

PP1 and *PP2* add strongly feminine sentence-final particles 'wa' わ(*PP1*) and 'noyo' のよ(*PP2*) after the verb 'gozonjinaindesu' ご(or 御) 存知ないんです. The use of the polite and strongly feminine form establishes Elizabeth's identity as female and cultured (Ide and Yoshida 2002: 466). On the other hand, the translator of *PP3*, Kōji Nakano, does not use any gender-marking sentence-final particles. Throughout the translations, *PP1* and *PP2* show a repetition of feminine sentence-final particles which emphasize Elizabeth's femininity and politeness. *PP3*, on the other hand, presents the least feminine personality because the use of feminine sentence-final particles is less frequent.

In addition, indirect expressions can often be seen in *PP1* and *PP2*. In these renditions, 'he' is translated in two ways: 'anokata [the person]' あの方 in *PP1* and *PP2*, and 'kare [he]' 彼 in *PP3*. The word 'anokata [the person]' あの方 in *PP1* and *PP2* specifies 'him' indirectly. The word 'ano' あの is a demonstrative 'that,' and 'kata' 方 can be literary translated as 'person' in English. However, there are two features in this word 'kata' 方. First, this is an honorific to express the speaker's respect for the object. Second, this word is used when the speaker wants to avoid uttering the person directly. These features function to let Elizabeth indicate the object (Mr Darcy) indirectly. In contrast, the word 'kare [he]' 彼 in *PP3* points to 'him' directly. By letting Elizabeth use these indirect expressions, the translators of *PP1* and *PP2* heighten Elizabeth's femininity.

Hence, the combination of highly polite forms, strongly feminine forms, indirect expressions, and the use of the *hiragana* character constructs the most feminized version of Elizabeth in *PP2*. *PP3* can be considered as the least feminized version in the three translations. Endo (1997: 171) points out that Japanese women's language has become less feminized since the post-war period in proportion to the rise in women's position in society. As a result, women sometimes use men's language and vice versa. She also presumes that the mutual utilization will increase in the future. Therefore, the less feminized personality in *PP3* might be said to be in line with the times.

Yamamoto's hypothesis that male translators have a tendency to use more female forms than female translators do can be further tested by comparison of *PP3* and three translations of *Emma* (*EM*, first published in 1816): *EM1* (translated by the female translator Shoko Harding in 1997), *EM2* (by the male translator Masashi Kudo in 2000), and *EM3* (by the male translator Kōji Nakano in 2005). *EM* was chosen precisely because, unlike *PP*, it has been translated by a woman as well as by two men. Moreover, *EM* was also written by Jane Austen, and published only three years later than *PP*, which means the usage of language in these novels can be considered as similar. Furthermore, bearing in mind the similar time-period in which they were translated (i.e. *PP3* in 2003, *EM1* in 1997, *EM2* in 2000 and *EM3* in 2005), it can be said that the use of women's language in the Target Texts is unlikely to show significant variance[5].

In this analysis, fictional conversations with close friends were chosen. Elizabeth's conversations with Jane, who is both her sister and best friend, were studied in the case of *PP*. For the survey of *Emma*, conversations with Miss Taylor have been chosen. She had been Emma's governess for 16 years but was 'less a governess than a friend' (*Emma* 2005: 3). I collected the data manually focusing on sentence-final forms and identified as five classifications: strongly feminine, moderately feminine, strongly masculine, moderately masculine, or neutral, by referring to Okamoto and Sato's classification (Okamoto and Sato 1992: 480–482). Sentence-final forms with no remarkable gender indexing

Table 1 Use of Gendered Sentence-final Forms (*PP3*, *EM1*, *EM2* and *EM3*)

Sentence-final Forms	Total Instances Used (%)			
	PP3 (M 2003)	*EM1* (F 1997)	*EM2* (M 2000)	*EM3* (M 2005)
Feminine forms	**75.52**	**60. 68**	**79.28**	**64.29**
-Strongly feminine forms	52.70	46.07	62.14	43.41
-Moderately feminine forms	22.82	14.61	17.14	20.88
Masculine forms	**0.00**	**0.00**	**0.00**	**0.00**
-Strongly masculine forms	0.00	0.00	0.00	0.00
-Moderately masculine forms	0.00	0.00	0.00	0.00
Neutral forms	**28.48**	**39.33**	**20.71**	**35.71**

Note 1: Total number of instances = 241 (*PP3* 2003), 178 (*EM1* 1997), 140 (*EM2* 2000), and 182 (*EM3* 2005)[6]

Note 2: The year of translation is employed the date that the novel translated for the first time.

Note 3: M in brackets indicates that the translator is male and F means that the translator is female.

Note 4: As all figures are rounded off to two decimal places, there is a systematic error when they are totalled.

are categorized as neutral forms. This methodology is also applied to the next study.

Compared with *PP3*, *EM2* and *EM3* (see Table 1), it is apparent that *EM1* uses the least feminine sentence-final forms, only 60.68 per cent. In contrast, the frequencies in use of feminine sentence-final forms in *PP3* and *EM2* are remarkable: 75.52 per cent and 79.28 per cent, respectively. *PP3* is the least feminized translation of *PP* as analysed earlier, so it can be inferred that *PP1* and *PP2* use feminine forms more excessively. These results lend support to Yamamoto's statement that male translators have a tendency to high frequency in the use of feminine forms. The hypothesis needs to be tested in further studies of such multiple target texts.

3. Women's language as linguistic ideology in translation

Even in novels originally written in Japanese, it has not been unusual to portray women's speech patterns in a stereotypical manner. The prominent female writer Ichiyo Higuchi became popular in the nineteenth century because she wrote with the supposedly authentic women's language. Higuchi used to write with a brusque style but changed it following the advice of a male writer, Tousui Nakarai, that it was not enough for women to write naturally, they should also write with a woman's stereotypical literary style. Consequently, her novel *Takekurabe* [*Growing Up*] (1885) had a great success, and Higuchi became the first woman writer in Japan fully to support herself by her pen. Higuchi's classic and elegant style reflects an ideal model of feminine speech style, which is created from a male perspective, and was striking within a male-dominated Japanese literary world. Her female writing style was highly praised and she later wrote a book on letter writing for women (Ueno 2003: 21–2, Urushida 2001: 84).

Similarly, as Inoue (2003) indicates, the translator's choice of language could be considered as 'a social representation of how women should speak'. Japanese readers supposedly hear the most authentic Japanese women's language from foreign female characters such as Scarlett O'Hara, Queen Elizabeth II, or even Minnie Mouse in translated novels, magazines, newspapers, or film subtitles and dubbing (Inoue 2003: 314–315). This supposedly authentic women's language is far different from lived experiences. Inoue defines the authentic women's language as 'vicarious language' (2006: 3). Women's language is neither simply a linguistic feature, nor real Japanese women's language. But this is 'a culturally salient category and knowledge' (ibid. 13) that women are supposed to know. Japanese people acquire the knowledge from texts such as translations, magazines, books, and newspapers (Nakamura 2007: 28). Most Japanese understand women's language; nevertheless, the majority of Japanese women do not actually use it in their conversations. In fact, Mizumoto (2005) demonstrates that most sentence-final particles, which indicate speakers' femininity, have almost vanished from the contemporary Japanese women under thirty. However, female characters in translation continue to use such gender-marked language (Nakamura 2007).

Japanese readers fill in the gap between literary language and real-life language in their mind when they read Japanese translation and fiction. Even if Japanese women do not use literary language or so-called authentic women's language, they are aware of the regulation on speech style, and regard that language as their own (Inoue 2003: 315). Furthermore, no matter which gender they belong to, Japanese readers take it for granted that female characters will use this stereotypical language in translation because female characters in translation have been using gender-marked language for a long time. This tendency has become a kind of convention in Japanese translation (Nakamura 2007). Japanese readers and translators are used to the Japanese literary convention and they are, in a sense, unconscious of the ideological aspect of women's language. Even a female translator will use typical female forms for characters in her translations. For example, the female translator of Michael Ende's *Momo* (1976) and Margaret Atwood's *Surfacing* (1993), Kaori Ōshima has confessed that she tends to be subconsciously affected by social expectations for women's speech style, and uses feminine forms when she renders women's voices.[7]

Japanese women's language has been assigned by male-dominant authority and politically determined throughout history. Modern Japanese women's language was promoted politically during the Meiji period (1868–1912). The Meiji period is an important era for Japanese modernization, given that it was during this time that Japan became an industrialised society. The role of women in modernization had to be clarified (Inoue 1994) and so a woman's role was codified through the education Japanese girls received. Such 'feminine training' was designed to express their femininity, and among the disciplinary measures was speech training: 'a soft voice, polite and feminine style of speech' (Lebra 1984: 42). Kindaichi (2006: 39) indicates that the typical usage of women's language which is seen in contemporary Japanese, such as a series of sentence-final particles, was established during this time.

There are some data which testify to this convention and show that even in Japanese translation of a contemporary novel, a female character's speech patterns do not reflect real Japanese women's dialogues. Table 2 is a comparison between the Japanese translation of *Bridget Jones's Diary* (translated by female translator Yoshiko Kamei in 1998) and a linguistic analysis of Japanese women's conversation conducted by Okamoto and Sato (1992).

In this analysis, both the fictional and actual conversations chosen occur in the context of close friendships. I study Bridget's conversations with three close friends: Tom, Jude, and Sharon. The Okamoto and Sato's survey is based on nine tape-recorded informal two-person conversations between three homemakers aged between 27 and 34, who are all close friends. All of the subjects are from middle- or upper-middle-class backgrounds, born in Tokyo and residing there at the time, speaking standard Japanese. I have compared 115 sentences in *BJD* to 390 sentences of authentic data of actual conversations in Okamoto and Sato's survey (1992). Although their professions are different and there is a six-year time difference of these data, Okamoto and Sato's study can be a benchmark to see the gap between emphasized feminine speech style in *BJD* and Japanese contemporary women's actual conversations.

Table 2 Use of Gendered Sentence-final Forms (*BJD* and Real Language Practices)

Sentence-final Forms	Total Tokens Used (%)	
	Okamoto and Sato (1992)	**BJD (1998)**
Feminine forms	**24%**	**45.22%**
-Strongly feminine forms	12%	28.70%
-Moderately feminine forms	12%	16.52%
Masculine forms	**14%**	**0.87%**
-Strongly masculine forms	0%	0.87%
-Moderately masculine forms	14%	0.00%
Neutral forms	**62%**	**53.91%**

Note 1: Total number of tokens = 390 (130 instances for each subject, Okamoto and Sato 1992) and 115 (*BJD* 1998).

Note 2: The year of translation/publication is the date that the novel was translated for the first time.

Note 3: Each subject in Okamoto and Sato's survey aged between 27 and 34.
Source of the data 'Okamoto and Sato':
Okamoto, Shigeko and Shie Sato. (1992) 'Less Feminine Speech among Young Japanese Females', in (eds.) Hall, Kira, Mary Bucholtz and Birch Moonwomon. *Locating Power: Proceedings of the Second Berkeley Women and Language Conference, April 4 and 5, 1992, Vol.1*, Berkeley and Calif; Berkeley Women and Language Group: 483.

Note 4: All figures are rounded off to two decimal places.

From the results compiled by Okamoto and Sato, we can see that Japanese women's language is mostly composed of neutral forms (62%). They sometimes use feminine forms (24%), and at times masculine forms appear in their conversations (14%). In the translation, Bridget uses mostly neutral forms (53.91 %) or feminine forms (45.22%), and it is extremely rare that she speaks with masculine forms (0.87%).

To analyse these two sets of data in detail, there are two considerable differences: in feminine forms and masculine forms. As for feminine forms, *BJD* uses nearly twice as many as found by Okamoto and Sato: 45.22 per cent in *BJD* versus 24 per cent in Okamoto and Sato. The difference is more remarkable when considering the balance between strongly feminine forms and moderately feminine forms in Okamoto and Sato, and *BJD*. While strongly feminine forms and moderately feminine forms have the same percentage, 12 per cent in Okamoto and Sato, there is a remarkable discrepancy between strongly feminine forms and moderately feminine forms in *BJD*: 28.70 per cent and 16.52 per cent respectively. The result indicates the translator's inclination toward strongly feminine forms. Not only does the translator use feminine forms much more than in real women's discourse, but she also heightens Bridget's femininity with strong feminine forms. The translator's language choice constructs Bridget's personality as being much more feminine than that of real Japanese women.

Regarding masculine forms, *BJD* seems to avoid masculine forms intentionally. Contemporary Japanese women used masculine forms at 14 per cent in Okamoto and Sato, whereas there is only one masculine form in *BJD*: 0.87 per cent. For instance, though Bridget uses swear words such as 'Bastard!' (126, 168), 'Bastards' (127), '[. . .] the bloody bastard' (ibid.), and 'Bloody bastard' (ibid.), most of them were modified: '*Rokudenashi!*' [A good-for-nothing] (Kamei 2001: 166), '*Rokudenashidomo!*' [Good-for-nothings] (Kamei 2001: 167), or '*Usuratonkachi no rokudenashi*' [A foolish good-for-nothing] (Kamei 2001: 167). Only once does, the translator use a masculine particle '*ga*' to emphasize Bridget's anger with the 'fuckwittage' (188) of men: '*Rokudenashidomo ga!*' [Loser!] (Kamei 2001: 245). The particle '*ga*' indicates Bridget's abusive language use (*Shinmeikai Japanese Dictionary* 2005: 214).

Table 1 verifies that male translators tend to overuse feminine forms for female characters' speech, and Table 2 signifies that even a female translator chooses supposedly 'ideal' feminine forms in her translation. The data in Table 2 support Ōshima's observation indicated above (Ōshima in Nakamura 2007: 52).

Stereotypes are often influenced by social expectations. If Japanese translation is affected by social expectations, it reinforces the spread of Japanese women's language as ideology. When Japanese women's language is repeatedly used in translations, the repetition helps to implant the 'vicarious language' (Inoue 2006: 4) in women's minds telling them 'how women should speak'. Stereotypically feminine expressions reflect gender bias, and help the bias to continue and be justified (Frank 1989: 109)[8]. At the very least, the repetitive use of stereotypes in translations may induce women to fit into a socially-mandated mould even if not in regard to speech itself but in terms of general behaviour and aspirations. Japanese readers are considerably used to stereotypical feminine speech in fiction and translation, and the influence of stereotypes on women's speech/views of themselves has not been discussed enough in Japan.

4. Conclusion

In conclusion, this paper has analysed the three Japanese translations of *PP* focusing on the femininity of Elizabeth, which is constructed by the translators' choice of language. Due to three characteristics: the highest degree of politeness, strong femininity, and indirectness, *PP3* can be regarded as the least feminized version of Elizabeth. Also, the analysis of sentence-final forms in the four Japanese translations of *PP* and *EM*, which have been translated by both male and female translators: *PP3* (2003), *EM1* (1997), *EM2* (2000), and *EM3* (2005), was conducted and it strongly suggests that male translators are prone to overuse women's language for female characters' speech in a novel as Yamamoto hypothesizes (2000). Furthermore, the last analysis of the translation of *BJD* and real women's discourse demonstrates that even a female translator is influenced by socially-expected stereotypes of female speech style, and overuses feminine forms in her translation. This fact indicates that even female translators are not able to break out of the expected norm. The markedly feminine figures in Japanese translation are created by social expectations, and translation functions to reinforce an ideal model of how women should speak. Even if in reality Japanese women do not speak with an apparently authentic women's language, the representation of women in Japanese translation may influence perceptions of women's role in society.

5. Notes

1. There used to be two different Japanese translations of *Le Deuxième Sexe*; the first version was by a male translator in 1953, and then a feminist group re-translated it in 1997 because of the previous

translator's biased interpretation and some mistakes: the change of structure, the mistranslation of some important words such as 'feminine,' the strong focus on experiences but less on theories, and so on. However, both versions are currently out of print in Japan.

2. '[I]t is individuals who "do" gender. But it is a situated doing, carried out in the virtual or real presence of others who are presumed to be oriented to its production. Rather than as a property of individuals, we conceive of gender as an emergent feature of social situations [. . .]' (West and Zimmerman 1987: 126).

3. The percentage of translated titles published in Japan was 13.8 per cent in 1971 falling to 9.8 per cent in 1991. These statistics can be compared to a mere 2.4 per cent in 1990 and 1.4 per cent in 2001 in the UK, and 2.96 per cent in 1990 and 2.85 per cent in 2005 in the US. Moreover, the impact of translations in Japanese publication is noteworthy. The proportion of translations in a top 10 yearly bestseller is 24 per cent in 1945–1954, 2 per cent in 1955–1964, 4 per cent in 1965–1974, 10 per cent in 1975–1984, 16 per cent in 1985–1994, and 20 per cent in 1995–2004 (*Nihonzasshikyokai* 2007: 294–5, Venuti 2008: 11).

4. *Katakana* characters are mainly used for loan words or telegrams.

5. There is another Japanese translation of *EM* on the current market in Japan. This version was translated in 1974 by a male translator Tomoji Abe, so this is excluded in this study because of the time difference in the date of publication.

6. Although the total instance numbers in *EM1* and *EM3* are almost the same, the number in *EM2* is approximately 40 less than the others. That is because *EM1* and *EM3* sometimes divide one sentence into two when the English sentence is a compound which uses a semicolon or a dash.

7. 'Even if characters use the same words, I sometimes translate them differently depending on the speaker's gender. Although I do not intend to be regulated by 'the Japanese women's language,' I regulate myself to choose words by affecting deeply rooted rules of 'femininity' subconsciously. This regulation works even more strongly when I render a text which is written by a female writer. In most cases, I try to restrain myself and make the strong words ambiguous. That means that I avoid harsh or provocative words and make them obscure' (my translation, Ōshima in Nakamura 2007: 52).

8. '[i]t is clear that language not only reflects social structures but, more important, sometimes serves to perpetuate existing differences in power; thus a serious concern with linguistic usage is fully warranted' (Frank 1989: 109).

6. Bibliography

Primary texts

Austen, J. ([1813]2003) *Pride and Prejudice*. London: Penguin Books.

Austen, J. ([1816]2005) *Emma*. Cambridge and New York: Cambridge University Press.

Fielding, H. (1997) *Bridget Jones's Diary*. London; Picador.

Harding, S. (trans.) (1997) Austen, J. *Ema [Emma]*. Tokyo: Aoyama Shuppansha.

Kamei, Y. (trans.) ([1998]2001) Fielding, H. *Burigitto Jōnzu no Nikki [Bridget Jones's Diary]*. Tokyo: Sony magazines.

Kudo, K. (trans.) (2005) Austen, J. *Ema [Emma]*, vol.1 and 2. Tokyo: Chikumashoten.

Kudo, M. (trans.) ([2000]2007) Austen, J. *Ema [Emma]*, vol.1 and 2. Tokyo: Iwanami shoten.

Nakano, K. (trans.) ([2003]2006) Austen, J. *Kōman to Henken [Pride and Prejudice]*, vol.1 and 2. Tokyo: Chikumashoten.

Nakano, Y. (trans.) ([1963]2007) Jane Austen. *Jifu to Henken [Pride and Prejudice]*. Tokyo: Shinchosha.

Tomita, A. (trans.) ([1950]2006) Austen, J. *Kōman to Henken [Pride and Prejudice]*, vol.1and.2. Tokyo: Iwanami Shoten.

Secondary texts

Beauvoir, S. (1949) *Le Deuxieme sexe* [*The Second Sex*, E.M. Parshley (trans.) (1997)]. Paris: Gallimard.

Butler, J. P. ([1990]2006) *Gender Trouble: Feminism and the Subversion of Identity*. New York and London; Routledge.

Chino, K. (2003) 'Gender in Japanese Art', in J. S. Mostow, N. Bryson, and M. Graybill (eds), *Gender and Power in the Japanese Visual Field*. Honolulu University of Hawaii Press, 17–34.

Endo, O. (1997) *Onna no Kotoba no Bunkashi [The Cultural History of Women's Language]*. Tokyo: Gakuyo Shobo.

Flotow, Luise von (1997) *Translation and Gender*. Manchester: St Jerome University of Ottawa Press.

Frank, F. W. (1989) 'Language Planning, Language Reform, and Language Change: A Review of Guidelines for Nonsexist Usage', in F. W. Frank and P. A. Treichler (eds), *Language, Gender, and Professional Writing: Theoretical Approaches and Guidelines for Nonsexist Usage*. New York; Commission on the Status of Women in the Profession, Modern Language Association of America, 105–33.

Furukawa, H. (2009 Forthcoming) '"Fabricated" Feminine Characters: Overemphasised Femininity in the Japanese Translation of Bridget Jones's Diary and a Japanese Novel Kitchen'. Norwich Papers, vol.17.

Godard, B. (1990) 'Theorizing Feminist Discourse/Translation', in S. Bassnett and A. Lefevere (eds) *Translation, History and Culture*. London and New York: Pinter Publisher, 87–96.

Hung, E. and Wakabayashi, J.(eds) (2005) *Asian Translation Traditions*. Manchester: St Jerome Publishing.

Ide, S. and Yoshida, M. (2002) 'Sociolinguistics: Honorifics and Gender Differences', in N.Tsujimura (ed)*The Handbook of Japanese Linguistics*. Oxford: Blackwell Publishers, 445–81.

Inoue, M. (1994) 'Gender and Linguistic Modernization: Historicizing Japanese Women's Language', in M. Bucholtz, A. Liang, L. Sutton, and C. Hines (eds) *Cultural Performances: Proceedings of the Third Berkeley Women and Language Conference, April 8–10, 1994*. Berkeley: Berkeley Women and Language Group, 322–33.

Inoue, M. (2006) *Vicarious Language: Gender and Linguistic Modernity in Japan*. Berkeley: University of California Press.

Inoue, M. (2003) 'Speech Without a Speaking Body: "Japanese Women's Language" in Translation', *Language & Communication*, 23, 315–30.

Kindaichi, H. ([1957]2006), *Nihongo [The Japanese Language]*. Tokyo: Iwanami.

Lakoff, R. (1975) *Language and Woman's Place*. New York and London: Harper and Row.

Lebra, T. S. (1984) *Japanese Women: Constraint and Fulfillment*. Honolulu: University of Hawaii Press.

Mizumoto, M. (2005) 'Terebi drama niokeru joseikotoba to genda firuta [Women's Language and Gendered Image in TV dramas]'. *Nihongo to Gendaa [The Japanese Language and Gender]*, No.5. www.soc.nii.ac.jp/gender/journal/no5/3_mizumoto.htm [accessed on 1 July 2008].

Nakamura, M. (2007) 'Sei' to Nihongo ['Gender' and the Japanese Language]. Tokyo: Nihonhoso Shuppankyokai.

New Encyclopædia Britannica, Vol.6. (15th edition 2002) Chicago; London: Encyclopædia Britannica.

Nihonzasshikyokai (2007) 'Nihonshosekishppankyokai Gojuunenshi [Fifty annals of the Japanese publication association]' www.jbpa.or.jp/nenshi/ (Japanese) [accessed on 4 March 2008].

Ohara, Y. (2004) 'Prosody and Gender in Workplace Interaction: Exploring Constraints and Resources in the Use of Japanese', in S. Okamoto and J. S. Smith (eds), *Japanese Language, Gender, and Ideology: Cultural Models and Real People*. New York: Oxford University Press, 222–39.

Okamoto, S. (2004) 'Ideology in Linguistic Practice and Analysis: Gender and Politeness in Japanese Revisited', in S. Okamoto and J. S. Shibamoto (eds), *Japanese Language, Gender, and Ideology: Cultural Models and Real People*. New York: Oxford University Press, 38–56.

Okamoto, S. (1995) '"Tasteless" Japanese: Less "Feminine" Speech among Young Japanese Women', in K. Hall and M. Bucholtz (eds) *Gender Articulated: Language and the Socially Constructed Self*. New York and London: Routledge, 297–325.

Okamoto, S. and Sato, S. (1992) 'Less Feminine Speech among Young Japanese Females', in K. Hall, M. Bucholtz and B. Moonwomon (eds) *Locating Power: Proceedings of the Second Berkeley Women and Language Conference, April 4 and 5, 1992, Vol.1*. Berkeley and California: Berkeley Women and Language Group, 478–88.

Reynolds, K. A. (1993) 'Onnakotoba to nihongobunka [Women's Language and the Japanese Culture]', in K. A. Reynolds (ed), *Onna to Nihongo [Women and the Japanese Language]*. Tokyo: Yusindo, 3–30.

Shinmeikai Japanese Dictionary. (6th edition 2005) Tokyo: Sansedo.

Smith, J. S. (1992a) 'Women in Charge: Politeness and Directive in the Speech of Japanese Women', *Language in Society*, 21, 59–82.

Smith, J. S. (1992b) 'Linguistic Privilege: "Just Stating the Facts" in Japanese', in K. Hall, M. Bucholtz and B. Moonwomon (eds) *Locating Power: Proceedings of the Second Berkeley Women and Language Conference, April 4 and 5, 1992, Vol.1*. Berkeley and California: Berkeley Women and Language Group, 540–8.

Simon, S. (1996) *Gender in Translation: Culture and Identity and the Politics of Transmission*. London: Routledge.

Spender, D. ([1980]1998) *Man Made Language*. London: Routledge and Kegan Paul.

Tanaka, L. (2004) *Gender, Language and Culture: A Study of Japanese Television Interview Discourse*. Amsterdam: John Benjamins Publishing Co.

Tanaka, S. (1986) *Kashikoi Hito ni Narinasai: Utsukushiku Ikitai Anata ni [Be a Wise Woman: To You Who Want to Live Beautifully]*. Tokyo: PhP kenkhusho.

Ueno, C. (2003) *Ueno Chizuko ga Bungaku wo Shakaigakusuru [Ueno Chizuko Analyses Literature from a Sociological Perspective]*. Tokyo; Asahisinbunsha.

Urushida, K. (2001) *"Onnarashii" bunsho ha kakonomono'* [It is Old Style to Write Womanly], in O. Endo (ed). *Onna to Kotoba [Woman and Language]*. Tokyo: Akashi Shoten, 80–90.

Venuti, L. (2008) *The Translator's Invisibility: A History of Translation*. London: Routledge.

West, C. and Zimmerman, D. (1987) 'Doing Gender', *Gender and Society*, 1 (2) 125–51.

Yamamoto, Y. (2000) *'Honyaku no wadai'*[About translations]. http://cosmoshouse.com/lit–trans.htm (Japanese) [accessed on 26 May 2007].

Part IV
Back to Basics

The Nature, Place and Role of a Philosophy of Translation in Translation Studies

10

Kirsten Malmkjær
University of Middlesex, UK

Chapter Outline

1. Introduction

In this chapter I step back and look beyond translation theory to the theory of meaning to see whether this discipline, in which translation has been a central issue since the middle of the twentieth century, might be of some help to us in both our theorising and in our practice. I also want to explore the idea that our practice may have something to feed back to the theory of meaning about the nature of that very phenomenon. However, my overriding aim is to highlight what I see as the nature, place and role of a philosophy of translation in Translation Studies, because it is far from obvious from the state of the discipline as we tend to depict it today that a philosophy of translation exists, or what its place and roles might be, if it did exist.

For example, as shown in Figure 1, the much rehearsed map of Translation Studies developed by Toury (1995: 10) on the basis of Holmes' ([1972]1988) famous paper, 'The name and nature of translation studies' has no place for a philosophy of translation.

That may not be surprising, because philosophies of x tend to exist outside of x itself – within philosophy, in fact. For example, the philosophy of language exists outside linguistics, within philosophy; the philosophy of mind exists outside of psychology, within philosophy; and the philosophy of science exists outside of science, within philosophy. This is partly because philosophy has retained its own philosophical interest in these areas at the same time as new disciplines have developed from them. The new disciplines have concentrated on developing and applying understanding that originated in philosophy to practice in society, while philosophy has maintained its interest in essences and fundamental questions. This is a perfectly healthy and generally fruitful division of labour – at least it seems to me to be so in the fields that I am most familiar with, linguistics and the philosophy of language. Nevertheless, I want to argue that the case of a philosophy of translation is different, for the following reasons:

1. Philosophers do not in fact see themselves as dealing with a philosophy of translation as such; for them, the question of translation is just one question, though a very central question, within the philosophy of language.
2. Philosophers are not especially interested in many of the issues that interest translation scholars, so we cannot expect to find in their writings any discussion of implications of their work for our discipline. These, we have to draw out ourselves.
3. The philosophical debate about translation has a direct bearing on the most fundamental questions in our discipline.

I therefore want to advocate that we lift the most pertinent aspects of the philosophical debate on translation into our own discipline and add the philosophy of translation to Holmes' map, or to whatever other map or outline that we might like to use to picture our discipline. The philosophy of translation is not identical with translation theory; it is more basic than that, and I would like to see it as a branch of Translation Studies in its own right, for reasons that I will outline in the following section.

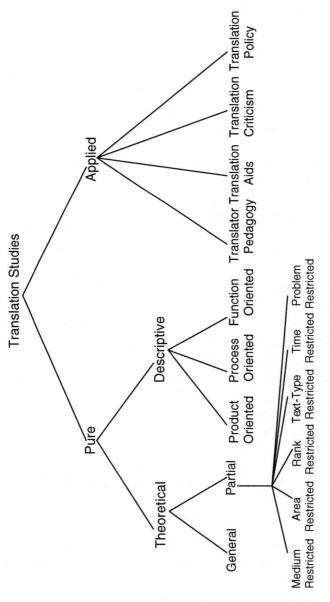

Figure 1 Holmes' and Toury's Conception of Translation Studies

2. Why bother with a philosophy of translation?

Translation Studies scholars working in the areas of Think Aloud Protocol Studies (see e.g. Tirkkonen-Condit and Jääskeläinen 2000) and TransLogging (see e.g. Lykke Jakobsen 1999) have made tremendous strides in recent years in describing the outward manifestations of the mental processes involved in translation. Others, examining large collections of translations with or without their source texts (see e.g. Mauranen and Kujamäki 2004), have shown that translated texts tend to exhibit features which make them stand out from non-translated texts. We have learnt from these studies a great deal about what happens in translators' consciousness as they translate and about what kinds of text they produce, and we know something of the connections between these two manifestations of translation. It may not be immediately obvious why we would need any other kinds of knowledge with the field of Translation Studies, particularly not, someone might argue, philosophical knowledge: surely, they might remark, translation is more likely to be illuminated by insights into and derived from translators' own mental activity *in medias res* than by speculation about translation in the minds of armchair-based philosophers.

However, I want to suggest two reasons why it is important to have a philosophy of translation. One is that it is reassuring to have a basic understanding of what translation is that underlies our various approaches to it and holds together our various theories of it and of its constituent concepts and descriptive notions. The other is that we need a philosophy of translation if we are to provide satisfactory answers to some of the challenges the discipline faces both from outside of itself and from within itself.

3. Challenges from the inside

i. Challenging the practice

The possibility of translation has regularly been questioned from within Translation Studies itself, usually with reference to partial untranslatability and often with reference to the argument that literary translation is impossible; but it is not uncommon to see the translation of certain every-day concepts and notions described as untranslatable too, usually on grounds of cultural differences.

Consider Jakobson, who declares that,

In poetry, verbal equations become a constructive principle of the text. Syntactic and morphological categories, roots, and affixes, phonemes and their components (distinctive features) – in short, any constituents of the verbal code – are confronted, juxtaposed, brought into contiguous relation according to the principle of similarity and contrast and carry their own semantic relationship. The pun, or to use a more erudite, and perhaps more precise term – paronomasia, reigns over poetic art, and whether its rule is absolute or limited, poetry by definition is untranslatable. Only creative transposition is possible: either intralingual transposition – from one poetic shape into another, or interlingual transposition – from one language into another, or finally intersemiotic transposition – from one system of signs into another, e.g. from verbal art into music, dance, cinema, or painting. (1959: 238)

Here, it seems to be assumed that a translation must be an equivalent text, in a sense of equivalence not specified, but obviously excluding 'interlingual transposition' from one language into another.

A less sophisticated statement of a similar position is to be found in Paris according to whom the original is the 'traditional limit' of translation and who thinks that 'how close we can get to it is a problem which torments, or should torment, all translators' (1961: 57). He concludes that 'it is obvious that Donne or Dylan Thomas lose everything when they lose their own language' (1961: 57–8).

This statement is so sweeping that counterexamples positively crowd the mind. For example, Thomas's 'Altarwise by Owl-Light' (Thomas 1952: 71) finds a very close equivalent in the Danish, 'Altervis ved Ugle-Lys' as far as paronomasia is concerned, and the fact that it has one syllable more than the original hardly disqualifies it as a translation.

Counterexamples like this and, more particularly, the fact that so many translations exist and are accepted as translations show the shortcomings of the definitional, Source Text oriented approach to Translation Studies adopted by Jakobson and Paris, which has in any case been dismissed by Toury (1980). But we can add extra strength to Toury's Target Text oriented argument by considering the curious position to which the argument for limited untranslatability commits its adherents.

In the very same article in which we find the quotation above, Jakobson also declares that

All cognitive experience and its classification is conveyable in any existing language. Whenever there is a deficiency, terminology can be qualified and amplified by loanwords or loan translations, by neologisms or

> semantic shifts, and, finally, by circumlocutions. (. . .) No lack of gram-
> matical devices in the language translated into makes impossible a literal
> translation of the entire conceptual information contained in the origi-
> nal. ([1959]1987: 431–2)

These two statements taken together commit Jakobson to two views that seem
untenable. First, if literal translation of 'all cognitive experience and its classification' is possible, and if poetry is untranslatable, our experience of poetry
must be something other than cognitive. But is not all experience cognitive?
What kind of experience is poetic experience supposed to be?

Secondly Jacobson seems committed to the unlikely view that there are
two quite different ways in which language relates to concepts in the case of
people who use more than one language. One view (for non-literary texts)
might be pictured like this:

CONCEPT

L1 term   L2 term   . . . L^n term

The other (for literary texts) might be pictured like this:

L1 CONCEPT   L2 CONCEPT L^n CONCEPT

L1 term   L2 term L^n term

It can surely not be the case that some concepts – those involved in processing literary texts – are language specific while other concepts are not. There is
no doubt that the translation of poetry can be challenging; but we must seek
a different explanation for the opportunities to excel that translators of poetry
and of literature are offered by their chosen text types.

Of the two models of the relationship between a bilingual's or a multilingual's
conceptual system and their languages, there are compelling arguments for the
former; the second model, which would make concepts language specific, con-
flicts with for example the neurolinguistics of bilingualism. According to Paradis,

> the conceptual component of verbal communication is not language-
> specific and there is a single non-linguistic cognitive system, even though
> speakers group together conceptual features differently in accordance
> with the lexical semantic constraints of each language. The lexical items
> are part of the language system, but the concepts are not. (2004: 200)

I will try, in the arguments that follow, to illustrate how the fact of the different groupings of conceptual features can affect translation, of course, it is also possible – in fact, it is overwhelmingly likely – that meaning is more than this relationship between concepts and terms, and this will probably have consequences for translation. The philosophy of language has much to say about this, too, but the translation case that I will come to illustrates one such aspect with particular clarity.

ii. Challenging the theory

The possibility of having a theory of translation has also been questioned from within Translation Studies, assuming that we think of George Steiner as a translation scholar. Steiner makes this challenge with reference to Quine's (1959; 1960) view of translational indeterminacy, remarking in a spirit of deep pessimism that

> the bare notion of a mature theory of how translation is possible and how it takes place, of a responsible model of the mental attributes and functions which are involved, *presumes* a systematic theory of language with which it overlaps completely or from which it derives as a special case according to demonstrable rules of deduction and application. I can see no evasion from this truism. But the fact remains that we have no such theory of language. (Steiner 1975: 279–280)

It is only by examining the theory of translational indeterminacy, which is the theory that has so unsettled Steiner, that we can lay this particular ghost to rest. It will also help us choose between Jakobson's two views of how concepts relate to languages.

4. External challenges to Translation Studies

The challenges that translation faces from other disciplines can be discussed under the headings, cultural, linguistic and ontological relativism (see Malmkjær 2005: 44–58).

iii. Cultural relativism

A good example of cultural relativism is the anthropologist, Bronislaw Malinowski's (1884–1942), view that

> a European, suddenly plunged into a Trobriand community and given a word-by-word translation of the Trobrianders' utterances, would be no nearer understanding them than if the utterances remained untranslated – the utterances become comprehensible only in the context of the whole way of life of which they form part. (1923; Sampson 1980: 225)

This would have the curious consequence that speakers of the various varieties of English should be unable to understand each other and it would mean that the efforts of, for example, African writers who produce English language literature are wasted if they hope thereby to communicate more widely than if they wrote in, say, Giguyu.

Clearly, this cultural relativist stance is closely related to linguistic relativism, best known, probably, from the work or Edward Sapir and Benjamin Lee Whorf.

iv. Linguistic relativity

In Sapir's formulation,

> Human beings do not live in the objective world alone, nor alone in the world of social activity as ordinarily understood, but are very much at the mercy of the particular language which has become the medium of expression for their society. It is quite an illusion to imagine that one adjusts to reality essentially without the use of language and that language is merely an incidental means of solving specific problems of communication or reflection. The fact of the matter is that the 'real world' is to a large extent built up on the language habits of the group. No two languages are ever sufficiently similar to be considered as representing the same social reality. The worlds in which different societies live are distinct worlds, not merely the same world with different labels attached. ([1929] Mandelbaum 1949: 69)

Sapir is clearly talking here about the *social* world, rather than of the physical world, which places him in a dilemma not unlike Jakobson's. In Sapir (1921, especially Chapter 5), he expresses firm universalist sentiments: We must have, he declares, a large stock of basic or radical concepts, the concrete wherewithal of speech. We must have objects, actions and qualities to talk about, and these must have their corresponding symbols in independent words or in radical elements. No proposition, however abstract its intent, is humanly possible without a tying on at one or more points to the concrete world of sense. In every intelligible proposition at least two of these radical ideas must be expressed, though in exceptional cases one or even both may be understood from the context. And, secondly, such relational concepts must be expressed as moor the concrete concepts to each other and construct a definite, fundamental form or proposition. ([1921] 1926: 98)

Whorf's relativism is similarly half-hearted. Even in the expression of what he refers to as 'a new principle of relativity', he leaves open the possibility of translation:

No individual is free to describe nature with absolute impartiality, but is constrained to certain modes of interpretation . . . All observers are not led by the same physical evidence to the same picture of the universe, unless their linguistic backgrounds are similar, or can in some way be calibrated. (Whorf 1940: 214)

But the possibility of radical relativism remains in the minds of a number of scholars of a relativist persuasion. For example Lakoff and Johnson maintain that,

People with very different conceptual systems than our own may under-stand the world in a very different way than we do. Thus they may have a very different body of truths than we have and even different criteria for truth and reality. (1980: 181)

This takes us neatly into ontological relativism, where the external challenge meets the internal one from Steiner.

v. Ontological relativism

Within the language sciences, relativism with respect to how other people view truth is the most radical form of relativism because of the central role that truth has traditionally played in the theory of meaning, and because the notion of truth has been closely intertwined with the notion of reference, which has traditionally be thought of as the point of contact between language and what it is about. The central players in this game are Willard van Orman Quine and Donald Davidson.

Quine's (see 1960) pessimism with regard to the theorizability of the notion of meaning arises from a worry that a listener can never be certain that a speaker means by an utterance the same as the listener would mean by it. Speaker and hearer may have radically different ontological commitments (Hookway 1988: 134) – that is, their ways of dividing up the world into categories of item may by so radically different that context cannot be used, as in e.g. Catford (1965), as a measure of translation equivalence. Therefore, the central questions in the theory of meaning are unanswerable. These questions are, in Davidson's terms, the following:

> Having identified [an] utterance as intentional and linguistic, we are able to go on to interpret [the speaker's] words: we can say what his words, on that occasion, meant. What could we know that would enable us to do this? How could we come to know it? ([1973] 1984: 125)

For an empiricist like Quine, the answer to the first question has to be 'relationships between words and the world'. As he puts it,

> Surface irritations generate, through language, one's knowledge of the world. One is taught so to associate words with words and other stimulations that there emerges something recognizable as talk of things, and not to be distinguished from truths about the world. (1960: 26)

But the answer to the second question is 'We cannot come to know the associations that obtain for the speaker between words and stimulations.' This is because when a speakers says, for example, 'Gavagai' in response to what the hearer takes to be a rabbit-stimulation (a rabbit running by), there is no knowing what the speaker's stimulation in fact is (1960: 51–2); the speaker might experience, not a whole enduring rabbit stimulation, but a rabbit stages stimulation, or a stimulation by temporal segments of rabbits, or un-detached rabbit parts.

5. Meeting the challenges

Quine's work suggests that the notion of meaning is an unhelpful starting point in setting up a theory of meaning; partly for this reason, Davidson (1967: 307–309) suggests a different starting point for the theory of meaning, the concept of truth.

Setting out from the notion of truth has the advantage that truth is 'a single property which attaches, or fails to attach, to utterances, while each utterance has its own interpretation' (Davidson [1973] 1984: 134). This means that we might be justified in declaring some utterances true without claiming to understand them. For example, if we hear a speaker, Kurt, who belongs to a speech community which we call German, saying *Es regnet* when it is raining near him, then, instead of assuming that this sentence means 'It is raining', we might more modestly take our observation of Kurt's behaviour (eventually together with evidence provided by a mass of other German speakers in similar circumstances) as evidence for the statement '"Es regnet" is true-in-German when spoken by x at time t if and only if it is raining near x at t' ([1973] 1984: 135), where x stands for any speaker and t for any time. Note that the notion of truth in use here is not of absolute truth; it is the notion of holding an utterance true, and speakers adopt that attitude to individual sentences only relatively to certain times and sets of circumstance. So it is a notion of truth that is relative to times, speakers, languages, utterances and sets of circumstances.

To make this theory function as a theory of translation requires us to assume enough similarity between speakers to make it likely that the utterer of the sentence in quotation (in this case 'es regnet') would agree with the description of the circumstances in which the utterance is held true *whether or not* the language of description is the same as the language of the sentence in quotation. In other words, regardless of the languages involved, utterer and interpreter must be able to agree, for any utterance U that '"U" is true if and only if C', where C is a statement of the circumstances in which 'U' is held true. In other words, the theory requires 'dis-quotation'; the second term in the equation is out of quotation marks; sentences are related to circumstances, not to other sentences.

But Quine's suggestion is that this dis-quotation operation is fundamentally and fatally (as far as the theory of meaning is concerned) unjustified because he denies us access to the description of the circumstances in which the speaker would hold the sentence true. But perhaps this denial is not justified:

> The methodological advice to interpret in a way that optimizes agreement should not be conceived as resting on a charitable assumption about human intelligence that might turn out to be false. If we cannot find a way to interpret the utterances and other behaviour of a creature as revealing a set of beliefs largely consistent and true by our own standards, we have no reason to count that creature as rational, as having beliefs or as saying anything. (Davidson [1973]1984: 137)

According to Davidson (1974), to assume that someone is making noises that are part of rational speech behaviour is to assume that they have something that they want to express. In other words, it is to assume that they want to express something which they hold true, which is the same as to assume that they have beliefs.

So any creature whose noises we bother to interpret is thereby credited with a notion of holding something true. If we were to deny the attitude of holding true to the creature, we would at the same time be denying that it had beliefs. But the cultural relativist certainly does not want to do that; s/he just wants to deny that the creature has any beliefs which we could gain access to. According to the cultural relativist, the reason why we cannot gain access to the creature's beliefs is that we cannot translate its language into our own; the creature has beliefs, that is, it has a notion of holding something true, but it is impossible to translate from its language into ours. In other words, the creature's language is true (for it), but not translatable.

The trouble with this theory is that there does not seem to be any way in which the truth predicate can be explained without reference to the notion of translation, without dis-quotation. As Tarski (1956) points out, the predicate, 'is true' functions in such a way that for any sentence S of a language there is a statement of the form, 'S is true if p', where p is the translation of S into the language of the theory. This is not because sentences must be true, it is because the truth predicate, 'is true' is a kind of shorthand for an infinite number of sentences related to the circumstances in which they are true: 'Truth is . . . a notion that we might reasonably want to have on hand, for expressing semantic assent and dissent, infinite conjunction and disjunction' (Leeds 1978: 121). It is encapsulated in the Tarski sentences, which express a theory of the truth concept. And this truth concept is inextricably tied into the notion of translation via dis-quotation: A sentence of the object language, in quotation, is related to a set of circumstances – expressed in a dis-quoted, operational sentence.

Tarski sentences assume translation. Davidson reverses the direction of explicitation; taking the attitude of holding true as given, the possibility of interpretation/translation follows. Either way, the notion of truth is inseparable from the notion of translation, and any theory that seeks to separate the two, as the theory of cultural relativism does in order to retain the idea that speakers have beliefs while maintaining the untranslatability of their language, is internally inconsistent.

This theory has a number of consequences for translation. For example, if truth is relative to times, circumstances and speakers, then, insofar as truth plays a central role in the meaning relationship, meaning, too, must be particular to such a set of circumstances. And since circumstances are unique to the moment, meaning is not replicable and we can forget about trying to recreate it in translation.

Let me now return to Paradis's claim that bilingual speakers employ,

> a single non-linguistic cognitive system, even though speakers group together conceptual features differently in accordance with the lexical semantic constraints of each language. (2004: 200)

In the following section, I would like to illustrate the notion of different groupings of conceptual features in different languages by way of an example of the kind that typically brings out the possibilities of differences at this level especially clearly.

6. On the different groupings of conceptual features

In the Viking Ship Museum in Bygdøy in Olso is the Oseberg Ship. It was built between 815 and 820 AD, and used as a grave ship for a high-ranking woman who died in 834 AD. It was excavated in 1904 on Oseberg farm in Vestfold, a county to the west of Oslo Fjord.

Among the things found on the Oseberg Ship was a piece of wood with the runic inscription:

ᛚᛁᛏᛁᛚᚢᛁᛏ
l i til u ism (litiluism)

The inscription is not clearly visible through the glass of the case where the wood is kept, but it can be seen on www.arild-hauge.com/innskrifter1.htm, which quotes Projektet Samnordisk runtextdatabas and provides the following information about what these runes might mean:

> Tolkningen er usikker, men den mest vanlige er *litilvíss (er) maðr*. Den siste 'm-runen' blir da tolket som *maðr* – 'mann, menneske' – og 'u-runen' blir lest som 'v', og oversettes *'Lite vet mennesket'*. (2004: 163)

> The interpretation is uncertain, but the most common is *litilvíss (er) maðr*. Here, the final 'm-rune' is interpreted as *maðr* – '*man, human being*' – and the 'u-rune' is read as 'v', and the text is translated as '*Lite vet mennesket*' [*Little knows the human being*]. (my translation)

So, what is written is something like (in English translation) 'littlewh', which is expanded interpretatively as 'littlewisehuman'; and the standard runological interpretation is a much further expansion into something like 'Little knows the human being'.

However, when I visited the museum on 15 June 2007, the inscription, in modern Norwegian, on the glass case where this piece of wood is displayed, in the finds wing of the museum, was 'lite klokt menneske' (little clever human). It is not difficult to see how that derives from 'littlewh' → 'littlewisehuman'. The English translation provided was 'unwise person' and the German was 'kleiner kluger Mensch' (little clever human). It is not difficult to see how both of those understandings are derivable from 'Lite klokt menneske', 'little clever human'. But neither is interpretable as the original is interpreted on the website, which is as a sentence:

Lite   vet   mennesket
Little knows   the human being
O   V   S   (sentence)
Each is only a noun phrase.

The Norwegian representation of the runic inscription has clearly been understood differently by the two translators into English and German, and the two interpretations are mutually exclusive; it is only possible for one of them to represent the Norwegian faithfully, as the metaphor has it, and probably neither does, in fact, represent what the author of the modern Norwegian had in mind, if he or she was knowledgeable about runic inscriptions, as it would be comforting to think that he or she was, since he or she had been entrusted with translating for the museum.

On the piece of wood with the runes, three concepts are referred to, according to the standard runological interpretation provided on the web site:

Limited quantity
Wisdom
Human being

The standard runological interpretation then arranges these concepts into a sentence by assuming predication, and by assuming that the characteristic that is of limited quantity is wisdom and that the concept of limited wisdom is ascribed to humanity by way of modification by the expression of the concept of limited wisdom of the noun phrase that refers to humanity. The notion of humanity in operation here is general.

The translation into modern Norwegian is ambiguous between this and a different interpretation: it is possible to understand this translation as a noun phrase denoting a particular human being; and it is this interpretation that has been embraced by both the translator into German and the translator into English. But as their two very different translations show, this interpretation leaves a second question unresolved, which is about the relationship between the concepts involved; in particular, about what it is that is limited in quantity: The wisdom or the human being. In other words, what is the scope of 'lite'? Is it only 'klokt' or does 'lite' reach across all of 'klokt menneske'?

There is simply no way of knowing, by only looking at the language here, what the correct interpretation of the relationships between the three concepts that the three terms refer to are, and this raises the question of what else is involved in meaning than the notion of holding true and the notion of reference between terms and concepts; and some light may be cast on this question by considering where translators might go to find help in cases like this.

A popular resource today is of course the internet, which increasing numbers of people are beginning to think of as the corpus to beat all others as a resource for information about general language, however that may be defined. Here, 'lite klokt' turns up again and again in contexts where something or someone is not very clever, as in the following example which is a headline to an article by Johan P. Olsen published in the newspaper, *Aftenposten*, on 19 March 2003:

Lite klokt å nøle med ny EU-debatt

This means that it is not very clever to delay the new debate about the EU.

In contrast, it is very difficult to find an example of 'lite klokt menneske'; the nearest I have found is

> Mitt postulat er at denne lite gunstige situasjonen er en konsekvens av at Mennesket som art er FOR intelligent, men FOR LITE klok

which came from http://debatt.aftenposten.no/item.php?GroupID=2&Thread ID=1389 (accessed on 16 November 2008). It means roughly 'My postulate is that this not very beneficial situation is a consequence of the fact that the human being as a species is TOO intelligent but TOO LITTLE wise' (meaning insufficiently wise).

Another source of guidance about how to translate is of course the context of texts. The original runic text appeared on a piece of wood that was found on the Oseberg ship, which was used, as mentioned above, as a grave for a high-born Viking woman – a queen, maybe. What would be the sense of placing in such a grave a piece of wood with either the German, or the English inscription, 'unwise person' or 'small clever person'? Neither makes any sense.

But the sense suggested by the web page makes perfect sense in such a context: The death of a highborn person might very well lead to a philosophical consideration of how little we know – to a reflection on the human condition. This, apart from being more appropriate to the context in which the text is used, also presents quite a different picture of the Vikings than the more trite interpretations do: It presents them as people who reflect in the abstract on vast topics such as wisdom and humanity and the limitation of the former, that is wisdom, in examples of the latter, that is humans, something which of course implies an ability to think beyond oneself to mysteries that are beyond us, to imagine that there is a lot more to be known, discovered and understood than we know, have discovered, and understand.

But whatever translation we end up with, we retain the three concepts in the original little text: limited quantity, wisdom, and humanity. So all is rarely lost in translation – in fact much more is gained from having translation than if there were no translation.

The philosophy of translation shows us that translation is always possible; but Translation Studies shows what else, apart from translation, is involved in translation.

7. Bibliography

Catford, J. C. (1965) *A Linguistic Theory of Translation: An Essay in Applied Linguistics.* Oxford: Oxford University Press.

Davidson, D. (1967) 'Truth and Meaning'. *Synthese* 17, 304–23.

Davidson, D. (1973) 'Radical Interpretation'. Reprinted from *Dialectica* 27, 313–28, in (1984) *Inquiries into Truth and Interpretation*, Oxford: Clarendon Press, 125–39.

Davidson, D. (1974) 'On the Very Idea of a Conceptual Scheme'. Reprinted from *Proceedings and Addresses of the American Philosophical Association* 47, in (1984) *Inquiries into Truth and Interpretation*, Oxford: Clarendon Press, 183–98.

Hauge, A. (2002) www.arild-hauge.com/innskrifter1.htm, Århus, Denmark. Projektet Samnordisk runtextdatabas 2004 [accessed on 30 November 2009].

Holmes, James, S. ([1972]1988)'The Name and Nature of Translation Studies'. Paper presented to in the translation section of the Third International Congress of Applied Linguistics, Copenhagen, 21–26 August 1972. In *Translated! Papers on Literary Translation and Translation Studies*, Amsterdam: Rodopi, 66–80.

Hookway, Christopher (1988) *Quine: Language, Experience and Reality*. Cambridge: Polity Press.

Jakobsen, A. L. (1999) 'Logging Target Text Production with *Translog*', in G. Hansen (ed.) *Probing the Process in Translation. Methods and results*. Copenhagen Studies in Language. Copenhagen: Samfundslitteratur, 9–20.

Jakobson, R. (1959) 'On Linguistic Aspects of Translation', in R. A. Brower (ed.) *On Translation*, Cambridge, MA: Harvard University Press, 32–9. Reprinted in Jakobson, R. (1987) *Language in Literature* (ed.) Krystyna Pomorska and Stephen Rudy. Cambridge, MA; London: The Belknap Press of Harvard University Press.

Lakoff, G. and Johnson, Mark (1980) 'Metaphors We Live By'. Chicago: University of Chicago.

Leeds, S. (1978) 'Theories of Truth and Reference'. *Erkenntnis* 13, 111–29.

Malinowski, B. ([1923]1953) 'The Problem of Meaning in Primitive Languages'. Supplement to C. K. Ogden and I. A. Richards, *The Meaning of Meaning*. London: Routledge and Kegan Paul.

Malmkjær, K. (2005) *Linguistics and the Language of Translation*. Edinburgh: Edinburgh University Press.

Mauranen, A. and Kujamäki, P. (eds) (2004) *Translation Universals – Do They Exist?* Amsterdam; Philadelphia: John Benjamins.

Paradis, M. (2004) *A Neurolinguistic Theory of Bilingualism*. Amsterdam; Philadelphia: John Benjamins.

Paris, J. (1961) 'Translation and Creation', in W. Arrowsmith and R. Shattuck (eds) *The Craft and Context of Translation*. Austin: University of Texas Press, 57–67.

Quine, W. van O. (1959) 'Meaning and Translation', in R. A. Brower (ed.) *On Translation*. Cambridge, MA.: Harvard University Press 148–72.

Quine, W. van O. (1960) *Word and Object*. Cambridge, MA: The MIT Press.

Sampson, G. (1980) *Schools of Linguistics: Competition and Evolution*, London: Hutchinson.

Sapir, E. (1921) *Language: An Introduction to the Study of Speech*. New York: Harcourt, Brace.

Sapir, E. (1929) 'The Status of Linguistics as a Science'. *Language* 5. Reprinted in D. G. Mandelbaum (ed.) (1949) *Edward Sapir, Culture, Language, Personality: Selected Essays*. Berkeley, LA; London: University of California Press, 65–77.

Steiner, G. (1975) *After Babel. Aspects of Language and Translation*. London; Oxford; New York: Oxford University Press.

Tarski, A. (1956) 'The Concept of Truth in Formalised Languages', in *Logic, Semantics, Mathematics*, Oxford: Oxford University Press.

Thomas, D. (1952) *Collected Poems 1934–1952*, London: J. M. Dent and Sons Ltd.

Tirkkonen-Condit, S. and Jääskeläinen, R. (eds) (2000) *Tapping and Mapping the Processes of Translation and Interpreting.* Amsterdam; Philadelphia: John Benjamins.

Toury, G. (1980) 'Translated Literature: System, Norm, Performance. Towards a TT-Oriented Approach to Literary Translation', in *In Search of a Theory of Translation.* Tel Aviv: The Porter Institute for Poetics and Semiotics, Tel Aviv University, 35–50.

Toury, G. (1995) *Descriptive Translation Studies and Beyond.* Amsterdam; Philadelphia: John Benjamins.

Whorf, B. L. (1940) 'Science and Linguistics', *Technol. Rev.* 42 (6): 229–31 and 247–8. Reprinted in Carroll, J. B. (ed.) (1956) *Language, Thought and Reality: Selected Writings of Benjamin Lee Whorf.* Cambridge, MA: The M. I. T. Press, 207–19.

Index